Wildlife, Conservation, and Human Welfare

Wildlife, Conservation, and Human Welfare
A United States and Canadian Perspective

Richard D. Taber, PhD
School of Forestry
University of Montana

Neil F. Payne, PhD
College of Natural Resources
University of Wisconsin-Stevens Point

KRIEGER PUBLISHING COMPANY
Malabar, Florida
2003

Original Edition 2003

Printed and Published by
KRIEGER PUBLISHING COMPANY
KRIEGER DRIVE
MALABAR, FLORIDA 32950

Copyright © 2003 by Krieger Publishing Company

All rights reserved. No part of this book may be reproduced in any form or by any means, electronic or mechanical, including information storage and retrieval systems without permission in writing from the publisher.
No liability is assumed with respect to the use of the information contained herein.
Printed in the United States of America.

FROM A DECLARATION OF PRINCIPLES JOINTLY ADOPTED BY A COMMITTEE OF THE AMERICAN BAR ASSOCIATION AND A COMMITTEE OF PUBLISHERS:

This publication is designed to provide accurate and authoritative information in regard to the subject matter covered. It is sold with the understanding that the publisher is not engaged in rendering legal, accounting, or other professional service. If legal advice or other expert assistance is required, the services of a competent professional person should be sought.

Library of Congress Cataloging-in-Publication Data

Taber, Richard D.
   Wildlife, conservation, and human welfare : a United States and Canadian perspective / Richard D. Taber, Neil F. Payne.
   p. cm.
   ISBN 1-57524-061-0 (alk. paper)
  1. Animal populations—United States—History. 2. Wildlife conservation—United States—History. 3. Human-animal relationships—United States—History. 4. Animal populations—Canada—History. 5. Wildlife conservation—Canada—History. 6. Human-animal relationships—Canada—History. I. Payne, Neil F. II. Title.

QL752.T32 2003
333.95'416'0973—dc21

2002034034

10 9 8 7 6 5 4 3 2

Cover art by William E. Page

This book is dedicated to our wives, Pat Taber and Jan Payne, for their selfless support and understanding, and to our students and other field biologists acting under often trying circumstances to strengthen the factual base for sustained positive relations between human and other forms of life.

CONTENTS

Preface ... ix

Acknowledgments ... xiii

1 Stone Age Settlers into North America ... 1

2 Human-Wildlife Developments in Eurasia: Farming and Animal Domestication ... 14

3 Ancient Warrior-Rulers ... 28

4 Medieval Europe ... 35

5 European Trade and Exploration ... 45

6 European Trade and Settlement ... 59

7 Wildlife Conservation in the Colonial Mother Country ... 76

8 Wildlife Conservation in North America: Regulation ... 82

9 Wildlife Conservation in North America: Land Use to 1945 ... 98

10 Wildlife Conservation in North America: 1945–1970 ... 114

11 International Wildlife Conservation ... 125

12 Broadening Wildlife and Habitat Conservation ... 141

13 Holistic Conservation on Public Lands ... 156

14 Developing Nationwide Patterns of Conservation ... 175

Appendix A Attitudes Toward Wildlife ... 191

Appendix B Common and Scientific Names of Animals and Plants Mentioned ... 195

Index ... 203

PREFACE

This volume attempts to put relations between human and wildlife populations into a frame of reference that includes human and wildlife history and the factors shaping relevant human behavior. In this effort we focus on the actual, treating the ideological only as it affects the actual. Our own ideological values place wildlife survival in a human-dominated world as a major goal, and we attempt to describe pathways leading to the realization of that goal.

The geographical focus is America north of Mexico. The United States and Canada provide examples of human societies from paleolithic to postindustrial. These nations have been notable for wildlife use, overuse, and restoration, and for their contributions to related international affairs. And while they both focus much of their wildlife concern on less developed tropical regions, they both have examples of wildlife in jeopardy within their own borders.

We human beings inhabit but one planet in the universe, and depend for our lives upon its natural resources. Throughout the world, human societies exhibit an uneven distribution of wealth, health, education, and technological proficiency. Such differences increase the possibility of exploitation of the have-nots by those who have. It also places a responsibility upon those who have—a responsibility to look beyond their own welfare toward the larger welfare of this planet and the diversity of life upon it.

Among the more secure humans exists an acceptance of this responsibility, an informed concern for the continued existence of wild animals within a global framework, and for use by humans for the future. Through nuclear fission we now have a global capability to return to prehistoric conditions; humankind can move toward a life of fulfillment or a life of deprivation. Hopefully, our civilization is willing and able to work rationally toward a life of fulfillment. Successfully approached, such a decision can raise the overall quality of human life and the lives of a multitude of equally worthy but less dominant species.

All living things have been shaped by a need to obtain nourishment and avoid harmful environmental pressures, in short, to survive and to reproduce. The processes needed for successful life are guided and empowered by chemical reactions. These reactions occur more rapidly in warm than in cold environments, and within warm bodies more rapidly than in cold bodies. For eons, the bodies of land animals grew cool at night, so reactions were sluggish; as the sun warmed them by day, they became warmer and more active. Most terrestrial animal life was confined to warm conditions of the tropical climates and warm seasons in temperate climates. With the appearance of birds and mammals, a new adaptation had evolved. Bodies were warmed by internal chemical reactions, allowing rapidity in all bodily functions. Warm-blooded animals could function efficiently even when the environment was cold. This opened the possibility of active and successful life not only in the tropics or the temperate summer but also in cold environments anywhere on earth. At the same time, the constant maintenance of a warm internal body required a constant availability of the fuel consumed in the production of heat, that is, nourishment.

Humans are mammals, warm-blooded, with the high nutrient needs that the maintenance of a high internal temperature dictates. When a human hungers or believes that its young hunger, food-seeking predominates over other behaviors. When hunger is satisfied, other needs guide behavior patterns.

Humans have existed for at least 200,000 years in our present general form and mental capacity. For almost all (99%) of that period, hunting and gathering have provided all human food. About a third of the prehistoric diet was meat. Ability to obtain food has affected the survival and successful reproduction of one human group over another. In most human societies, the genetic predisposition toward the search for food has been augmented by cultural encouragement. Our hunting-gathering ancestors, we feel sure, undertook the search for food as a way of satisfying both physiological hunger and their desire for community approval.

Cultural approbation is a human value; perhaps a continuing need like food served as nourishment for the psychic as well as the physiologic. In our attempt to understand human behavior toward wildlife, it is useful to accept the concept of a human need for cultural approbation, perhaps not as compelling as the human need for food, but still significant in guiding human behavior.

This leads us to a rough differentiation among three guiding human values with regard to wildlife:

Immediate material satisfaction is accomplished by taking wildlife without consideration for any long-term consequences for the wildlife population: to satisfy the need for food; to obtain wildlife products for immediate monetary profit; to defend oneself against animal attack; to satisfy the hunting drive or to take awesome game for peer esteem.

Sustained material satisfaction can be sought through the control of human behavior for future benefits: to avoid waste of game; to adhere to conservative customs; to refrain from degrading habitats; to instruct the younger generation in prudent ways; or to propitiate the game to assure its reappearance or avoid its malevolence.

To describe satisfaction outside material concerns we have no one unequivocal word, so we must coin and define one; let us use *nonmaterial*.

Nonmaterial satisfaction stems from values beyond material considerations. It can be expressed as equating the value of other animal lives with those of humans; protecting those lives as a human duty; protecting them from human-caused suffering; or employing those animals as messengers to the supernatural world.

Any one person can obtain all three sorts of satisfaction at one time or another as circumstances vary: acute hunger seeks immediate short-term satisfaction; when less immediate need exists, sustained material satisfaction can be sought; and when material requirements are assured, the values beyond material needs can be pursued. How a full belly can change a person's perspective was well put by a thoughtful Arab, who said that when he was hungry, he could see only the dates on the trees, but when he had eaten, he saw the oasis in all its glory. In the following chapters we will attempt to clarify the consequences of these three sorts of human satisfaction for wildlife populations.

These populations are of grave current concern as we realize that we are driving some to extinction despite our earnest desire to control and reverse this trend. If we tally up all the known species of birds and mammals in the world, we find that since about 1600 some 8684 species of birds and 4226 species of mammals were recognized, many comprising several subspecies. Since that time 94 species of birds and 36 species of mammals have become extinct, largely through human actions. Though severe and irreplaceable, these losses are only the tip of the extinction iceberg; 253 species of birds and 316 species of mammals in the world are in imminent danger of extinction today. The principal threat to their continued existence is human activity.

The human-nature relationship has existed as long as people have inhabited the earth, and will continue as long as the human species continues to inhabit the earth. It has changed constantly as human cultures and nature's responses have changed, often slowly, but sometimes rapidly. We are currently in a period of rapid change in human-nature relationships, both in our power to cause damage and in our power to repair damage.

Humans live within—and are part of—ecosystems. Humans depend upon the web of services these ecosystems provide. It is generally recognized that, like wildlife, human society depends for its greatest welfare on healthy ecosystems. Our alteration of natural ecosystems has resulted in risks and costs that we can recognize and remedy. With its chronological organization, this volume is an attempt to understand the human behavior that has led us to the present, and the behavioral strengths that can be used to direct us toward a harmonious coexistence with other creatures of this earth.

Richard D. Taber

ACKNOWLEDGMENTS

When the senior author was in his early teens, during the economic depression of the 1930s, he lived in rural northern California, where people hunted and trapped for immediate material satisfaction without much concern for legal restrictions. At age 14 he read Aldo Leopold's *Game Management,* which opened the prospect of wildlife husbandry—restoration and sustained use. Some 12 years later he was a graduate student under Aldo Leopold, who had been developing concepts about the non-material aspects of human relations to wild nature. Then, as a graduate student under Aldo's son Starker Leopold, he was encouraged to pursue the idea of treating the three main ways that humans approached wildlife—immediate material gain, prudent husbandry, and non-material value—in a broad historical way. He here expresses his appreciation for this early encouragement.

Gradually he gathered and organized information on this topic with the help of professional colleagues and other wildlife enthusiasts. By the early 1970s, as public environmental interest rose, he offered a course, *Wildlife and Human Welfare,* for the College of Forest Resources, University of Washington. So began the writing of this book. But due to other more demanding interests, the manuscript lay dormant for some years.

Both authors became colleagues and friends while the junior author worked for the senior author at the University of Washington from 1973 to 1975 when they joined in a cooperative study. More recently, they have combined their efforts to update, re-write, write, and polish to get this book published, although it had to wait until both had retired from their faculty duties.

The junior author acknowledges his debt to his academic mentors Burd S. McGinnes, Henry S. Mosby, and J. Juan Spillett, and to his Newfoundland employer Frank Manuel. This work has been helped immensely by secretarial assistance through the Montana Cooperative Wildlife Research Unit at the University of Montana and the College of Natural Resources at the University of Wisconsin-Stevens Point, Alison Perkins and Cheryl Felckowski serving as decipherers *extraordinaire.* Both authors thank the fine folks at Krieger for their editing and other timely help.

Chapter 1

STONE AGE SETTLERS INTO NORTH AMERICA

If we compare the Old World (Europe, Asia, Africa) with the New World (North America and South America), one significant difference is that we humans evolved to our modern form in the Old World over millions of years, continually interacting with wildlife populations, while no humans existed in the New World for almost all that time. The long mutual history of human and wildlife populations in the Old World had consequences for wildlife. Human hunting, ever more persistent and effective, exerted a selective pressure on its prey, whereby the individuals with a tendency to evade human hunters lived to pass on those traits, while those less predisposed to avoid hunters were killed. The first hunters in the human evolutionary line were naturally less efficient than human hunters later became, so the selective pressure of human hunting on prey was increased only gradually over many thousands of years. As a result, most prey species were selected to survive human hunting and in fact did coexist with increasingly expert human hunters for long periods in the Old World. In turn, the origins of human intelligence seem to be linked to the acquisition of meat; both hunting it and sharing it developed social and cognitive skills. Indeed, our hunting heritage might also have caused our bipedalism, stereoscopic vision, tooth structure, tool use, and language.

By some 100,000 years ago our human line had produced people much like ourselves in form—our own species, *Homo sapiens*. Over many thousands of years, these ancestors of ours developed a tool which, constantly improved, made continually more rapid cultural elaboration possible—the power of human speech. With the ability to communicate came the invaluable opportunity to pass from one generation to another, from one individual to another, from one group to another, the lessons of past experience, the advances of invention and insight, the many threads of communication that integrate the members of a community. Humans in groups share values held by their group in common, and also learn from the generation before. The written word is relatively recent in human history (about 3400 BC, and never in the American Indian-Inuit cultures of North America until after 1492 with arrival of Europeans), so values have long been learned orally, often by way of myth and religion. The strong possibility exists that the greatest contribution of wildlife to humanity might very well be nothing less than the awareness of cause and effect developed from early dependence on wildlife, in other words, human consciousness itself. Biological processes create

1

and shape culture. Response to cultural change, in turn, alters the biological processes.

By roughly 50,000 years ago, this ability to impart learning had raised human cultures to comfortable levels of existence. People were able to obtain and process food, shelter themselves from the elements, protect themselves from enemies, and generally understand the world around them.

The tangible environment that they could see and feel was but a small part of the total world of their belief. A spiritual otherworld existed from which life came and to which it returned, a world revealed in glimpses in dreams and visions, a world described and explained in stories passed from generation to generation. The spiritual world that surrounded them was powerful, a source of good luck or bad. Good luck could be sought through proper actions, the behavior dictated by accepted custom. Bad luck could occur when prescribed behavior was neglected, manifested by sickness, accident, or failure in the hunt. Reasons for bad luck could always be found. Behavior favoring good luck was continually reinforced. As speech was perfected and hunting became more and more a dependable way of life, every wild species was known to have magical powers, some more, some less, which required a particular pattern of human behavior with respect to it.

By roughly 50,000 years ago, humans like ourselves were skillful hunters who presumably reinforced their prospects for success by practicing the approved rituals: mimicking a successful hunt before starting out, responding to the warning or encouraging signs of nature, communicating grateful and respectful feelings toward the prey appropriate for its spiritual powers. According to this way of thinking, if propitiation is spiritually successful, the game just killed and departed to the spirit world will be willing to return to life to be hunted again. A spiritual aspect of the game is its ability to pass its characteristic attributes into the body of the human who eats it.

Long-continued hunting by humans usually has a selective effect on game populations, favoring survival of the more wary and elusive. Many thousands of years of human hunting might well have exerted selective pressure on the human as well as the game populations. The human hereditarily inclined toward the pursuit of game was perhaps more successful in leaving descendants than the human with less hunting spirit. Large herbivores so abundant in open habitats are not easily killed by a lone hunter. Early human hunters of open grassland hunted in teams, maneuvering to herd game into nets or snares or over cliffs or into water where spearmen waited. The individual hunter had to submerge his individuality and become an effective member of a group if the communal hunt was to succeed and the tribal culture survive. The cooperative bond between males developed in the primate ancestors of humans, and could have been a central factor in the rapid evolution of humans as team-hunting predators. Like members of the modern sports team, which is the apparent derivative, members of a hunting team adapt their individuality to needs of the team. Their rewards are the communion of spirit within the team and the approbation of the larger society of females and dependents which the team serves. In the population sense, effective teamwork has greater survival value than ineffective teamwork does. Our ancestors were enthusiastic hunters and hunting enthusiasm has commonly been demonstrated by humans to the present day.

By 50,000 years ago, humans had developed a highly successful hunting life. Success stemmed from developments in belief, in social organization, and in techniques. Belief reinforced confidence that the game properly propitiated would be taken and the hunters would not be injured. Organization would form and direct the hunting team and provide the support and approbation of its dependents. Technique was too various to be described in a word: knowledge, weapons, eventually dogs.

Knowledge came from tradition and daily observation of game, its sign, and its behavior; for important prey it was profound.

Weapons and traps were traditionally known in many forms for many purposes. American Indians did not develop a bow-hunting culture until AD 500 (ancient Europeans did at least 30,000 years ago). For the largest mammals that were by then preferred quarry, a key invention before the bow and arrow was the spearthrower (atlatl). This simple extension of the human arm increased the speed and distance of the throwing arc and the velocity and striking power of the spear. An additional advance was the detachable spearhead. When the prey was impaled, the shaft could be withdrawn and rearmed for another throw or thrust. These are but two examples among many.

Among potential game species, the largest were the most valued. One individual would provide ample meat for the band and a host of other useful raw materials, such as skin, bone, horn, tendons, and fat. Signs of the largest game would arouse the greatest excitement and its death the most elaborate rites of propitiation. Successful hunters of the largest game would enjoy high status and acclaim. Young boys would dream of emulating them.

The big game hunter had strong community support. His hunting partners cooperated in traditionally successful hunting tactics. When a large prey animal was wounded, the hunters' dogs could pursue and harass it, bringing it to bay while the hunters drew closer for a more focused attack. More daring hunters could immobilize the largest prey by dashing in with a stone axe to cut the tendon—the hamstring—of its hind leg.

Herding game could be moved toward, and over, convenient cliffs or driven by fire into an area set earlier in the anticipated path of escape. Circumstances suggested the tactics to be used, and earlier success or failure guided the hunters' decisions.

Early European sailors often could smell North America before they could see it, due to smoke from American Indian-caused fires. Fire was long used by humans, not only for warmth and as an aid in preparing food, but also as a way of modifying hunting grounds to advantage. The principal prey animals, of any size, eat the most favored of the vegetation they can reach, within a few feet of the ground for most. By killing shrubs and small trees, fire removes competition for light and moisture of plants growing close to the ground. After a fire the food for game is often much improved in both quantity and quality, as grasses fertilized by ash put out new growth, seeds germinate to produce seedlings, and competing plants die. Further, by killing trees, fire increases the availability of seasoned firewood. When humans invade a new region, the event is often marked by a layer of charcoal in the soil. But like lightning fires, fire from Indians generally went uncontrolled, often resulting in undesirable habitat changes and massive killing and waste of wildlife.

Successful human hunting cultures spread as populations increased and the need for additional hunting grounds increased accordingly. Movements of bands into territories adjacent to ancestral homes continued over thousands of years, gradually extending human occupancy to regions far from their African homeland. Movement to new territory was easiest when that territory was not occupied already, but as populations became larger competition for hunting grounds increased.

Two aspects of relationships between bands were freedom of visitation and defense of territory. Protected by the signs of peace, visitors would be welcome for their news, for their addition of new knowledge, for their possibilities as new band members; they had much potential for contribution. But in each territory, each band defended the resources upon which band survival depended.

The resource-territory is controlled and thus owned jointly by the band. The band exerts this ownership by forcibly defending its territory or by granting use to others within its territory after acceptance of formal application. This phenomenon is not confined to people of the Stone Age; we can find it in contemporary societies as well. In the territorial buffer zone between warring groups, hunting pressure was lightest and the surviving game was able to increase and restock the more heavily hunted areas.

Human territoriality has several consequences for wildlife. Resident species that are taken for human uses tend to be less abundant close to human dwellings, more abundant farther away and most abundant in the contested region where one tribal territory fades into another, particularly when the tribes are enemies. The "border refuge" effect occurs also among humans in later cultural stages. For example, the buffer zone between warring Chippewa and Sioux tribes in Minnesota prevented competing hunters from occupying the best game region intensively enough to deplete the deer supply. When a lengthy truce occurred, the buffer, in effect a protected zone for deer, was destroyed, causing famine. A strikingly parallel concept exists with wolf packs.

We have emphasized hunting because this account focuses on the human relation to wildlife. The predatory aspect of human culture affects wildlife and requires an intimate knowledge of the ways and uses of wildlife. Human predatory culture also leads imaginative humans to develop a rich inclusion of wildlife into their magic, religion, and mythology—the realm of belief that explains in supernatural terms whatever is beyond, yet related to, everyday experience. Each human community learned its complex of beliefs from its elders and embellished the tales in the telling, each separate community gradually becoming different from distant communities in its beliefs, practices, and often language. Within any community, then, was a unanimity of belief and custom that provided the social comfort that derives from predictability. As a hunting band of perhaps 25 to 50 individuals grew larger, it split into two, and through repeated splits a tribe was formed. It had common language, customs, and beliefs. Its units could meet in times of ample food to exchange gifts, information, and young marriageable members, and enjoy appropriate social and religious ceremonies. Another tribe with different ways might well compete for territory as hunting grounds became more crowded. So through territorial defense a continuing enmity between tribes was maintained. Due to the influence of such customs as abhorring waste and broadening the food base through increased knowledge, invention, and control of human population size through tribal conflict, periodic famine, and perhaps infanticide, humans came into some balance with the natural world from which they drew their material and spiritual support.

Opportunities for human expansion into new territories were affected by weather, which controlled vegetation and game, and by human cultural adaptability. Weather was characterized during the Interglacial Ages (Pleistocene) by recurrent cold periods of glacial advance and the following warmer periods of glacial retreat. By the time of the next to last extremely cold period 50,000 years ago, human cultures were richly adapted to practically any environment, particularly those that provided enough large mammal prey. As the climate warmed, human hunting bands were culturally equipped to follow the retreating ice northward toward Siberia. There the largely treeless tundra supported such potential human prey as woolly mammoth, reindeer, bison, and muskox. The mainstay of the human diet was meat; current estimates put daily consumption per person at about 5 pounds. Meat beyond immediate needs could be preserved by drying, smoking, freezing in winter or in frozen ground (permafrost), or mixing with fat and berries (pemmican).

As with other species, human population density tends to rise with increasing availability of limiting resources, and to decline as such resources dwindle. For the hunting-gathering band, a renewable resource consisted of the usable plant and animal products available within their aboriginal environment. Typically, the area over which a group foraged was limited by human mobility and the difficulty of transporting possessions and young on moves, or resources back to camp, as well as the presence of neighboring groups. This placed a limit on the size of the foraging area, which set a limit on how many humans could be supported by that foraging area. With something like 25 to 50 humans making up the band, a self-supporting community of parents and children, gatherers and hunters, the human population of the entire earth during the Middle Pleistocene has been estimated at about 1 million, or 0.03 human per square mile. Since humans were biologically successful creatures increasing in numbers, human population pressure caused them to spread. Spilling slowly out of Africa perhaps 100,000 years ago, modern humans had spread over Eurasia and even Australia across 55 miles of sea by 40,000 to 50,000 years ago.

During the warmer period following the intense cold of 50,000 years ago, humans spread far north, becoming even more efficient in their adaptations. Bone took the place of scarce wood in supporting their dwellings and also took the place of stone in spearheads at times. Winter snows saw snowshoes and sleds. With the bone needle they stitched clothing tailored enough for an active hunter, as well as skin-covered huts and boats. A boat also could be fashioned from birch bark or a log, and bundles of reeds could serve as a raft, allowing early hunters to exploit fishing opportunities, expand territory, and disperse farther.

Winters in the far north are long and dark. Around a fire fueled by dried animal dung and peat, the people talked. They told stories, they recounted the traditional tales of how the world came to be, and its plants and animals, and its humans. They transmitted and embroidered the many aspects of the otherworld that could sometimes be experienced in dreams and visions. They passed on from generation to generation the beliefs that gave the confidence of understanding.

As common customs bound each individual to the others, the social bonds grew stronger within each group as people carried out traditional activities in identical ways. As it had for thousands of years, the continuous cohesion of the band led all members to think of themselves less as individuals than as members of their band, and of a particular group within their band. Each, then, strove continuously to conform to the most respectable customs and be guided by the most respectable values of the band.

Human populations in northern Asia prospered, the surplus moving ever northward as the glaciers retreated. As early as 35,000 years ago big game hunters of northern Eurasia flourished. But another glacial advance began as temperatures dropped once more. As the cold increased and the glaciers crept south, the sea level dropped. More and more of the earth's water was being locked up as ice. The shallow waters of the Bering Sea between Siberia and Alaska became progressively shallower, and from about 25,000 to 10,000 years ago, the former seabed was exposed as marshy land. So, as increasing cold had been forcing the northernmost humans and their prey southward, new land was emerging to the southeast. This new land, Beringia, was soon colonized by the large animals that had long been human prey—reindeer, mammoth, muskox, and bison among them. Human populations expanded into these new hunting grounds and had spread to Alaska over the thousands of years that followed. Over still more thousands of years the large invading mammals from Asia, including humankind, had spread south into the lands below the edge of the continental glaciers.

About 17,000 years ago the continental ice glaciers had reached their maximum southward extent, well into the northern part of the present United States. Then as they began to melt and retreat, they revealed a cold landscape with many marshes and ponds. The peaty soil supported a low-growing cover of mosses, lichens, short-stemmed forbs and grasses, and stunted shrubs. A few scattered spruces grew in warmer spots. Large mammals adapted to this abundant forage included the American mastodon (also at home in the heavier coniferous forests to the south), the woolly mammoth (of the cold northern tundra of Old World and New World), and the newly arrived muskox and reindeer (caribou).

The ice retreated and the taiga moved north, as did plant communities south of the tundra. These were dominated by grasses in the arid west and by evergreen (coniferous) forests in the rainier east. These, too, supported large mammals. Many large mammals occurred in the grasslands and associated shrubby streambank habitats. Among the most striking and presumably most valued by human hunters were the mammoths (woolly, Colombian, and imperial) and the giant bison. The American mastodon was the comparable attractive game in the swampy coniferous forests of the continental east.

Currently, experts differ as to whether the first immigrants to North America and South America came by boat as early as 40,000 to 50,000 years ago, perhaps from Polynesia (see p. 45), whether they walked across the land bridge of Beringia, which was possible 10,000 to 25,000 years ago, boated along the edge of it (finding evidence made difficult by encampments now under water), or even crossed the North Atlantic pack ice. DNA studies indicate that Asian origins for four lineages account for more than 95% of indigenous Americans, but that a fifth DNA lineage, mostly in Canada's Ojibwa people, occurs in Europeans. Moreover, according to experts, North America needed over 50,000 years to become one of the most linguistically complicated areas in the world.

In any case, by some 12,000 to 15,000 years ago, big game hunters had spread throughout North America and even South America, leaving traces of their travels that reveal several significant aspects of their relations to the natural world that supported them. First of all, they entered the New World fully equipped and experienced for the hunt of the largest mammals. Secondly, they spread rapidly through the continent leaving scanty traces as though the favored game was quickly eliminated from each newly entered region. There is no doubt that hunting bands spread quickly through the continent and had a part in the extinction of the largest mammals; some skeletal remains contain undoubted spearheads.

The big game hunters continued to expand their range. During this expansion their most favored game, it seems evident, was the largest in general and on occasion the most unusual. These would excite the most attention and approbation among hunters and their dependents. Nothing in the belief and behavior of the hunters other than an abhorrence of wastage would constrain this hunting. And so, as humans hunted, climate became warmer and drier, and newly invading Asian species probably competed and introduced diseases and parasites, the largest mammals became extinct.

The most relevant aspect of these extinctions for us is that it was within human power to kill large beasts and continue to kill them beyond the power of the beasts to maintain their populations. In doing this, hunters would exploit a resource beyond its capacity to recover and be acting out a paradigm—more intensive use as the used population declined and the remaining members became more valuable to the human mind. Then, as now, the rare thing was attractive by virtue of its scarcity.

By 11,000 years ago, the unmistakable appearance occurred in North America of Paleo-Indian hunters using distinctive (Clovis) projectile points. That also seems to be when extinct genera such as mammoths and horses suddenly disappeared along with other large mammals. In the North America of at least 10,000 to 12,000 years ago, human hunters appeared among a fauna never before hunted by humans. After extinction of a relatively small number of animal species during North American settlement from Asia, a rich fauna continued to exist for thousands of years in habitats fully occupied by humans who were supported to a significant degree by continual predation upon that rich fauna. In other words, no continual loss of species occurred in North America after it was settled by American Indians and Inuit despite continuous human use. When hunting has made survivors more difficult to find, most hunted species will be less vigorously pursued, as hunters turn to more abundant game. The exception to this generalization is the species that is so valuable to the hunter, either for utility or approbation, that it will continue to be pursued down to the last, and it becomes extinct. This probably was the case with the conspicuous giant mammals.

By about 8000 years ago the last of the continental glaciers had melted away and the tree line had moved northward under the warmer conditions. By about 5000 years ago the continental vegetation formed roughly the pattern we see today.

Supported by an ancient oral tradition, intelligent observant humans had no difficulty in adapting to every sort of continental environment. Naturally enough, they were most abundant where the landscape was most productive, and suffered shortage when adverse conditions reduced available productivity. Enough food was the primary need, and short rations and even starvation were familiar facts. When meat was needed, hunters were keen to find game and fishermen to catch fish. Satisfaction of human hunger took precedence over any other consideration.

About 6300 years ago American Indian tribes in Mexico were improving their food supply through early domestication of plants, namely, maize, and later, squash and beans. Slowly created from the selection and perhaps crossing of the wild ancestors, maize (corn) had the greatest impact on Indians north and south of Mexico. For one thing, tribes that produced enough portable food, such as parched corn, had a military advantage over those that did not.

From about 5000 to 3000 years ago local cultures became ever more closely adapted to local natural resources in order to support the growing human populations. Along the seaboards, shellfish, fish, and marine mammals were human mainstays. In the forested eastern and western interiors, deer, bear, turkey, fish, bulbs, and nuts provided food. In the grasslands, grazing mammals, exemplified by bison but including a host of other potential human prey, were mainstays.

By 3000 years ago tribes were beginning to learn about growing maize in the southeastern United States, where the climate is naturally most suitable, and the southwestern United States, where irrigation supplemented inadequate rainfall. But traditional tribal life was long maintained and generally included seasonal movements from one sort of environment to another. The notion of staying in one spot long enough to grow, protect, and harvest a crop was not attractive enough for immediate adoption.

As long as natural products sufficed, brisk intertribal trade carried valuables widely, and young men could hunt and defend the tribal territory, all was well.

When the human population rose above what could easily be supported, territory could be expanded only at the expense of the neighbors.

For human societies, intertribal warfare and intertribal trade are generally compatible. Warfare and hunting require similar weapons, and in Paleolithic culture, weapons are made of wood, bone, and stone. Not every stone is suitable for chipping to a cutting edge, so the demand for suitable stone, which occurs only in certain places, was never-ending. Flint and obsidian chunks were valuable, and traded far from their points of origin. Lack of suitable stone from which to make cutting tools and weapons was a serious impediment to the success of the hunter-warrior and one that he was anxious to correct.

The individual tribe protected its territory, the region from which it drew sustenance. Sometimes a tribe occupied only certain lands, excluding all others. At times, several tribes might claim large tracts of land, even though not permanently controlled or occupied. These might serve them as hunting grounds, even though hostile tribes might be encountered. War could be part of the hunt.

A growing dependence on maize agriculture spread from south northward, ultimately as far north as the climate permitted, but maize did not become important food until about 1000 years ago. Maize raised the ability of the land to support people. The increased population required not less, but rather more wild meat and fish, and more wild products such as skins. Since farming required human presence to clear land and then plant, tend, protect, and harvest the crop, the old custom of seasonal movements to harvest seasonal natural foods began to be replaced by year-round habitation. Larger permanent human aggregations generated social mechanisms to control the frictions of crowding—mechanisms that led toward increasing power in the hands of ever fewer leaders. These developments connected with farming were of course centered on suitable regions, particularly the midwestern, southern, and southeastern regions of summer rains, and the southwestern areas in which Mexican advances in irrigation were adopted.

Over time the array of natural products supporting each tribe grew. Big game hunting specialists had produced generations that used not only big game but also fish, fowl, small mammals, and many other foods. Hunger drove the hunt, down to the last vulnerable prey. But just as catastrophic human losses were ultimately replaced by new human populations, so prey losses were replaced by dispersal from surviving populations. As far as we know today, the more or less continuous use of fish and wildlife populations by American Indians and Inuit over thousands of years did not result in any further wildlife extinctions.

In addition to material aids, the Paleolithic hunter had spiritual support. In the spiritual world every hunter has a magical animal helper, i.e., a totem of a species revealed to him in a childhood fasting dream. The hunter could bring his totem to his aid with its particular song. In addition, each game species has a "master" which notes how that species is treated. Therefore the game that is killed is treated respectfully. The animal's death is mourned and it is addressed in familial terms. To do otherwise would cause the spirit "master" of the particular type of animal to withhold game from the hunter.

No doubt the spiritual beliefs of North American Indians imposed some measure of control over expedient hunting fervor. The fact that most game survived through this span of time suggests that the human population was relatively stable from continual warfare and other sources of human mortality, and that the reproductive powers of game increased as its population decreased, a term known as compensatory reproduction.

Thus, the link between living and slain wild creatures was central to religious, magical, and mythological belief. Each wild species had its otherworldly master looking out for its welfare and avenging its mistreatment. The living creature represented the invisible magical world in corporeal form, and returned to that world at death, aware of the nature of its death and the appropriate response to unacceptable treatment.

Wildlife was believed to be so linked to the spirit world that animal behavior could signal coming events; good or bad luck in the hunt could be foretold in the actions of wild species. Oracular messages could be communicated through interpretation of the behavior of animals dreamed. In many such ways human lives were guided by beliefs and behaviors concerning the visible and invisible worlds in which each wild species existed.

Millions of humans lived successful and, on the whole, leisurely lives, supported by their religious beliefs and practical skills. They did this without iron tools or weapons and without any domestic animals larger than the dog. Each tribal member was brought up to conform to the customs of the tribe. Every boy was raised to be a hunter and a warrior. Intertribal warfare, generally of small scale, gave approved roles to young men.

American Indian and Inuit cultures were (and are) closely integrated with the natural world and its wildlife components in many ways. In a material sense, nature produces food and fiber, and the aboriginals of North America were culturally adapted to obtain and use wild products efficiently and creatively. Natural products also included many things useful in an esthetic way: rattles from deer hooves, feathers for headdresses, skins for drumheads, porcupine quills and ermine tails for ornamenting clothing, colored earths and animal fat for painting one's person and possessions. The list goes on. Agriculture was slow to develop partly because the plow and wheel were not invented in the New World, and North America lacked domesticable animals to feed and to help with chores.

American Indian cultures were not always in balance with their environment. Entire tribes have completely disappeared, partly if not mostly due to environmental degradation, e.g., the Cahokians (population 40,000 in AD 1200) in a huge city near St. Louis and the Hohokam (AD 1100 to 1400) near Phoenix.

From our reconstruction of the first peopling of America north of Mexico, we can derive some generalizations that appear to have relevance for both human behavior toward humans and human behavior toward wildlife, generalizations to which we will return later.

Some relationships between humans:
- Humans tend to form social groups with customary beliefs and behaviors; communication within a social group is freer than communication between social groups.

- Human social groups feel a degree of ownership in the areas they occupy and the natural products of those areas, and are inclined to defend these from other humans.

Some relationships between humans and wildlife:
- Humans have deep interests in wildlife. One of these is the pursuit of game and its respectful use.
- In human minds, human needs justify the taking and use of wildlife.
- Humans have a long ancestry as increasingly skilled predators on wildlife.

While the people from northeastern Asia were spreading over their new lands in the Americas, their relatives in Eurasia experienced cultural changes that would eventually have marked consequences for America north of Mexico. The American Indian and Inuit view of time was cyclic, the year moving through its moons of different seasonal events, and the human generation moving through its span, taking the place of the generation before and being replaced by the generation to follow. Had there been no further human penetration of America, this aboriginal way of life, and the coexistence of humans with the many native plant and animal species, might have continued to the present day. But the people who remained in Eurasia when the Bering land bridge was being crossed had thenceforward a quite different history that eventually would exert new forces on the North American scene.

Bibliography

Archer, M. 1984. Effects of humans on the Australian vertebrate fauna. Pages 151–161 *in* M. Archer and G. Clayton, editors. Vertebrate zoology and evolution in Australia. Hesperian Press, Carlisle, Australia.

Bolen, E. G., and W. L. Robinson. 1999. Wildlife ecology and management. 4th edition. Prentice Hall, Upper Saddle River, NJ.

Bower, B. 2001. Maize domestication grows older in Mexico. Science News 159:103.

Campbell, B. 1995. Human ecology. Aldine de Gruyter, Hawthorne, NY.

Champagne, D., editor. 1994. The native North American almanac: A reference work on native North Americans in the United States and Canada. Gale Research, Detroit.

Cohen, M. N. 1977. The food crisis in prehistory: Overpopulation and the origins of agriculture. Yale University Press, New Haven, CT.

Diamond, J. 1997. Guns, germs, and steel: The fates of human societies. Norton, New York.

Elaide, M. 1995. The encyclopedia of religion. 10:471–474. Simon and Schuster Macmillan, New York.

Fagan, B. M. 1995. People of the earth: An introduction to world prehistory. 8th edition. Harper Collins College, New York.

Farb, P. 1968. Man's rise to civilization as shown by the Indians of North America from primeval times to the coming of the industrial state. Dutton, New York.

Flannery, T. F. 1999. Debating extinction. Science 283:182–183.
Frobenius, L., and D. C. Fox. 1937. Prehistoric rock pictures in Europe and Africa. Museum of Modern Art, New York.
Fromkin, D. 1999. The way of the world, from the dawn of civilization to the eve of the twenty-first century. Knopf, New York.
Gilbert, F. F., and D. G. Dodds. 2001. The philosophy and practice of wildlife management. 3rd edition. Krieger, Malabar, FL.
Gray, G. 1995. Wildlife and people: The human dimensions of wildlife ecology. University of Illinois Press, Urbana.
Grinnell, G. B. 1907. Tenure of land among the Indians. American Anthropologist (N.S.) 9(1):7–11.
Hickerson, H. 1965. The Virginia deer and intertribal buffer zones in the upper Mississippi Valley. Pages 43–65 *in* A. Leeds and A. Vayda, editors. Man, culture, and animals: The role of animals on human ecological adjustments. American Association for the Advancement of Science, Washington.
Hunter, M. L., Jr. 1996. Fundamentals of conservation biology. Blackwell Science, Cambridge, MA.
Jennings, F. 1993. The founders of America. Norton, New York.
Jochim, M. A. 1976. Hunter-gatherer subsistence and settlement: A predictive model. Academic Press, New York.
Klein, R. G. 1989. The human career. University of Chicago Press, Chicago.
Krech, S., III. 1999. The ecological Indian: Myth and history. Norton, New York.
Kurtén, B., and E. Anderson. 1980. Pleistocene mammals of North America. Columbia University Press, New York.
Lee, R. B., and I. Devore, editors. 1972. Man the hunter. Aldine, Chicago.
Leeds, A., and A. Vayda, editors. 1965. Man, culture, and animals: The role of animals on human ecological adjustments. American Association for the Advancement of Science, Washington.
Marquis, T. B. 1965. Wooden Leg: A warrior who fought Custer. University of Nebraska Press, Lincoln.
Martin, C. 1978. Keepers of the game: Indian-animal relations and the fur trade. University of California Press, Berkeley.
Martin, P. S. 1984. Prehistoric overkill: The global model. Pages 354–403 *in* P. S. Martin and R. G. Klein, editors. Quaternary extinctions: A prehistoric revolution. University of Arizona Press, Tucson.
Martin, P. S., and R. G. Klein, editors. 1984. Quaternary extinctions: A prehistoric revolution. University of Arizona Press, Tucson.
Masters, P. M., and N. C. Flemming, editors. 1983. Quaternary coastlines and marine archaeology: Towards the prehistory of land bridges and continental shelves. Academic Press, New York.
Mech, L. D. 1977. Wolf-pack buffer zones as prey reservoirs. Science 198:320–321.
Mowat, F. 1975. People of the deer. Seal Books, Toronto.
Nelson, R. W. 1983. Make prayers to the raven. University of Chicago Press, Chicago.

Nitecki, M. H., and D. V. Nitecki, editors. 1986. The evolution of human hunting. Plenum, New York.
Oswalt, W. H. 1973. Habitat and technology: The evolution of hunting. Holt, Rhinehart and Winston, New York.
Parfit, M. 1997. A dream called Nunavut. National Geographic 192(3):68–91.
Price, T. D., and G. M. Feinman. 1993. Images of the past. Mayfield, Toronto.
Price, T. D., and J. A. Brown, editors. 1985. Prehistoric hunter-gatherer: The emergence of cultural complexity. Academic Press, New York.
Read, H. 1955. Icon and ideas: The function of art in the development of human consciousness. Faber and Faber, London.
Service, E. R. 1966. The hunters. Prentice Hall, Englewood Cliffs, NJ.
Stanford, C. B. 1999. The hunting apes: Meat eating and the origins of human behavior. Princeton University Press, Princeton, NJ.
Stringer, C., and R. McKie. 1996. African exodus: The origins of modern humanity. Holt, New York.
Taylor, C. F. 2001. Native American weapons. University of Oklahoma Press. Norman.
Tiger, L. 1969. Men in groups. Random House, New York.
Trigger, B., editor. 1978. Handbook of North American Indians. Volume 15. Smithsonian Institution, Washington.
Trigger, B.C., and W. E. Washburn. 1996. The Cambridge history of the native peoples of the Americas. Cambridge University Press, New York.
Trut, L. N. 1999. Early canid domestication. American Scientist. 87:160–169.
Vereshchagin, N. K., and G. F. Baryshnikov. 1983. The ecological structure of mammoth fauna of Eurasia. Zool. Zh. 62:1245–1251.
Ward, P. D. 1997. The call of distant mammoth: Why the ice age mammals disappeared. Copernicus, Sacramento.
Wenke, R. J. 1990. Patterns in prehistory: Humankind's first three million years. 3rd edition. Oxford University Press, New York.
West, F., editor. 1996. American beginnings: The prehistory and paleoecology of Beringia. University of Chicago Press, Chicago.

Chapter 2

HUMAN-WILDLIFE DEVELOPMENTS IN EURASIA: FARMING AND ANIMAL DOMESTICATION

Some 40,000 years ago successful people like ourselves were expanding into new European hunting grounds as the climate warmed and glaciers receded. During the following thousands of years the climate grew cold once more, glaciers expanded, and sea levels dropped. By the coldest part of this last glacial period some 25,000 years ago, the sea levels around Eurasian shores had dropped some 300 feet, exposing vast areas of new land soon colonized by plants. Plants attracted grazing animals and grazing animals attracted and supported expanding populations of human hunter-gatherers, the skilled, successful people of the late Stone Age.

For long, our ancestors had been steadily improving their ability to make a good living from the land. They were able to increase their potential food supply through use of fire to benefit grass and grazing mammals, and they were capable of encouraging useful plants by weeding around them and planting some of their seeds in new favorable places. A band could improve the territory over which they moved seasonally from crop to crop, and bands that did so were more likely to prosper than those that did not. As the shoreline receded and new land appeared, human population surplus had new habitat to support it.

Suddenly (in geologic terms), around 12,000 years ago the end of the cold period saw massive ice-melt and a rise in sea level. In temperate North America where new uplands for human expansion were plentiful, the rise in sea level affected communities only around the seacoast. But in temperate Eurasia the upland was already occupied by humans living by hunting and gathering, augmented by (from the human perspective) landscape improvement. Flooding of the continental shelves pushed a good portion of the temperate Eurasian population upslope into lands already occupied by humans. This population crisis was accompanied by increasingly intense development of agriculture and animal domestication as people strove to produce more food from less space.

Some 12,000 years ago—2000 years before the end of the last glacial period —as human populations increased, some hunter-gatherer groups in the Middle East began to experiment with deliberate growing of wild cereal crops and to domesticate some wild mammals to expand human food supplies. During the next 8000 years agricultural food production spread throughout suitable parts of

Eurasia. Agriculture and animal domestication increased human food and human reproduction over the norm among hunter-gatherers. Mainly through infanticide and a long lactation period which prevents ovulation, nomadic hunter-gatherers spaced their children at 4-year intervals, for a mother had to carry and nurse her toddler until it was old enough to keep up with adults as the band moved seasonally about its territory to take advantage of seasonal production. In contrast, farm women did not have that burden since the permanent village was near the farmed fields. The number of persons who could be supported from fields within walking distance of the village was much larger than the number in the average hunting-gathering band; whereas such a band averaged about 25 to 50, an agricultural village averaged, and averages today, more like 125 persons.

Traces of early human agriculture are now found widely through temperate Eurasia, dating from 10,000 to 12,000 years ago or so, and, it seems probable, associated with the sudden flooding of so much of the temperate human habitat. It was certainly associated with domestication.

Domestication occurs through selective pressure applied by humans to change wild plants and animals to forms better fitted to human needs. If seed-gathering loses seeds that drop off in harvesting but gains those seeds that remain in the head and so are stored for the next seeding, then the tendency for seeds to remain in the head is genetically encouraged and domestication of that plant has begun. If, among the young of wild sheep caught and tamed, some are more tractable or have a more desirable woolly coat and are kept for breeding, and the unruly or straight-haired ones are eaten, then domestication of sheep has begun. In short, domestication forces a plant or animal from the form adapted to its needs in the wild toward a form adapted to human needs.

Long before the rise of agriculture the gray wolf had been domesticated. Mitochondrial DNA of wolves and domestic dogs indicates that dogs originated more than 100,000 years ago. It is reasonable to speculate that the great spread of highly successful Paleolithic hunters, which began some 30,000 to 40,000 years ago, was supported by the addition of the domesticated wolf dog as man's hunting partner. With the probable addition along the way of some genes from the four species of jackal, this domesticate provided the genetic source of that bewildering variety of contemporary beasts we collectively call dogs. The tamed wolf or domesticated dog could well have crossed Beringia, along the Bering Strait into the New World, with the first Americans. For Paleolithic people, the dog was an extremely valuable addition to the human economy.

Among the adaptations, discoveries, and inventions of humans spreading through Europe and Asia, the taming of the wolf was of prime importance. Skilled in hunting big game, Paleolithic bands attracted scavenging carnivores to their wastes. Over centuries, wolves came to be tolerated, their young raised for food and pets in prosperous times, their keen powers of scent appreciated. With a tamed wolf under his control, a hunter could enhance his chance of finding game, bring wounded game to bay, and find game that had died in hiding. Bred near the camp, tamed wolves produced litters from which the most tractable and teachable young were kept. The process of domestication began long ago, namely, selecting from among the wolf's genetic potentialities those configurations useful to humans.

Domestication of wildlife progressed from about four methods. First, the dog was selectively bred from the wolf, which probably was brought home as a pup by early humans because of the love for young creatures as pets, the mutual social-economic service of cleaning up leftover debris from killing game, the similarity of hunting techniques and ultimate use in the hunt, and its availability as human food.

Second, human big game hunters, keen observers of prey behavior, could anticipate and sometimes control the movements of herds of ungulates, to kill what was needed. Beginning with the guiding of hoofed animals, with the help of dogs, clever humans could move on to protecting their game from predators, and eventually to capturing and selecting among young prey animals those that would be permitted to live and reproduce. The domestication of sheep, goats, and reindeer occurred this way and appears to be preagricultural.

Third, additional animals were domesticated after plants were farmed, as byproducts of the domestication of plants. Animals such as cattle, buffalo, pigs, elephants, deer, and perhaps rabbits and camels were attracted to crops, and some were ultimately tamed and domesticated by early humans.

Fourth, in quite recent times further deliberate domestications occurred usually with an economic purpose in mind. Mink, tropical fish, the canary and other such birds, catfish, alligators, probably chickens (for eggs), and even snails, silkworms, and honeybees are examples.

The potential for domestication is enhanced by certain physiological and behavioral qualities. Such species should (1) be hardy; (2) have a dominance social hierarchy so that humans are accepted as leaders; (3) be easy to tend, i.e., placid, gregarious (easily controlled by a herdsman), versatile in feeding habits, and not highly adapted for instant flight (in contrast to antelope, gazelle, and most deer); (4) breed freely in captivity; and (5) be useful to humans. Gradual elimination of individuals with characteristics undesirable to humans, even from an unconfined population, can lead toward domestication. Few species of wildlife qualify for domestication; few have been domesticated.

In the Old World, widely distributed, potentially tamable wildlife species occurred, such as the dog, sheep, goat, wild boar, and wild ox, but in the New World, only the llama, alpaca, guinea pig, and turkey were domesticated—and then only regionally in South America and Central America. The bison was never domesticated in the Old World or the New World, although other more dangerous bovines were, such as the gaur of India and Assam.

The first hoofed animal to be domesticated in the Near East for food and other products seems to have been the sheep, about 10,500 years ago, although some evidence indicates it was the pig. The domesticated sheep, which probably arose from the Asiatic mouflon, had a greater propensity for fat accumulation than the goat, and fat, a concentrated potential source of human energy, was highly esteemed by humans. The fat-tailed sheep is still extant. Sheep also can be milked, but the genetic complex that proved more valuable was that which led to production of wool. The potential for wool production exists in the gene pool of wild sheep, but is not expressed; it seems that heavy wool is maladaptive for wild sheep. The course of domestication for tamed wild sheep was shifted by genetic selection from adaptations to the natural environment to adaptations to human need. Humans kept the woollier individuals for breeding while the less woolly were slaughtered. In time, domestic sheep were major producers of an annual crop of valuable animal fiber.

The domestication of the goat, which probably arose from the bezoar goat, closely followed domestication of the sheep, and provided the farming people of western Asia with milk much like human milk in composition. This was not only a valuable supplement to human milk, permitting a higher rate of infant survival and human population growth, but it formed a good dietary combination with the grains, harvested from wild grasses, that were becoming more important as human mainstays.

The domestication of the pig occurred probably about 9000 years ago (or maybe even earlier than the sheep) from the wild boar, and the domestic hog is still so closely related to the wild one that it retains the same scientific name. The pig has many virtues as a producer of meat. It can be kept in confinement and fed scraps from the human table, or it can, with the aid of dogs, be herded into the forest, where it busily digs in the humus for insects, earthworms, mice, mushrooms, nuts, and fleshy roots. It has an extremely high reproductive rate (up to two litters of 10 or 12 piglets each year), and it grows rapidly. In addition, it yields much lard, which has many uses in human technology, and its meat keeps well when smoked as ham and bacon.

The cow and the pig apparently started their careers toward domestication by raiding early agricultural crops. Domesticated from wild cattle, the cow ultimately replaced the goat in many places as a source of milk, but its first important addition to human technology was as a draft animal about 6600 years ago, when agriculture had become widespread in the Near East. The ox (castrated bull) moves slowly but is immensely powerful. It can drag logs of firewood or sledges of building materials to the settlement. With invention of the wheel about 5500 years ago, it could haul burdens of every sort, including whole families on seasonal moves or in search of new territories in which to settle.

The horse evolved in the New World and apparently spread westward to Eurasia across the Bering land bridge into the Old World before dying out in the New World. The domestication of the horse from the wild horse occurred in the Old World about 5000 to 6000 years ago, at first for food, later to pull wheeled vehicles, later still to ride. Onagers and asses were domesticated somewhat before then.

Like the horse, the camel evolved in North America, but died out there after some populations had crossed Beringia at the Bering Strait into the Old World, and others the land bridge of Central America into South America. The dromedary (one-humped) and bactrian (two-humped) camels of Eurasia were domesticated possibly as early as 6000 years ago. Of six species of camel on earth, the dromedary and bactrian camels occur in the Old World. Of the four other species of camel, all in the New World, the llama and alpaca were domesticated in South America perhaps as early as 7500 BC as descendents of the guanaco, which is wild, as is the vicuña.

Domestication of the chicken occurred at least 4000 years ago in Southeast Asia from red jungle fowl, mainly for egg production and secondarily for meat.

The largest animal to be domesticated was the elephant. The Asian elephant was domesticated at least 4000 years ago, the African elephant somewhat later. Interaction between humans and elephants involved (1) predation for food, probably the earliest form of exploitation; (2) predation for ivory, which has been important in human economics since early civilization; and (3) taming for use in warfare, burden, and circuses and zoos.

In addition to the dog (from the wolf), sheep and goats were domesticated in Eurasia in preagricultural times; cattle, water buffalo, yak, banteng, and pig in early agricultural times (originally encountered as crop-robbers); Asian elephant, African elephant, dromedary camel, bactrian camel, horse, ass, and onager mainly for transport and labor; and cat, ferret, and mongoose for pest destruction. Humans probably got the idea of taming wild animals from hunting them, so that meat and other valuable materials could be stored "on the hoof" until wanted, and so that, at a later stage, the animal's muscle power could be used for transport and industry.

No clear evidence exists about the date of reindeer domestication. Human dependence on wild caribou in circumboreal regions began during the Pleistocene and continues today, making it perhaps the single most important species in the entire anthropological literature on hunting. Indirect evidence suggests domestication occurred at least 3000 years ago, but its domestication at 7000 to 12,000 years ago, as some writers suggested, is unlikely. Wild caribou and domesticated reindeer are the same species. During glacial periods when tundra ecosystems extended far to the south, Paleolithic hunters of Europe and Asia became skillful predators of the abundant reindeer. They could have brought reindeer calves into camp and tamed them on occasion, and found them useful in the hunt. Tamed reindeer could serve as a screen behind which the hunter could hide while stalking the wild herds. Estrous females could serve as lures to bring wild rutting males close to the hidden hunter. And the tamed stag, its antlers equipped with snares, could be sent out to challenge and hold the combative wild reindeer stag. Like other herbivores, tamed reindeer are strongly attracted by sodium and nitrogen. Human wastes, rich in sodium and nitrogen, accumulate in soil and vegetation around human settlements, so it is easy to imagine tamed reindeer flourishing and producing young which, through elimination of the less tractable, became domesticated in time. Human welfare gained immeasurably from this. In time, domesticated reindeer became not only a completely controlled source of meat and hides, but also of milk. Reindeer also were used as pack animals and to pull sledges. With increased mobility and material security afforded by reindeer domestication, human populations could become more dense and could exist in formerly marginal or hostile environments. Productivity of the tundra ecosystem formerly passed into wild herbivores and thence into control of human hunters. Eventually such productivity was captured in the bodies of domestic herbivores completely accessible for a wider variety of human uses at the time or season of human choice.

Agriculture has experienced four revolutions: (1) domestication of plants about 12,000 years ago in widely separated locations—China, Mexico, Iraq (the Fertile Crescent along the Tigris and Euphrates rivers), South America; (2) exploration and discovery, beginning in the 15th century; (3) Industrial Revolution; and (4) technology which spawned pesticides, fertilizers, and hybrid crops, and a vast increase in human population.

About 12,000 years ago, then, intelligent industrious humans enhanced the desirable large-seeded annual grains by removing competing plants (weeds), scaring away competing seed-eating animals (pests), and, at last, preparing seedbeds and sowing the desired crop in the Near East region. From the host of plants whose uses were familiar to these humans through generations as gatherers, they domesticated wheat, barley, oats, flax, and some starchy vegetables, as well as the woody wine grape, olive, date, fig, apple, pear, and cherry, among others. (Earliest domesticated crops north of Mexico were corn, beans, squash, pumpkins, sunflowers, and tobacco.) Lands most suitable for cultivation were unforested and relatively level, covered by a mantel of soil fine enough to plant, hoe, and hold moisture in the crop root zone. Where such conditions were found, or could be created by cutting and burning encumbering vegetation, cultivation spread. The first plows were used about 4000 BC. Lands too steep, rocky, dry, wet, forested, etc., could be put to other human uses: production of wood, wild game, and, with domestication of additional wild herbivores, grazing of livestock. With a measure of food storage, clever humans had leisure to think about increasing food production. (The first beer was drunk around 6000 BC.) With greater food production, the human group could increase and prosper.

With dogs, sheep, goats, pigs, cows, and horses, and the beginnings of grain agriculture, human populations in the Near East and western Asia enjoyed a broad and stable resource base that permitted rapid increase of human population density. Farming tribes became ever more numerous and powerful, spreading into "new" areas suitable for settlement, areas that no doubt had long been occupied by other humans still pursuing the hunting-gathering way of life.

Like other primates, humans tend to be members of groups, and as such tend to be hostile to humans belonging to other groups. That caused problems after humans developed civilization by densely settling river valleys. Use of irrigation techniques compounded problems by further concentrating humans in narrow corridors along rivers.

Other conflict must have occurred too. Hunting peoples could survive mainly in parts of the landscape least suitable for agriculture—marshes, deep forests, desert edges, and mountains. They probably would raid the crops and hunt the livestock of farming peoples. But their resource base would become ever more slender as farming people increased in population and occupied more and more of their hunting grounds. Moreover, the most productive agricultural soils had also supported the most productive wildlife populations.

Domestic animals would further erode the resource base of hunting peoples. Domestic herbivores could outcompete wild herbivores for food. With domestication, a selection toward greater efficiency of the digestive tract occurred (at the cost of such once important qualities as agility and alertness), and herding by their intelligent and well-informed human masters took them to another suitable pasture when one was exhausted. Farming people continued to hunt wild animals also. The total effect of these pressures on wild prey was to reduce its availability to hunting tribes and so further reduce their resource base.

In the face of invasion by farming people, then, hunting people fell back to less productive parts of the landscape, and their numbers shrank proportionally. Farming tribes defended their lands and flocks against these "wild men," set fire to marsh or forest that concealed them, destroyed their huts and foodstores, and killed surviving men and enslaved women and children whenever they could

The new agricultural way of life developed in a rather warm dry region, but as it spread north and west toward Europe, it encountered increasingly cool moist climates, and consequently denser forests. The spread of agriculture into these new lands was like a river of many channels, moving into the lighter soils where the forest was more open, and flowing past densely forested swamps and mountains too steep to cultivate, moving northward and up the mountains until stopped by growing seasons too short for crop production.

The earliest forest farming was of the slash-and-burn type. On a plot of ground, small trees and brush were cut down with stone axes, larger trees were girdled, and on warm summer days, the dead dry plant material was burned. Seeds were sown, and perhaps a herd of sheep or a drove of pigs was run back and forth to plant and cover the seed. One or two crops were grown, and then soil fertility was so depleted and competing weeds so abundant that the plot was abandoned for farming for years, while other plots were being subjected to the slash-and-burn routine. All of these plots had to be within reasonable distance of the village so that crops could be protected from raids by wild and domestic animals.

Domestic hoofed mammals, livestock, modified the natural environment. Sheep grazed in grassland, goats browsed in shrubby areas, and pigs rooted in the forest. Gradually the grubbing of pigs, eating acorns and uprooting seedlings, opened the forest floor, transforming it into a grassy sward, a parkland with large trees but no forest reproduction. Bit by bit, these large trees became old and died or were girdled and killed by men seeking firewood, and the parkland became a meadow. Some of it could grow crops, some of it could graze sheep and cattle. The goat is a browser and can even climb into low trees to feed, finding much food in the regenerating burned forest, where its feeding kills the woody sprouts, increasing invasion of grass. By reducing the number of trees and shrubs on hills too steep to cultivate, goats help create the grass-forb pastures suitable for sheep. Thus the resource base of these early farmers was strengthened and human populations increased.

Spread of this subsistence agriculture and domestication of animals had important effects on wildlife populations. The reduction of forest by fire, with its replacement by grass or shrub, had gone on at a modest rate for thousands of years before, but it intensified as human populations and intensity of human land use increased. In addition, heavy grazing by domestic animals on steeper slopes tended to weaken the ability of plants to protect soil during rains, and help moisture percolate into soil. Thus, more and more water ran down slopes during rainstorms, carrying away soil, and leaving less water to charge the soil and seep into the aquifer. Heavy grazing and trampling had three main effects: (1) larger perennial plants were replaced by smaller annual plants; (2) with trampling of the soil surface, topsoil was eroded and the exposed compressed stony surface resisted intake of rain, so less moisture was stored in the root zone each spring for potential plant use during the growing season, which, along with loss of fine soil, reduced potential plant productivity; and (3) a lower storage of water underground meant lower water levels in lakes, ponds, springs, rivers, streams, and wetlands, especially during the dry season. Altogether, reduction of forest and heavy grazing of hillsides warmed and dried the ground-level environment. The result was the invasion of plants and animals from warmer drier regions into landscapes dominated by subsistence agriculture and livestock husbandry.

The spread of farming and grazing also led to reduced populations of larger forest animals. As more forest was converted to open land, some patches of forest became isolated. Animals frequenting them became more vulnerable to hunting as cover was reduced, and increasing human populations produced more hunters and dogs. Ripening crops were attractive to wild herbivores, which were killed whenever possible to reduce crop damage and to avoid breeding with domestic stock. Domestic flocks were raided by wild predators, such as wolves, which became universally recognized as enemies of humans raising livestock.

Development of an agricultural way of life affected human values concerning wildlife. The long-term value of game animals, as the common property of the hunting-gathering band, began to fade, with its cultural taboos against wasteful killing and sharing of hunters' kill throughout the band. At the same time, the urge to hunt and the immediate value of the prey to the hunter remained high. Though no longer essential for human survival, hunting in agricultural times still provided valuable meat and skins. In place of the hunting team of the whole hunter-gatherer band, smaller hunter groups within the agricultural village competed with one another for game. Since game was no longer essential for human survival, though welcome enough on the table, community customary measures to maintain game populations were no longer enforced by customary pressures. Larger game mammals within a day's travel of the village disappeared.

While traditional human prey, large hoofed mammals, disappeared as self-sustaining populations near farming communities, populations of smaller wild creatures flourished. Ripening crops were a concentrated food source, and attracted large populations of resident small grain-eating mammals and flocks of seed-eating birds from afar.

Farmland provided a spectrum of habitats for wildlife species capable of using them. Fields were small and crops varied, as the village had to raise all the different crops that filled its needs: fiber such as flax or cotton, grain, vegetables, vines and trees for fruit and seeds. Fields often were fenced so that livestock could be kept out while crops were ripening or kept in to glean the aftermath; fruit-eating birds perched on these fences, their droppings containing seeds which sprouted into hedges of berry vines, wild cherries, hawthorns, and a host of similar plants. Shrubby fence rows supported a rich fauna of small birds and mammals, which sheltered in thorny thickets and ventured out to feed in field edge. These fence rows were protected travel ways along which even larger mammals such as hares could move from one field to another with changing seasons.

With time, the old slash-and-burn style of agriculture came to be replaced in part by a more stable pattern involving use of animal manure for fertilizer. Dung left by penned livestock was spread on arable fields, and so their fertility was maintained or even increased. Soil fertility was reflected in quality and quantity of plants growing there, both cultivated plants and weeds that flourished on field edges, in fallow fields, and among crops. These weeds often were species which had existed wild in the region where farming arose, often as pioneer plants on newly disturbed areas. Often their strategy for survival was to produce many seeds and then die back until the next growing season brought another cycle of quick germination, growth, seed production, and death of the parent plant. The numerous seeds produced by weeds of subsistence farms supported small seed-eating birds and mammals such as mice, sparrows, finches, and doves, which, in turn, formed prey for the smaller predators.

Once harvested, grain is potential food for any grain-eating animal that can adapt to the environment in which it is stored. Three of the various rodents that eventually became so adapted, living in human dwellings and eating stored foods, were house mouse, black rat, and Norway (house) rat. These have now spread throughout the world from their original home in Southeast Asia, being transported in boats and wagons, always benefiting from the warm indoor climate and food abundance that make human dwellings such suitable habitat. By consuming stored food and by spreading disease, these rodents have had, and are still having, a tremendous negative impact on human welfare. Even to the present day, house mice or rats often abound in the subsistence farming village, particularly where human dwellings and shelters for domestic animals are close together and waste disposal tends to be casual. On the other hand, commensal rats and mice provided ancestral stock from which were derived domesticated laboratory rats and mice so useful in human medicine today. By some 3600 years ago the wild ancestor of the cat, the wild cat, had been domesticated to act as a predator on commensal rodents.

About 4000 to 5000 years ago, when the horse, ass, and camel of Eurasia were domesticated, pastoral cultures could develop. A pastoral culture revolves around the welfare of herds of domestic animals—cattle in some cases, sheep and goats, even reindeer in others. The horse, ass, ox, and camel in various environments, as well as reindeer in the far north, often serve as beasts of burden for humans and their chattels when pastoralism involves seasonal movements from one pastoral region to another. Typical of such seasonal patterns even now is the move up into the mountains, ascending to the upland pastures by summer, followed by the move down to snow-free lowlands for winter.

Originally the herdsman was also a farmer, and drove his herds forth from the village in the morning and back to the village at night. Close pastures were most important and most heavily used. As time went on, herdsmen took their animals farther away from their villages to seek better pastures. Some herdsmen left sedentary village life altogether to lead a nomadic pastoral life, sometimes traveling long distances between seasonal pastures, living in tents wherever their travels took them, and sometimes sowing a crop on the way to summer pasture and harvesting it on the way back in fall.

Pastoral man tends to count his wealth in his herds. To have them prosper and increase is his constant desire. But variable rains from year to year mean variable levels of plant productivity; pastures can withstand more livestock grazing in wet years than dry years. Maintenance of heavy use in years of low productivity can weaken forage plants.

The continual weakening of forage plants through overuse shifts the balance between grasses and woody plants in favor of the latter. If the seeds of a woody plant fall and germinate in a healthy grassland, the grasses will exhaust the soil moisture in the upper levels of the soil during the first summer, and the seedling will die. But if the same seed were to germinate in a weakened grassland, it might well survive the first summer, strike its roots deep, flourish, and eventually shade out surrounding grasses.

Pastoralism ordinarily leads to increased woody vegetation in grasslands. Not only are fires less frequent with heavy pastoral use because there is actually less fuel to carry a fire under heavy grazing, but weakening of perennial grasses not only permits seedlings of woody plants to survive but also allows invading annual plants to replace perennial herbaceous plants. The changes constitute wildlife habitat shifts of great magnitude. Wild grazing animals and those requiring dense grasses for shelter decline, while animals which eat woody vegetation (browsers), shelter in shrubs, or live on seeds increase.

Wildlife also was altered by human hunting and predator control. Pastoral people are generally skilled in use of weapons. Skill with weapons was necessitated by chronic skirmishing between rival groups for pasturage, and by the need to protect the herds from predatory animals and raiding neighbors. Like farmers, pastoralists also might hunt game for food and recreation. Characteristic of some pastoral cultures is use of trained animals to aid in the hunt, not only dogs, but predators that hunt by sight, notably large birds of prey and cheetahs. In addition, artificial drying of the environment, caused by heavy grazing and trampling, was imposed on huge areas too dry for agriculture, changing grasslands to semideserts, and semideserts to deserts, with corresponding shifts in ecological productivity and associated plants and animals.

A human culture that spreads due to its success in promoting the welfare of its members often comes into contact with another human culture and competes for some essential human resources. Thus in its early days, pastoralism spread into regions too cold or dry for agriculture, at the expense of hunting-gathering cultures still occupying those regions.

To summarize, early agriculture and pastoralism resulted in a shift in human values regarding animals; no longer essential for food and skins, wild animals became less valued by the community, though still of intense interest to the individual hunter. Crops and herds were basic to human survival, and wildlife depredating on them became human enemies. Human uses of the land reduced habitat quality for wild grazing animals.

Refugia still existed for some wild populations in regions little affected by ever more intensive farming and pastoralism in particular places, mainly marshes, inaccessible mountains, deserts, and still dense forests. From such reservoirs of habitat, young game animals dispersed into neighboring farming regions. Long after some of these had been domesticated, their wild ancestral populations still existed and still produced a surplus that roused the hunting enthusiasm of young farmers.

People might have turned to agriculture only when other alternatives were declining or unavailable. The diet of farming humans tended to be rich in starch and low in proteins, fats, and many different vitamins and trace elements, compared to the diet of hunting-gathering people. This is clearly shown in the changes in human body size with the shift to agriculture; people became smaller as quantity replaced quality in their food supply. Studies of prehistoric diets suggest a general decline in quality and perhaps length of human life when farming began, from the average age at death at about 26 years during preagricultural times to 19 during postagricultural times. Even height declined from 5'9" for men and 5'5" for women to 5'3" for men and 5' for women by 5000 years ago in farming communities. More calories per day were required to farm than to hunt. In turn, food production led to further increase in human populations which resulted in more sedentary human settlement, more substantial housing, elaborate storage facilities, and special implements for clearing land and cultivating and harvesting crops, as well as tending animals. From these new technological developments emerged greater interdependence, long-distance exchange of raw materials and finished artifacts, and development of various products to benefit human welfare. Nonetheless, by concentrating human populations, farming produced malnutrition, starvation, epidemic diseases, and deep class division.

Compared to Stone Age hunting and gathering bands, early farmers were more numerous and more sedentary. Each village was surrounded by a territory including fields and uncultivated lands. A sense of village ownership existed over the uncultivated lands and their wild products, plant and animal, just as a sense of ownership by a hunting band existed over its territory. The wild resources of the band were usually treated as if owned in common, and their harvest was limited to the needs of the band. The wild resources of the village were treated as if owned by any villager who could harvest them. Wild products, such as game, were valuable and any surplus beyond the needs of the hunters' families could easily be sold or bartered within the village.

For the farm family, seasons of intensive labor and seasons of relative leisure occur. In fall, when crops had been gathered and weather grew cooler, young men were free to hunt and trap, combining the ancient enthusiasm for the chase with valuable game, if they were lucky. As long as wild lands existed, particularly extensive marshes, so did the chance of finding game. But unrestrained pursuit of wild game steadily reduced its numbers. The more vulnerable species, the species most valued and hotly pursued, and those with low rates of reproduction were the first to disappear. Typically around a farming village, the larger game animals were scarce or missing.

The larger predatory mammals such as wolves adapted to the loss of their wild prey by turning to domesticated prey. The village livestock and often the village children had to be protected from wild predators.

As farming populations grew, an apparent need existed for more farmland or more efficient farming. More farmland could potentially be gained by draining marshes, and greater farm production by controlled irrigation. Both of these, on any large scale, would require the cooperative effort of many skillfully directed workers—a requirement met through the development of empires.

Bibliography

Banfield, A. W. F. 1961. A revision of the reindeer and caribou, genus *Rangifer*. National Museum of Canada Bulletin 177, Biological Service 66.
Barker, G. 1985. Prehistoric farming in Europe. Cambridge University Press, Cambridge, England.
Bibby, G. 1961. Four thousand years ago. Knopf, New York.
Burch, E. S., Jr. 1972. The caribou/wild reindeer as a human resource. American Antiquity 37:339-368.
Campbell, B. 1995. Human ecology. Aldine de Gruyter, Hawthorne, NY.
Clutton-Brock, J. 1981. Domesticated animals from early times. University of Texas Press, Austin.
Clutton-Brock, J. 1987. A natural history of domesticated animals. Cambridge University Press, Cambridge, England.
Cohen, M. N. 1977. The food crisis in prehistory: Overpopulation and the origins of agriculture. Yale University Press, New Haven, CT.
Cohen, M. N., and G. J. Armelagos. 1984. Paleopathology at the origins of agriculture. Academic Press, New York.
Cohen, M. 1989. Health and the rise of civilization. Yale University Press, New Haven, CT.
Crosby, A. W. 1986. Ecological imperialism: The biological expansion of Europe, 900-1900. Cambridge University Press, New York.
Diamond, J. 1987. The worst mistake in the history of the human race. Discovery 8:64-66.
Diamond, J. 1997. Guns, germs, and steel: The fates of human societies. Norton, New York.
Fagan, B. M. 1995. People of the earth: An introduction to world prehistory. 8th edition. Harper Collins College Publisher, New York.

Fox, M. W. 1978. The dog: Its domestication and behavior. Garland STPM Press, New York.
Fromkin, D. 1999. The way of the world, from the dawn of civilization to the eve of the twenty-first century. Knopf, New York.
Gauthier-Pilters, H., and A. I. Dagg. 1981. The camel: Its evolution, ecology, behavior, and relationship to man. University Press, Chicago.
Gebauer, A., and T. D. Price, editors. 1992. Transitions to agriculture in prehistory. Prehistory Press, Madison, WI.
Graham, E. H. 1947. The land and wildlife. Oxford University Press, New York.
Gray, G. 1995. Wildlife and people: The human dimensions of wildlife ecology. University of Illinois Press, Urbana.
Harris, D., and G. Hillman, editors. 1989. Farming and foraging. Clarendon Press, Oxford, England.
Hemmer, H. 1990. Domestication: The decline of environmental appreciation. Cambridge University Press, Cambridge, England.
Hughes, J. D. 1975. Ecology in ancient civilizations. University of New Mexico Press, Albuquerque.
Hyams, E. 1971. Plants in the service of man. Dent, London.
Hyams, E. 1972. Animals in the service of man. Lippincott, New York.
Jennings, F. 1993. The founders of America. Norton, New York.
Kurtén, B. 1968. Pleistocene mammals of Europe. Aldine, Chicago.
Laetsch, W. M. 1979. Plants: Basic concepts in botany. Little, Brown, Boston.
Lange, K. E. 2002. Wolf to woof: The evolution of dogs. National Geographic 2002 (January):2–11.
MacLeish, W. H. 1994. The day before America. Houghton Mifflin, Boston.
Mason, I. L., editor. 1984. Evolution of domesticated animals. Longman, New York.
Meyers, N. 1983. A wealth of wild species: Storehouse for human welfare. Westview Press, Boulder, CO.
Olsen, S. J. 1985. Origins of the domestic dog. University of Arizona Press, Tucson.
Reed, C. A. 1969. The pattern of animal domestication in the prehistoric Near East. Pages 361–380 *in* P. J. Ucko and G. W. Dimbleby, editors. The domestication and exploitation of plants and animals. Aldine, Chicago.
Rindos, D. 1984. The origins of agriculture: An evolutionary perspective. Academic Press, New York.
Rowan, A. N., editor. 1988. Animals and people sharing the world. University Press of New England, Hanover, NH.
Serpell, J., editor. 1995. The domestic dog: Its evolution, behavior and interactions with people. Cambridge University Press, Cambridge, England.
Smith, B. D. 1994. The emergence of agriculture. Scientific American Library, New York.
Tudge, C. 1996. The time before history: 5 million years of human impact. Scribner, New York.
Vilà, C., P. Savolainen, J. E. Maldonado, I. R. Amorin, J. E. Rice, R. L. Honeycutt,

K. A. Crandall, J. Lundeberg, and R. K. Wayne. 1997. Multiple and ancient origins of the domestic dog. Science 276:1687–1689.

Woody, T. 1949. Life and education in early societies. Macmillan, New York.

Zohary, D., and M. Hopf. 1993. Domestication of plants in the Old World. 2nd edition. Oxford University Press, Oxford, England.

Zuener, F. E. 1963. A history of domesticated animals. Harper & Row, New York.

Zvelebil, M., editor. 1986. Hunters in transition. Cambridge University Press, Cambridge, England.

Chapter 3

ANCIENT WARRIOR-RULERS

Farming and herding supported ever-increasing human populations that spread into "new" lands over thousands of years and developed new inventions and techniques. Tribes still carrying on in the ancient Stone Age culture were pushed off the most productive lands by the numerous well-armed and well-organized newcomers, to survive, if at all, in regions too swampy, mountainous, dry, or forested for a productive or even supportive farming-herding way of life. If not actually killed or enslaved, these less technologically advanced tribesmen could to a degree be controlled through trade. They could become dependent upon products of the more advanced culture, for which they bartered the natural products of their remaining territories. As the sedentary farm-village life encouraged technical inventions such as weaving, pottery, use of dyes, and early metallurgy, the farm village had products for which the neighboring hunting-gathering tribes would barter their wild meat and skins.

For Stone Age man, whose duties were hunting and warfare, any item of trade that increased his efficiency in these activities was eagerly sought. Copper, then bronze, then iron, became available to advanced human culture in the Old World some 10,000, 5000, and 3500 years ago, respectively. As knives, spearheads, arrowheads, axes, etc., these metals would be in great demand in exchange for ivory, furs, and other valuable wildlife products.

Trade weakened the ancient balance between wild and human populations that had so long existed through the centuries when hunting and gathering was the only way of human existence. This weakening took two forms which we can still see in a few remote corners today. First, the tribal member bartering, let us say, for the first metal spearhead gained individual status for his possession, a possession his alone, not shared equally by all; in order to get this spearhead he had to obtain trading goods—wildlife products—beyond the immediate needs of his tribe. Second, as one tribe obtained metal weapons, enemy tribes needed to obtain them also, or be bested by an imbalance of power between mutually hostile tribes (precisely as the modern day nuclear detonations of hostile neighbors India and Pakistan in 1998).

A primitive arms race demanded ever greater supplies of trading stock, which usually consisted of wild products. The wild species from which these products came were therefore now subject to ever heavier human predation. The more avid the tribesmen were for products of the advanced culture, the weaker the ancient customs of community sharing and customary husbandry of renewable resources became. Wherever trade was intensive, valuable natural products were exploited ever more heavily, and eventually declined. Among such products were wild meats, furs, skins, feathers, and the like; as trade became more pervasive, populations of wild species providing these products were sometimes exploited beyond their capacity to recover without protection.

In this way agricultural communities brought hunting-gathering tribes into a market economy that demanded increasing pressures on wild plant and animal populations, and weakened ancient human customs of community viability. In addition, trade could not be conducted in isolation. Tribes that had survived with little outside human contact were now visited often by traders from far away, traders who could bring with them the diseases of denser human aggregations, from the common cold to tuberculosis, measles, and smallpox, to name a few.

Ever-increasing technological advances that produced items for trade with more primitive tribesmen also encouraged trade within the more civilized communities themselves. Through local inventions and discoveries, communities produced novel items for which adjacent and gradually more distant markets developed. These items and natural local products could be traded for other goods in locally short supply.

Trading routes began to link markets by land and water. Goods in transit could be stolen by force of arms. Mobile pastoral tribes were skilled in arms through generations of skirmishes over grazing rights and combat with predatory animals, and could become raiders of the trade routes or soldiers hired to protect goods in transit. Warfare, which had been one duty of every man in hunting-gathering societies, developed into a profession with its own special skills and values. With military power, the strong could take from the weak whatever they desired, from caravan goods to neighboring lands. Upon invading new lands and conquering their defenders, the victors often became the ruling class, producing a powerful elite of warrior nobles.

Rulers over subject peoples could accomplish new feats of land and water management, directed toward increasing the production of life-sustaining crops. With forced labor at their command, an emerging class of engineers could drain marshes, dyke against floods, and control the scope and seasons of irrigation. The basic relationship developed and applied in these activities has been described as *command and control*, through which orders flow from the center of power and are obediently carried out through a chain of command by the lowest and least politically powerful of the people.

With this new warrior-ruler class came a new value related to wild animals. This was the value of the hunt as training for the young warrior and practice for war. For purposes of the hunt there had to be suitable beasts to pursue. Most suitable, and often available, were the large predatory mammals, but generally military rulers also restored wild populations of hoofed game that had long been considered as common community property and depleted by uncontrolled hunting by farmers and herdsmen. For rulers to impose protection of game they decreed their own, they had to maintain a continuous effort to prevent or at least control the traditional custom of free hunting and trapping within the village territory—the common lands.

Skill with weapons was a physical and social necessity for noblemen of ancient times. Success in battle depended in part on weapons practice gained in hunting, and part of the mystique of the ruler was based on his actual or supposed performance with bow and arrow, spear, sword, lance, and dagger. The particular weapon used by aristocratic hunters varied with time, place, and quarry, but all such hunting of a serious nature included two important elements: the chase and the confrontation. The chosen animal was driven by beaters, dogs, or fire, and was routed from cover and often held by dogs or nets until the huntsman could challenge, engage, and dispatch it.

Generally, in all the ancient civilizations of Eurasia, the aristocracy started training their youth for war by means of the hunt. In China, between 2000 and 3000 years ago, young boys of noble birth learned the rudiments of horsemanship and archery by riding on sheep and shooting birds and rats. Older, they hunted foxes and hares. As their skill and hardihood developed, they could be groomed for military leadership. Hunting was part of the regular training of older boys of the upper classes in most early agrarian cultures.

The concept of hunting as training for war was established as early as 4000 or 5000 years ago. A clear distinction was drawn between those sorts of hunting that were useful in this regard and those that were not. For untold thousands of years ordinary people had taken wild animals by a great variety of means, using traps, snares, nets, pitfalls, and anything else that would produce results. But for warfare these were not too pertinent. Only a particular sort of hunting was useful for training soldiers, the sort that required skill with weapons, control of assistants and mounts, demonstration of courage, and success. Success in difficult endeavors was attributable to luck, i.e., good fortune beyond the ordinary expectation. Good luck could be thought to come through the support of "the gods." The lucky warrior had supernatural support, according to the belief among his troops. His continued success built their confidence.

Records of early hunting mostly did not exist. By the time we meet the Jews of the Bible's Old Testament, about 3800 to 2200 BC, they already plant and harvest and raise sheep, goats, and cattle. They no longer hunt for a living, but their language suggests they once did. Still, the people of Israel certainly knew about hunting, because they ate hart (red deer) and roe deer. They also used slings, nets, traps and snares, bows and arrows, and pits to acquire wild protein as well as to engage in a warrior life-style. Moreover, about 2350 BC, Nimrod, founder and ruler of the Babylonian empire, became a mighty hunter and warrior-leader-conqueror, lending his name as a current synonym to "hunter." In the Apocrypha, hunters decoy partridge, snare gazelles, and regularly eat game. But most hunters were Gentiles. The New Testament says much about fishing, nothing about hunting. But Egyptian hunting records can be traced to 2025 to 2475 BC, with a government office dealing exclusively with marshes and waterfowl hunters, implying management. Early hunting records also were left by Greeks, Etruscans, and Persians (even Aztecs of Mexico).

From what records of early times do exist, we know that as sport and as exercise for war, hunting was not only the delight but also the duty of rulers. In early empires, greatness of kings was measured as much by their hunting ability as by their success in battle. With challenge as a goal of the hunt, the most dangerous animals naturally became the most sought after by the aristocracy. Although Babylonian kings hunted elephants, wild horses, and many other large animals, the lion was their favored antagonist. In Babylonia (in present-day Iraq), by destroying these ferocious beasts, the king was protecting his people, just as he would in destroying human invaders.

Evidently, the kingly duty of lion-slaying for community safety was of such symbolic importance that it had to be carried out even when lion populations had been severely reduced. The Babylonians went so far as to assure a supply of these threats to the realm by breeding lions and maintaining them in zoos until such time as they were released for use in the royal hunt.

Lions were the first choice of almost all noble huntsmen in the ancient world. And we see a clear illustration of the difference between common and elite modes of hunting in ancient Ethiopia where, instead of using a pit or some other relatively safe method to catch the lion, the noble huntsman faced the lion in its den while his followers brought the lion to madness with whips until it charged and impaled itself on his spear. Not until this moment did the lesser hunters join in to finish off the wounded prey. Even after horses or chariots were in common use, hunting dangerous animals on foot was evidently quite usual in ancient times as a demonstration of courage on the part of the aristocratic leader. The Asiatic lion was naturally distributed from southern Europe to India, but was reduced century after century by persistent human pursuit. Today only a few hundred survive in the wild in the Indian forest of Gir.

Because until quite recent times and often enough today rulers have been soldiers, and soldiers rulers, it is useful to look in more detail at ways in which organized pursuit of wild animals can benefit the hereditary soldier-ruler aristocrat. Warfare demands organization and strict governing of disciplined troops. Accordingly, the aristocratic hunt was formal. A body of procedure covered every aspect of the chase, participating huntsmen and assistants were assigned ranks and positions in the same manner as soldiers, and rigid protocol was observed. The chase promoted skill in handling mounts (chariots, horses, camels, elephants) and control of auxiliaries (falcons, dogs, cheetahs, soldiers) through appropriate communication (messengers, signal flags, and horns). The chase also demonstrated divine support through personal daring and success in dangerous encounters, and recorded success in the form of trophies as symbols of the vanquished.

Combat also demands tactical skills. The hunt leader's proficiency in this area was tested by his ability to control actions of scattered groups of disciplined men. Toward this end, systems of signaling by horn and flag reached high degrees of perfection. Appropriate signals controlled the start of the hunt and various maneuverings of groups of huntsmen, and communicated the actions of the quarry.

The aristocratic warrior needed skill not only in expertly handling groups of men and vehicles, but also steeds. The horse was inseparable from the huntsman-soldier of the ancient world. Israeli history of the Bible's Old Testament does not record use of the horse in hunting, or of the dog, although the Old Testament indicates an interest by kings in hunting, with numerous references alluding to the game sought and the weapons used to obtain it. Assyrians and Persians started using horse-drawn chariots in warfare and hunting about 4000 years ago. Later, the riding of horses was developed. From that time forward fine horsemanship often has been required for military leaders. The traditional union of spirited horse and aristocratic rider was evidently formed early and lingers today. Thoroughbred horses were introduced into Crete from Syria about the 16th century BC.

As the intensity of land use and density of human populations increased, an inevitable depletion in numbers of wild animals occurred around population centers. Rulers wanted plenty of appropriate game for their own hunting and took measures to control hunting by common people and to improve conditions for production of game. Aristocratic hunters of olden times could not travel far for their sport; hostile neighbors and slow transportation kept them confined to areas fairly close to home. Their efforts to improve and maintain their game, then, were focused on the same local region within which many of their subjects lived.

The first reaction to reduced wildlife populations would be the control of professional animal trappers and hunters, so that nearby game could be reserved for the rulers. This dramatized a basic conflict in cultural values. On the one hand the customary opinion was that use of all wildlife within the territory of the community was open equally to all members of the community; on the other hand the opinion of the ruling class was that wildlife suitable for nobility should be restricted to it. This conflict has persisted in only slightly different forms to the present day.

As royal game became scarce in ancient days, certain lands were set aside as hunting preserves for exclusive use by nobility. These preserves or parks, often called paradises in those times, were generally close to the royal dwellings and were of the choicest uncultivated land available. They were kept well supplied with a diversity of suitable game, often including species imported from afar. In Persia (present-day Iran), for instance, royal paradises were stocked with lions, tigers, boars, stags, peacocks, pheasants, wild asses, gazelles, and ostriches. Nebuchadnezzar's famous hanging gardens of Babylon were actually a hunting preserve in the form of a man-made mountain. Chinese nobility had huge parks containing elaborate hunting lodges (palaces, actually) to which the royal household in full retinue would move to devote summer months to the chase. Aristocracies of Egypt, Macedonia, Greece, and imperial Rome also had special hunting preserves, necessitated by the general increase in human populations, persistence of secret common hunting, intensity of land use, and consequent deterioration of wildlife habitats. Powerful rulers could take lands out of cultivation or settlement in order to create or enlarge their hunting grounds.

Accomplishments of rulers were remembered and recounted orally, and written when writing had been developed (about 3400 BC). But of the common people, who left no written record, we can make only some reasonable judgments. Where common people lived in settled communities, they shared common cultures and beliefs, learned orally and through experience, and were resistant to pressures from outside their communities. They maintained the ancient attitude of a degree of ownership of the territory around their villages. Their diet, largely of starchy grain, could potentially be improved by adding wild meat. Wild game increased by the establishment of royal hunting preserves, and was a constant temptation. Hunting and trapping in the common territory was an ancient right by oral tradition. That the ruler now forbade it was something new and repugnant. Common people managed to take game despite the new laws if enforcement was lax and the community supported and protected the successful hunter. This pattern of common attitude was expressed freely when no protective laws were enforced, and often surreptitiously where enforcement was severe.

Development of empires in eastern Mediterranean lands was accompanied by a change in ways that nature and the supernatural were viewed. The tribal belief was that a spirit resides in each person and also in each natural object. As with North American Indians (see chapter 1), this led to the concept that the spirit, say, of a game animal, could recognize whether that animal had or had not been properly treated with respect and propitiation as it was hunted and killed. This belief was reinforced by admonitions of the elders, and guided and constrained the hunter.

In contrast, religions that arose in the Near East during development of more complex societies began to teach that man has a spirit but that animals do not. The Judeo-Christian religion, which is most relevant to this account, produced a Bible that clearly stated that God gave humans alone a soul and, further, gave them dominion over all other creatures, which implies stewardship and which usually has been ignored.

Introduced into the comprehension of common people, such religious teachings eroded the respect and awe that had traditionally guided the prudent, respectful attitude toward wild nature. By this new teaching, if no spiritual world of game animals really existed, no retribution through bad luck or sickness could result from their mistreatment. Coming as it did from people who were powerful with their metal weapons and other amazing trade goods, such teaching could be taken as gospel.

The Mediterranean empires rose, declined, and were replaced by other imperial powers. When an empire was strong, the central power could impose military force to gain such imperial objectives as conquering new territory, and promoting and protecting trade. Violence between communities within the empire impeded both productivity and trade, so the empire promoted internal peace.

The ancient empire most relevant to this account is that of Rome, which flourished from 500 BC to about AD 500. One of the causes, if not the main one, for the decline and fall of the Roman Empire was the failure to blend economy and society, including deforestation, overgrazing, erosion, and pollution, to the natural environment. Also, the entertainment industry of Rome included the display and killing of vast numbers of animals in amphitheaters, destroying more wildlife than most other aspects of Roman culture. When Titus dedicated the Colosseum, he celebrated by having 9000 wild animals killed in 100 days; 11,000 wild animals were slaughtered to celebrate Trajan's conquest over Dacia. Many people were employed in this enterprise, resulting in the extirpation of large mammals, reptiles, and birds in the entire Mediterranean Basin.

Still, the tranquil Roman countryside provided habitat for some wild animals, and Roman law covered different sorts of human ownership of these. The landowner could be granted exclusive control of animals within his property. This provided a basis for hunting preserves for the rich. Outside these particular areas, wild animals were considered the property of no one, that is, they were common property. Long after the collapse of the Roman Empire itself in AD 476, such laws lingered in western Europe as a basis from which later legislation arose.

Bibliography

Alison, R. M. 1978. The earliest records of waterfowl hunting. Wildlife Society Bulletin 4:196–199.

Anderson, J. K. 1985. Hunting in the ancient world. University of California Press, Berkeley.

Balee, W., editor. 1998. Advances in historical ecology. Columbia University Press, New York.

Berger, A. 1928. Die Jagd aller Volker in Wandel der Zeit. Verlag Paul Parey, Berlin.

Bibby, G. 1961. Four thousand years ago. Knopf, New York.

Fagan, B. M. 1995. People of the Earth: An introduction to world prehistory. 8th edition. Harper Collins College, New York.

Graham, E. H. 1947. The land and wildlife. Oxford University Press, New York.

Halley, H. H. 1965. Halley's Bible handbook. Zondervan Publication House, Grand Rapids, MI.

Hudson, A. J. 1993. Origins of wildlife management in the western world. Pages 5–21 *in* A. W. L. Hawley, editor. Commercialization and wildlife management: Dancing with the devil. Krieger, Malabar, FL.

Hughes, J. D. 1975. Ecology in ancient civilizations. University of New Mexico Press, Albuquerque.

Ponting, C. 1992. A green history of the world: The environment and the collapse of great civilizations. St. Martin's Press, New York.

Tober, J. A. 1981. Who owns the wildlife? The political economy of conservation in nineteenth century America. Greenwood Press, Westport, CT.

Whisker, J. B. 1981. The right to hunt. North River Press, Croton-on-Hudson, NY.

Woody, T. 1949. Life and education in early societies. Macmillan, New York.

Chapter 4

MEDIEVAL EUROPE

Much of modern North American wildlife conservation has its roots in western Europe, so historical developments there are relevant for this account.

As mentioned, climatic warming melted the glaciers and raised sea levels some 10,000 years ago. That was soon followed by animal domestication and agriculture in the eastern Mediterranean region. The same climatic change in western Europe made England an island and transformed the mainland landscape from tundra to forest. The evergreen coniferous forests moved up the mountain slopes as the ice melted back, and in the lower lands was replaced by broadleaved hardwood trees such as oak and beech.

By 3000 BC Stone Age humans were beginning to be influenced by the distant discoveries in Mediterranean regions, learning to grow some of the domesticated grains and keep some of the domesticated animals. With only stone ax, wooden shovel, and shoulderblade hoe, they had only a modest ability to clear and till the soil, so their efforts were confined to regions of thin soil. The greater part of the country, where soils were rich and deep, supported such a heavy forest on such wet and clayey soils that human technology of the time could make only slow headway toward clearing. The uncultivated region of forest and marsh that began to close around the common village fields was the village common territory, called the *waste*.

The waste was a primary land resource, as important to early European economy as land under cultivation. Its products and uses were varied; firewood, honey, mushrooms, fruit, and nuts could be gathered during appropriate season, swine could be driven into the woods to fatten on acorns and beechnuts, wild game could be taken with dogs and traps. Meat in the human diet was largely from wild game, for domestic flocks and herds were small. Few sources of winter food for livestock were known at that time, and in fall all domestic animals except the breeding herd were slaughtered. Meat was preserved by pickling and smoking. Thereafter, until the first spring lamb, all fresh meat came from wild animals of the waste. From the waste too came hides and warm furs. Hunting and trapping were regular fall and winter occupations of husbandmen. That portion of the waste lying around each settlement was considered within the territorial ownership of that village, its products the common property of village residents. This concept of communal ownership is the same as that of the hunting-gathering band.

Territorial ownership in the waste could be relatively vague so long as it remained extensive relative to cultivated areas. The early European clansman presumably felt that he had part ownership in the waste and its resources. With long acceptance, his customs regarding its use became law, which was respected and considered to be apart from and above any individual. This concept of law as something above all men, even the leader, came from the early Germanic tribes and contrasted with the Asian acceptance of the ruler's word as law.

Another European cultural characteristic, widely shared with other cultures, was a belief in divine intervention in human affairs, manifested as good luck or bad. Tangible evidence of continued good luck was demonstrated by success in war, gambling, and the hunt. Ancient rites of propitiation for the slain animal were maintained basically to bolster the hunter's luck. The ancient conservation custom of killing only for useful ends was encouraged by spiritual belief. Ignored was the balancing of the kill with the ability of the prey to recover, as hunters competed with each other. Through trade, valuable natural products such as furs flowed from the more remote regions to the more settled. The closer to human settlements, the more likely that game or furbearing species of wildlife would be locally extirpated. But for long, the ancient forests of the waste supported in their immensity such creatures as the now extinct aurochs (the primaeval cow), the forest bison, the brown bear, and the red deer.

Further Mediterranean discoveries diffused north into Europe and began to change the scene. Iron was obtained from abundant ore to become widely available for axes to clear the forest and ultimately plowshares to turn the heavy forest soils. More oxen and horses were raised to pull the plows. New domesticated plants appeared from the south, notably beans and peas, adding proteins to human diets and nitrogen to farmed soils. As the forests were cleared and their rich soils farmed, human populations increased, and the extent of the waste declined. Conflicts between human groups increased.

Two thousand years ago, when imperial Rome was employing its legions to force ever more regions into its system of tribute-paying provinces, western Europe was full of vigorous barbaric tribes often at war with one another for territory and slaves. Julius Caesar and his kind brought the lands north through present-day France and England into the Roman fold, with military governments that built roads, discouraged tribal wars, and promoted trade. With the decline of Roman rule about AD 500, this measure of central governmental power faded and local autonomy, with local violence, grew. So began the Dark Ages, i.e., the Middle Ages (AD 400 to 1400) of so-called intellectual stagnation, when a year or two of peace in any locale was novel enough to record.

Rome's imperial policy of encouraging enmity between tribes (though not to excessive violence) ensured that violence would rule when imperial power withdrew. The Roman legions were a force that ensured central control, but the disciplined military strength disappeared from western Europe when Rome withdrew. The former Roman provinces of Britain and Gaul soon broke into petty states like those beyond the Roman pale. Expansion of agriculture led to greater size, wealth, and density of human populations and to increased complexity of social structure. Need for common defense against roving bands of raiders, which were a common feature of early medieval times, had led to *feudalism*—the mutually advantageous arrangement whereby commoners supported a warrior leader and his men-at-arms and were in turn protected. Each village clustered around the baronial castle, a fortress to which livestock could be driven and villagers could withdraw when under attack. Each village was almost completely dependent on its own resources, both domestic and wild, for the necessities of life.

Each small kingdom had its ruler, a baron, i.e., lord, who was personal owner of all land in his domain. By awarding land called a fief to each of his local rulers, the baron could make them vassals who, in return, would pledge their loyalty and lead a military force on his behalf. A similar arrangement, privilege in return for service, developed between the vassals and the common folk who actually lived on lands allotted to them by the king, grew the food, provided the labor needed to support the military class, and were to an extent protected from the constant threat of lawless raiders.

The king of any particular nation depended upon his local rulers to provide military defense of the realm, and was forced to leave local affairs to local rulers. Emphasis on military force drove military efficiency, and by about AD 800 the improvement of armor, stirrups, and warhorses had produced the mounted knight, well able to prevail over the unmounted, unarmed commoners of his domain. Vassals had to provide a certain number of knights to serve the baron for a certain number of days. A vassal divided his own fief for his knights. The church, too, owned large fiefs and was part of the feudal system. For centuries the local rulers, the barons, enjoyed freedom from control by their central government and from any constraint on their domination of the local commoners who depended on them for protection. An oral tradition, presumably, kept alive the ancient concept that any injured person could appeal to the king for justice, but it would be centuries more before the kingly power in western Europe was adequate to affect the common welfare. Feudalism began in the 700s, reached its peak in the 800s to 1200s, and began to disappear by the 1400s.

Rough protection was better than none, so human populations increased, and more and larger villages were established. As cultivated land and meadow became commonplace, forest and marsh shrank. What had been apparently endless areas of waste were now reduced by human encroachment. Thus, within a few centuries the seemingly endless broad-leaved forests of western Europe were transformed into a landscape not very different from that of today.

Extensive conversion of the natural forest to farm and meadow had marked effects upon wild animals. The creatures of the deep forest lost habitat and came into contact with humans more often as the shrunken forest was used ever more intensively for fattening swine and gathering wood as well as for hunting. And now the forest-dwelling animals had more opportunity than before to venture forth and feed upon cultivated crops (red deer, forest bison, aurochs) or prey upon domestic animals (bear and wolf). The larger forest animals were steadily reduced by human predation and shrinkage of habitat. For example, the European bison and aurochs (or wild cattle) were abundant in European forests of AD 500, being caught in pitfalls. But over the next centuries the aurochs declined as loss of its habitat continued and hunting pressure increased. The last wild aurochs were gone by about AD 1500 and the forest bison barely survives under protection today.

On the other hand, increased habitat was provided for a whole new fauna of the forest edge and open land. Animals which had been characteristic of the warmer south now began to spread into the newly opened northern lands or were introduced; fallow deer, pheasants, partridges, rabbits, and a host of other species extended their ranges northward.

In addition to augmenting the food supply, wildlife supplied other material benefits to the economy. Hunting brought in hides and furs that were put to innumerable uses. Cold stone manor houses and castles, designed for military defense, were made livable in winter for the ruling class with skins of bears, wolves, and bison. Furs served as rugs and coverings of every sort. Layers of skins piled on the floor were both bed and bedding in a medieval castle. Leather was used for clothing and equipment, and clothing of the warrior rulers and their kin was made of fur or heavily decorated with it.

As in ancient times, the desires of warrior rulers gave rise to specialized uses of the hunt, which aimed at developing the essential soldierly qualities in young noblemen, as well as the pageantry proper for elite activities, as is well reflected for us in many medieval paintings, tapestries, and other artworks. The material objective of the hunt for the medieval aristocrat could be the killing of a game animal or the destruction of a predator threatening the villagers and their peaceful flocks. In either case it entailed pursuit with dogs, maneuvering bodies of men with bugle calls, and finally bringing the animal to bay. This amounted to immobilizing the prey until the noble huntsman could arrive and personally engage it. The quintessence of this was the slaying of the adult male boar, a formidable animal. To dismount, take the boar spear, and approach this maddened animal with proper demeanor called forth all those qualities of control and courage that constituted the aristocratic ideal, an ideal that the American author Ernest Hemingway, centuries later, was to describe as "grace under pressure."

In addition to the male wild boar, suitable aristocratic game in Europe included the adult male red deer (the stag), large forest bovids (bison and wild ox), the brown bear, and the wolf. In the elaborate hunting parlance of the time, animals unsuitable by virtue of season, class, age, or sex were dismissed as "folly" or "rascal." This division of game into suitable and unsuitable prey and other associated hunting protocol required a special vocabulary, mastery of which was indeed one of the marks of the aristocrat.

By AD 1100 the clearing of new land for cultivation had proceeded so far that enough waste no longer existed for all traditional community use. Large "aristocratic" game especially needed extensive areas of woods, and as trees on common lands were cut, the royal sport suffered.

Rulers wanted game to hunt, and their subjects wanted game to hunt and to eat, causing conflict. The customary law of the village was that the village waste was open to all villagers for their traditional uses. In England, such lands were termed "commons." The game of the commons traditionally belonged to the village members because of their customary access to the land on which the game was found. According to this concept, community ownership of the common land gave every member of the community the right to take game into possession from the commons. This meant that as the village population grew, and the waste or commons was more intensively used, competition between co-owners for game increased. Under this system, game declined as human populations and intensity of land use increased. Nevertheless, the concept of common ownership in and access to game still remained in the minds of the common people.

Rulers adopted a legal remedy for the decline of game; they harked back to the ownership of all lands by the king. The wording varied in different nations of western Europe, but the effect was the same; the king was owner of the kingdom, as lord proprietor. This concept was at variance with the customary laws of local communal ownership and also with the feudal contract under which the ruler had no legal rights other than those mutually agreed upon by all parties. The assumption of land under the concept of lord proprietorship flourished best, therefore, when the ruler was strong and able to impose his will in the face of opposition from commoners; preempted domains were maintained largely by military strength. William the Conqueror, for example, considered himself lord proprietor of the England he conquered in 1066. With his Norman warriors, he took over existing wild habitats for his royal sport and set aside new ones, evicting the human inhabitants. Like other rulers of the time, he shared his owner's prerogatives with his military commanders, who thus could act as owners of their estates under his favor. The royal hunting grounds were called *forests*, while those of the lesser aristocracy were called *chases*; both were protected from common hunters ("poachers" now) by special guardians and severe penalties. In addition, game preferred by the ruling class was forbidden to common hunters wherever it occurred. This so-called "royal" or "high" game included all the larger wild mammals.

Despite establishment of royal forests such as the real Sherwood Forest in the 1100s of mythical Robin Hood fame, in those early days much ground still existed in common ownership, used jointly by local people for, among other things, taking wildlife not specifically reserved by the ruler. There, bird netters, rabbit snarers, fur trappers, and their friends could legally enjoy pursuit of smaller game. The common person, then, could be a legal taker of much wildlife on the common lands, but a poacher if he took royal game or took any game in the royal forest.

An important difference can be traced between deterrents to poaching in England and on the continent. With his successful invasion of England from Normandy in 1066, William brought with him the punishments for poaching that were familiar in his homeland: hanging, blinding, maiming, and the like. But while such punishment characterized game protection on the continent for another five centuries or so, in England a steady reduction in their severity occurred. By the time of the Magna Carta (1215), no person could be deprived of life or limb for poaching; deterrents continued to become milder. The written record of medieval times is the work of the rulers and, more notably, their chroniclers, the common folk being largely illiterate and otherwise employed.

But some measure of reaction of the common people to rule from above—the rule of command and control—can be read between the chronicler's lines.

King Henry reigned in England two centuries after the Norman conquest of 1066, entrusting care of the extensive royal forests to his forest officers. If tenants or neighbors of the forest transgressed strict rules protecting forest trees and game, the duty of forest officers was to arrest and fine them. But to discover the facts, forest officers had to inquire among the four townships surrounding the site of the crime, townships charged with providing witnesses as part of their common responsibility. The community had various ways to protect its citizens from the enforcers of King Henry's law, mainly by neighboring townships reporting no knowledge of any transgressions, even though evidence had been found in the king's forest.

On the one hand is the local community, loyal to its members up to what is an accepted point. On the other is legal authority. At this time and place, a person who was convicted of killing a deer in the king's forest was heavily fined or, if he could not pay (which was common), was bound in prison for a year and a day. Then, if he could find pledges for his fine, he could come out free, but if not, he was exiled from the kingdom.

If the community considered the punishment excessive, it did not support the law. Laws not widely supported are of little effect. The community opinion is of central importance in matters of what is considered a crime, and what is accepted by the community as proper punishment. If the community does not accept the directives from above, it can often find ways to evade their dictates. And if the strength of the organized or integrated community is engaged in preserving and guarding what the community regards as its own, whether individual or community property, it has considerable likelihood of success.

For a medieval member of the upper class, the "terms of venery," i.e., the act, art, or sport of hunting, were part of his youthful instruction, a knowledge that marked him as one of "gentle breeding," the ancestor of the English "gentleman" of a later time. The gentlemanly code prescribed the proper, socially acceptable way of doing practically everything. It served as a bond of recognition within the upper class and a source of reprobation when the code was violated. Where the code applied to the human taking of wild game, it clearly restricted the hunter to "fair chase" of approved prey, and censured the common man's snare, net, and trap. The English sporting code has continued to guide opinion on what is and is not proper taking of wildlife to the present day. In its defense, its practical effect is to enhance the sporting, challenging aspect of hunting. At the same time, it is contemptuous of many traditional ways of taking game that are an appropriate part of many local cultures.

The tendency of aristocrats to control poaching by force might have been weakened in England by the potential of common people to retaliate. One may suppose that the longbow and the bodkin-pointed (armor-piercing) arrow had something to do with curbing the violence of noblemen. Developed first in Wales, the powerful longbow required long muscular training for its draw, training that was encouraged and required for military purposes by English rulers. English archers massacred the armored knights of France at Crecy in 1346, Poitiers in 1356, and Agincourt in 1415, and so perhaps gave pause to English knights at home, tempering their violence toward common poachers.

When deterrents slacken, poaching goes on apace, since the ancient and traditional values of hunting excitement and food-getting can then guide human behavior with reasonable safety. And to these older values, another can be added: revenge against overbearing rulers. Legislation, however stringent, has no effect on the poacher unless its enforcement is accurate, swift, and ruthless. It appeared that the rulers of England could not afford to be ruthless, just as the leaders of a modern nation under representative government cannot afford, for long, to be ruthless.

Nevertheless, English legislators continued their efforts to reserve hunting rights for the ruling class. These efforts were supported by the continued transfer of ownership of common lands into privileged hands. Legislation supporting this process was justified by the undoubted fact that the production of food and fiber was more efficient under large well-capitalized ownership than under common subsistence ownership, and by the fact that an island nation often at war needed self-sufficiency.

The concept of husbandry of wild animals gained strength as wildlife habitat came to be more under private control. The lawyers argued that although theoretically wildlife belongs to the Crown, no one really owns it, so anyone exercising the right of ownership over it by curtailing its natural freedom, supplementing its food supply, or protecting it from predators establishes a title to it which converts it more or less into a domestic animal.

This introduced a new legal concept from which it was but a step to the assumption that only a person of substance could own wildlife. Passed about 1400, the Game Law of England prohibited anyone who did not own land worth at least 40 shillings a year from taking or destroying other gentlemen's game. So, for the first time in England, wealth became a prerequisite to hunting rights.

The common man of Europe had a long tradition of preying on wild animals. The series of legislative measures which culminated in the Game Laws of England had reduced by degrees both the commoner's hunting ground *and* his hunting right. By the 13th century in England, most manorial lords had obtained from the king a grant of *free-warren*, which prevented anyone from entering their lands for hunting and fishing. But as the rulers erected legal barriers to protect game for their own use, common hunters continued their customary hunting and trapping, though now illegal. The 14th century saw several peasant uprisings, which were attempts to improve the commoner's life by regaining common lands and ancient rights. In 1381, Wat Tyler spoke for the uprising that he led when he insisted that all forest and game laws be repealed. All warrens, woods, waters, and parks were to be part of the commons, for all, rich and poor, to use for hunting, fishing, and hawking. They hanged him, of course, but these demands reflect the peasant conviction that hunting and fishing should be common rights.

Over ensuing centuries, the political position of the English commoner gradually improved, and as it did, the penalties for poaching became milder and therefore less of a deterrent. Although poaching was legally a crime, in practice it became something of a rural sport. Poaching was widespread in England through the Renaissance (14th to 16th centuries) and beyond, and under only mild control; it was also a problem for the aristocratic landowners of continental Europe, who continued to rely on deterrents of the severest sort.

It was severe exercise of police power by continental aristocrats, one supposes, that led eventually in France to revolution and the termination there of aristocratic control over the hunting of wild game. But the effects of a violent revolution upon wildlife are often catastrophic. The widespread distribution of weapons, the citizens' impatience with any restraint, perhaps even some feeling that the hitherto protected animals themselves represent the hated former rulers, all combine to ensure a period of slaughter. In France, the predictable result held true in the period following the Revolution (1789 to 1799); species especially vulnerable by reason of their habitats or their value were locally exterminated and populations of all other species useful for food or fur were seriously reduced.

Throughout most of the remainder of Europe, however, land and hunting continued to be controlled to a large degree by the ruling class. One positive consequence of this was the maintenance of wildlife habitat and the protection of game populations from human predation. Most large mammals survived somewhere in Europe: forest bison, brown bear, wild boar, red deer (elk), moose, wolf, etc.; only the wild ox (aurochs) and forest horse (tarpan) became extinct.

Feudalism began to disappear partly due to a remarkable invention that altered the social system and wildlife populations not only of Europe, but also of North America and throughout the world. The ancient pre-Christian Chinese invented it in the 800s, and it spread westward through contact with Arabs, eventually reaching Europe in the 1200s. It was a mixture of charcoal, sulphur, and saltpeter (potassium nitrate). Gunpowder.

The first guns were cannonlike weapons used by Arabs in North Africa during the 1300s. The feudalism of Europe relied partly on stone castles to defend the estates of aristocrats. These castles could not withstand assault from heavy cannonballs fired by gunpowder.

As Europe moved from feudalism toward a more modern mercantile culture, ownership of extensive land holdings (estates) and high social rank were tied together. As money became more important, land came more and more under ownership of a new aristocracy of wealth acquired from development of trade, manufacture, and ultimately colonialism. From small beginnings in the 1500s, the maritime nations of western Europe began to prosper; among the most prosperous, by virtue of money to invest, were large landowners. Estates were managed to protect and increase game. Game hunting continued to be a high-status pursuit. Estates also were managed to improve agriculture, livestock, and forestry in a way compatible with game. For three centuries European estate owners generally were those who could afford to manage their lands for both amenity and material return. In aristocratic families, generation after generation grew up with a keen interest in sport and nature, grounded in the husbandry of crops and animals.

Bibliography

Baillie-Grohman, W. A. 1925. Sport in art: An iconography of sport during four hundred years from the beginning of the fifteenth to the end of the eighteenth centuries. Blom, New York.

Balee, W., editor. 1998. Advances in historical ecology. Columbia University Press, New York.

Bennett, H. S. 1948. Life on the English manor. Cambridge University Press, Cambridge, England.

Bise, G. 1978. Medieval hunting scenes ("The hunting book" by Gasten Phoebus). Productions Liber SA, Fribourg-Geneve.

Bubenik, A. B. 1976. Evolution of wildlife harvesting systems in Europe. Transactions of the Federal-Provincial Wildlife Conference 40:97–105.

Buchanan, B. J., editor. 1996. Gunpowder: The history of an international technology. Bath University Press, Bath, UK.

Cabart, J. 1957. Outline of the development of hunting law on the territory inhabited by the western slavs. Vedecke Prace. Vyckumncho Ustavu, Lasa A. Myslivosti. Ve Zbaslavi, Csazv.

Chalmers, P. R. 1936. The history of hunting. Lippincott, Philadelphia.

Clagett, M. 1954. The medieval heritage: Economy, society, polity. *In* Chapters in western civilization. Volume 1, 2nd edition. Columbia University Press, New York.

Crosby, A. W. 1986. Ecological imperialism: The biological expansion of Europe, 900–1900. Cambridge University Press, New York.

Dagg, A. I. 1979. Wildlife management in Europe. Otter Press, Waterloo, Ontario.

Dahmus, J. H. 1968. Middle Ages: A popular history. Gollancz, London.

Faulkener, W. G. 1596. Hawking, hunting, fowling, and fishing, with the true measures of blowing. Reprinted 1972. Da Capo Press, New York.

Garnier, R. M. 1895. Annals of the British peasantry. Svan, Sonnenschein, London.

Hall, B. S. 1997. Weapons and warfare in renaissance Europe: Gunpowder, technology, and tactics. Johns Hopkins University Press, Baltimore.

Harper, F. 1945. Extinct and vanishing mammals of the Old World. Special Publication Number 12, American Commission for International Wildlife Protection, New York Zoological Park.

Hemingway, E. 1954. The sun also rises. Scribner, New York.

Herlihy, D. J. 1980. Attitudes towards the environment in medieval society. Pages 100–116 *in* L. J. Bilsky, editor. Historical ecology: Essays on environment and social change. Kennikat Press, Port Washington, NY.

Hudson, R. J. 1993. Origins of wildlife management in the western world. Pages 5–21 *in* A. W. L. Hawley, editor. Commercialization and wildlife management: Dancing with the devil. Krieger, Malabar, FL.

Larson, L. M. 1935. The earliest Norwegian laws: Being the Gulathing law and the Frostathing law. Columbia University Press, New York.

Leopold, A. 1933. Game management. Scribner, New York.

Strutt, J. 1898. The sports and pastimes of the people of England. Chatto and Winders, London.

Taber, R. D. 1961. Wildlife administration and harvest in Poland. Journal of Wildlife Management 25:353–363.

Thompson, J. W. 1931. History of the middle ages. Norton, New York.

White, L., Jr. 1962. Medieval technology and social change. Clarendon Press, Oxford, England.

White, T. H. 1936. England have my bones. Putnam, New York.

Wolf, M. L. 1995. An historical perspective on the European system of wildlife management. Pages 254–263 *in* W. F. Sigler, editor. Wildlife law enforcement. 4th edition. Brown, Dubuque, IA.

Chapter 5

EUROPEAN TRADE AND EXPLORATION

From about AD 800 to 1100, Scandinavia—Norway, Sweden, and Denmark—made up the leading sea power of Europe in an era when the English, French, and southern Europeans scarcely sailed beyond sight of land. Even without aid of compass—not invented until the late 12th century by the Chinese—the Scandinavians were comparable in navigation only to the Polynesians in the Pacific. The Scandinavians sailed to the Faroes even before AD 800, to Iceland by 870, to Greenland around 985, and finally about the year 1000 farther west into North America, where Leif Ericsson landed in Newfoundland. Attempts to establish a colony in North America from about 1000 to 1014 at L'Anse aux Meadows, Newfoundland, were repelled by Inuit or American Indians, who thus would enjoy American isolation for almost another 500 years without major impact on their own populations or the wildlife resource.

Since the failed Viking attempt to establish in North America, it remained undiscovered by Europeans until the Spanish supported the Italian Christoforo Colombo (Christopher Columbus) who "discovered" and laid claim to the "Indies," i.e., the West Indies in 1492. Five years later the English supported another Italian, Giovanni Caboto (John Cabot), who "rediscovered" the island of Newfoundland in 1497. In 1534, Jacques Cartier entered the Gulf of St. Lawrence and made the French claim to Canada. Thus began the decline and demise of aboriginals, estimated at 2 million to 10 million north of Mexico, and many wildlife populations, as Europeans colonized and spread throughout North America.

Following the early Scandinavian explorations, other coastal European nations became more proficient sailors and harvesters of the sea. By about 1400 much legal access to wildlife as game in western Europe was controlled by the ruling class, but common property in oceanic wildlife still prevailed. While terrestrial wildlife was protected and managed by landowners aiming toward sustained material satisfaction as well as nonmaterial satisfactions of the hunt, oceanic wildlife was sought with immediate material satisfaction in mind, since fish, seals, and whales were free to whoever could take them.

On the western coast of Europe the development of trade and a cash economy opened the way for capital investment in expanded whaling efforts. With enough financial support from investors, special whaling ships could be built equipped with boats from which whales were harpooned. Such ships had facilities for treating and storing commercial products such as blubber and whalebone, and provided a crew and supplies for long voyages. The stockholders in the enterprise, the investors, naturally wanted the greatest short-term financial return. Their aim was immediate material satisfaction. The result was competition, ship by ship, nation by nation in the North Atlantic where whales and their prey were abundant due to cold water rich in oxygen.

Oceanic opportunities were demonstrated by entrepreneurs such as the Basque whalers who, by 1540, were operating off Newfoundland and Labrador, where they built whaling stations between 1550 and 1600 for the valuable whale oil that provided illumination in that era, and for the tough and springy whalebone (baleen). Returning to their homestead in the Basque region of Spain and France, they brought not only oil and whalebone, but tales of furs to be had by trade with the natives. By the early 1700s hundreds of ships from various European nations were involved.

Inuit had been harpooning whales in leads, or openings in the ice pack, and Indians of the northwest coast had been whaling from cedar boats. Over centuries the numbers of whales taken in all these efforts contributed to human welfare in terms of meat, fat, oil, baleen, and bone. The impact of the hunt on the large populations of whales was negligible.

The one species of great whale not associated seasonally with polar waters, although it can be found there, is the sperm whale of temperate and tropical oceans. The sperm whale dives to great depths in its pursuit of prey like the giant squid or cuttlefish, and has a blunt profile due to the presence of a large case, or receptacle, filled with oily matter that is thought to be an adaptation for the changes in water pressure associated with deep feeding. Sperm oil, actually a liquid wax, proved even more valuable than whale oil, and a mysterious product called ambergris much more valuable yet. Ambergris is a waxy secretion in the intestine of sperm whales; it is most profitably used in manufacture of perfumes.

Through the early 1700s sperm whales were hunted on a small scale along the eastern coast of North America by English colonists who were learning how to deal with this large aggressive creature. In mid-century the King of England declared a bonus, or bounty, for successful colonial whalers in an effort to encourage his minions to catch up to the successfully whaling Dutch. This made the hunt more profitable, so whalers ventured farther in their search. By 1800 New England whalers were hunting sperm whales in the far Pacific.

In 1557 English traders were hopeful of discovering a northeast passage to China—the reverse of the successful Portuguese route along the African coast—and prepared to trade English woolen goods along the way as they sailed north and reached the White Sea. On the voyage they made two fruitful discoveries. One was the abundance of Atlantic right whales around Spitzbergen. The other was the eagerness of the Russians to trade furs for woolen goods.

Through the following centuries, north Atlantic whales were avidly pursued, mainly by the English and Dutch. In 1600 one Dutch whaler returned over 200% profit from baleen and oil in a single voyage. Not surprisingly, the preferred right whales (which floated when dead, and thus were the "right" whales) and then other species gradually declined, being slow breeders, not to fully recover in modern times even under full protection.

European Trade and Exploration

Commercial exploration led repeatedly to the discovery and subsequent commercial exploitation and extirpation of wildlife. Whales belonged to whatever group of humans could control access to them, and so were the property of the rulers of whaling nations, soon including England and Holland. Each European coastal nation had a number of economic whaling units consisting of sources of capital plus the ships and crews such capital could equip and support for the voyage. Each national ruler could benefit from successful whaling enterprises by demanding a share in the profits but could not control competition between whaling units for the largest catch. Obviously it was most profitable for each investment group to have its ships catch as many whales as possible over the shortest period of time. The money so gained could then be reinvested in whaling if that showed the most promise, or some quite different venture. Competition between different groups for a common resource will eventually reduce that resource to what might be termed *commercial extinction*, that low level at which it no longer attracts investor capital. If a wildlife population is reduced to commercial extinction, it might survive, or it might be in such a narrow bottleneck of numbers that adverse factors gradually drain it toward extinction, such as inbreeding depression or inability to locate mates in the vastness of the oceans, especially for slow breeders (e.g., blue whales). Untroubled by such concerns, early whalers simply looked for new populations to hunt when old ones declined.

People then sought immediate material satisfaction, resulting in the well-financed liquidation of a vulnerable wildlife resource for maximum profit without concern for long-term consequences. Whereas the tribesman in olden times might have been constrained from excessive killing by customary conservative doctrines within his tribe, the capitalist, something new, was not socially constrained. In fact, his nation (say England) might applaud his heavy exploitation of whales as an aid to dominance over a competing rival nation (say Holland) also taking whales.

In addition to discovering right whales, English merchants voyaging to the White Sea discovered Russians eager to trade furs for woolen goods. Hitherto, the route by which furs reached the English market was by way of the Baltic Sea, a route controlled by profit-seeking middlemen. By taking the White Sea route around northern Scandinavia, the English could barter directly with the Russians for furs, obtain more for their trade goods, and vastly increase their profits in the home market.

During the same era in their far northwest, the Russians also were exploring new territories for fur. They moved across Siberia, exhausting a variety of local furbearers as they went. By the early 1700s they reached and began to explore the Bering Sea region. When their first Bering Sea expedition was shipwrecked, they turned to wildlife to support themselves in their extremity, and completely destroyed the species that had saved their lives, the gigantic sea cow. The history of the first exploration of those northern waters comes down to us from the expedition naturalist, young Wilhelm Steller. Wrecked on an island off Kamchatka in 1741, the Russians providentially discovered huge manatees, up to 24 feet long, placidly browsing on marine plants in shallow water offshore. They were easy to catch and each Steller's sea cow, as they came to be called, provided a huge amount of meat. The expedition survived the winter. Thereafter, each sea cow, up to the very last, was worth a determined effort to kill it for meat, and was easy to find along its shoreline habitat. Within 20 years the Steller's sea cow had been hunted to extinction.

The Russian fur harvest was under central control, and had potential for a husbandry of the fur resource so that a sustained annual take to sell in China could potentially have been maintained. But even under a complete monopoly, the desire of local managers for the highest possible annual catch overrode long-term considerations. By pushing farther and farther, the Russians attempted to maintain their annual harvest of fur. Even with an eventual expansion into Alaska and south to present day California, they could not maintain a profitable harvest and so withdrew.

Having killed the last Steller's sea cow, the Russians continued their explorations of the Bering Sea during the 1700s and discovered the island breeding rookeries of the northern fur seal and the populations of sea otter along the coasts of the Aleutian Islands and southward along the coast of North America. Fur seal and sea otter skins were valuable in trade. Because the sea otter's pelt is the epitome of warmth and beauty, it was especially esteemed by the prosperous (and suspicious) Chinese, who let the Russians trade at a single post, Kiakhta, from the 1730s.

In 1768 the English sent Captain James Cook on a voyage of exploration to the Pacific. An accomplished navigator and cartographer, he explored widely on this and two more expeditions, fixing many a coast and island on the world map and observing and recording the natural world. First published in 1784, Cook's record brought to the commercial world detailed information on the exact location and approximate abundance of the baleen whales of the Antarctic, the fur seals of the south Atlantic, and the sea otter of the northwest coast of North America. Further, Cook told how eager the American Indians of the coastal northwest were to trade sea otter pelts for any scrap of metal, and then how these pelts proved extraordinarily valuable in the Chinese port of Canton.

It was said that the sea otter pelt was worth its weight in gold. Along the coast from the Aleutians southward, its commercial hunt was first pursued by the Russians, who pushed south from Alaska in search of fur, ultimately appearing in California. This was perceived as a threat by the ruler of Spain who was the putative owner of California. By 1745 to 1765 Russian probes had concerned the government of Spain enough to order its Mexican colonial government to develop settlements and ports in California. Among other things, these served the ships from Spanish holdings in the Philippines. Perhaps through Cook's report, by 1784 Spanish colonial administrators in California in their turn became alert to the potential value of sea otters in the China trade. They envisioned an exchange between sea otter pelts flowing to China and mercury flowing to the New World for use in gold mining. For the next half century, the local authorities in California attempted to keep other nationals from exploiting the California sea otter population.

Keeping competing forces at bay when there was so much money to be made was impossible. Spain had a sort of claim to the Puget Sound region by virtue of early exploration, but by the 1790s Boston vessels were there, freely pursuing a lucrative triangular trade. Stocking up in Boston with copper or brass plates (known as "clicks") worth $1.50 apiece, they sailed around Cape Horn or through the Straits of Magellan and north to the Pacific Northwest coast. There they traded five clicks for a good sea otter pelt worth $50 in the Chinese port of Canton, their next destination. The money obtained for pelts was immediately invested in a valuable cargo of silk, tea, porcelain, and the like, to be transported back to Boston or to Europe and sold at an extremely healthy profit.

By the early 1800s Yankee skippers were contracting with the Russians, still established at Sitka, for Aleut hunters in Russian employ to take sea otters directly and so eliminate the need to trade for pelts. In 1811 some 8000 sea otter skins were taken in this cooperative effort. That same year, while Mexico was revolting against Spain, and California was cut off from supplies, an American ship with a cargo from China turned up and enjoyed a good exchange with local dignitaries for (illegal) pelts taken from sea otter populations supposedly guarded in central and southern California. In 1822 the revolution ended and Mexico was independent; the Mexican governor of California, then part of Mexico, thought of collaborating with the Russians in an otter-China trade that might help support his government. This was actually in effect until 1829 when the Russians became reluctant to share the profits. Meanwhile Mexican citizens were free to hunt, and American trappers were beginning to filter in to become citizens. But while the shore-based otter hunting could be controlled to some degree and conservation regulations such as protection of pups were in force, a final threat appeared. Otter pirates operating out of Hawaii raided the California coasts, and in a few years too few sea otters remained to repay the harvest effort. In 1841 the Russians abandoned their southernmost port, Ft. Ross, on the coast of northern California because the local supply of marine mammals (not only sea otters but also fur seals) was exhausted by overhunting. The discovery of California gold in 1848 probably diverted potential otter poachers. Even so, the California sea otter was thought to be extinct by the end of the century.

Fortunately, reports of its demise were premature and a surviving population has been growing. A contemporary threat is oil, which mats otter fur, subjecting the otter to body heat loss to the cold sea. Oil on the sea comes from offshore drilling and from accidental spills. In 1989 the oil tanker *Exxon Valdez* grounded and leaked in Prince William Sound off the coast of Alaska, killing an estimated 5500 sea otters.

One of Captain Cook's observations, interesting to investors, was of the abundance of fur seals and elephant seals (giant seals) on their rookeries on islands off the southern tip of South America, and the south island of New Zealand. Duly published, this led to a sort of fur seal and elephant seal rush. Unlike whaling, which required special skills and equipment to catch and process the whale, seal hunting required only that the hunter get to the rookery. With only modest investments needed, many ships participated. Between 1820, when large-scale sealing began in the southern Atlantic islands of South Georgia and the south Shetlands, and 1825, the southern fur seal and the elephant seal (taken for oil) had been reduced by American sealers, among others, to commercial extinction. In only two seasons, 1820 to 1821 and 1821 to 1822, 90 vessels had taken 1,520,000 fur seals and 940 tons of elephant seal oil. Thenceforth, only a little local hunting kept populations of southern fur seals and Juan Fernandez fur seals (once thought to be extinct) and southern elephant seals at low population levels.

By 1825 the concentration of whaling efforts had been in the Pacific for 15 years. Some 640 U.S. whalers and many from other countries hunted there for the California gray whale, among others. Whalers long at sea and hungry for fresh food found that the huge Galapagos tortoise, being cold-blooded, would stay alive for a long time without food or water, so they took these tortoises aboard as a nonperishable supply of fresh meat. A search of the logbooks of 79 New England whalers who touched at the Galapagos in the early 1800s for this purpose shows that they took off 10,373 tortoises. Much depleted, the Galapagos tortoises escaped complete extinction at this time only because commercial exploitation had made them too difficult to find.

By the 1840s the western coastline of North America was beginning to support American immigrants. The overland flow was mightily augmented by shipborne immigrants during the gold rush in 1849, during which California became a state of the United States. Many a whaling ship bound for the north Pacific was abandoned when its crew jumped ship in San Francisco Bay. But after a few years whaling in the north Pacific was resumed. Two species of baleen whales migrated seasonally into the rich waters of the north Pacific: California gray whale and bowhead whale. Both had been hunted for centuries by Inuit, American Indians, and Aleuts of Canada and the United States.

Commercial whalers reduced the populations of the California gray whale and pushed farther north in pursuit of the bowhead, penetrating the Bering Sea in 1840. Commercial whaling continued thereafter for some 30 years. Providentially for the whales, the investors who supported whaling were faced with a dilemma in the late 1800s. Steam was replacing sail, and such nations as Norway, with few natural resources, were investing in efficient new whaling ships. With investment opportunities of many sorts, the United States found further whaling ventures unprofitable not only because they would require a major shipbuilding effort but also because whale oil, widely used for illumination, was being replaced by the petroleum product kerosene (or in British terms, parafine). As whaling by the United States declined in the north Pacific, the California gray whale began its recovery. The bowhead whale that summered in the shallow Chukchi Sea of the north continued to be taken in a small way by Inuit hunters in the open leads of the spring ice. This modest use of an already depleted population could theoretically keep that population at a low level, but in actual fact this has not been demonstrated for the bowhead.

Two other oceanic mammals of the north Pacific had been pursued incidental to whaling and also fishing. These were the northern fur seal and the sea otter.

European Trade and Exploration 51

Though threat from whalers declined through the late 1800s, the threat from fishermen increased as commercial fishing efforts of the United States, Canada, Japan, and Russia grew ever stronger. In addition, it took but a small investment to join in the fur seal and sea otter hunts. Continued competitive pressure on fur seal and sea otter populations raised concerns in the United States and Canada that by the early 1900s resulted in one of the early attempts to achieve sustained rather than immediate material gain, the Fur Seal Treaty (see chapter 14).

A wildlife population reduced to commercial extinction is not worth investing in intensive exploitation. It can experience one of three outcomes:
1. The remaining population might be so valuable and vulnerable that it becomes extinct through small-scale harvest (e.g., Steller's sea cow) or inbreeding.
2. The remaining population might be kept at a low level from continued light use by local humans or other predators, as appears to be the case with the bowhead whale of the North Pacific, or inability to locate mates (e.g., the blue whale).
3. The remaining protected population might recover to higher, more secure levels. This is the case with the California gray whale. It once appeared to be the case with the fur seal and the sea otter, but the modern threats of oil spills and commercial fishing nets leaves the question open.

The mammals yielding up their valuable pelts were many, including lynx, fox, sable, beaver, and ermine. Of these, the beaver, being an herbivore, existed naturally in the most dense and productive populations. In addition, it was easy to locate by its dams, cuttings, and lodge. Hence, beaver was a mainstay of the fur trade. When sumptuary laws limited the use of fur to adorn men's clothing according to social class (fur-wearing being largely a masculine prerogative in medieval days and beyond), but left the matter of fur hats to the wearer's discretion, the terms *beaver* and *hat*, in England, became synonymous. With increasing prosperity in western Europe, the value of furs increased, and hence the pressure on populations of furbearing animals. This led the Russians to push farther and farther east through Siberia in search of more animals. It also increased the value of the few furs that western European fishermen and whalers were then obtaining from the natives of North America.

Captain Cook was a busy man, leaving his mark wherever he went. In 1778 his explorations took him to the Hawaiian Islands, opening the way to the extinction of 90% of the indigenous species of birds, most noteworthy the majority of the 28 species of Hawaiian honeycreepers found nowhere else, mostly from massive habitat destruction probably combined with the introduction of predators such as mongoose and roof (black) rat, a mosquito capable of carrying avian diseases, and various other introduced species (870 plants, 2000 invertebrates, 80 vertebrates). Cook annoyed the Hawaiians and so they killed him the next year. The islands already had been populated by Polynesians who themselves had eliminated some species of honeycreepers by habitat destruction, hunting for food and feathers, and the inadvertent importation of Polynesian rats.

The vicissitudes of European trade influenced wildlife populations in quite another way, through the rise of oceanic exploration and contact with naive island life. In Roman times a lively shipborne commerce existed across the Mediterranean linking land and sea routes to India and China. With the rise and expansion of Islam, from about 700 AD, and the closing of Near East ports to Europeans, new land routes were developed around the northern shore of the Mediterranean, linking Italy to the bazaars of Constantinople, where, among much else, the dried musk gland of the Asian musk deer used for making perfume could be found. Prospering, Italy emerged early into the Renaissance. A drive to promote the Islamic religion pressed on, and in 1453 Constantinople fell, closing the European trade link to the Orient.

Southern Europeans were anxious to reestablish trade with the "Indies," and had a good idea by this time that the world was round; they sailed west from ports in Portugal and Spain. While the Portuguese explored ever farther along the coast of Africa, bringing home elephant ivory, the Spanish supported the Italian navigator Columbus in his due-westward voyage, and laid claim to the West Indies in 1492. In 1493, the pope arbitrated competing claims between these two nations by decreeing that "new" lands east of a north-south line 100 leagues west of the Azores should belong to Portugal, and those west to Spain.

Secure in the papal blessing, the Portuguese pressed on around Africa to the great island of Madagascar, north along the eastern African coast, and then, no doubt with guidance from Arabian navigators, sailed across the Indian Ocean, first reaching the Asian trading ports they sought by 1498. Soon regular sailing routes were developed for an increasing commercial traffic. Since no small sailing ship of the time could travel far without stopping for water, wood, meat, and often repairs, convenient landing places were sought along the way. Islands with fresh water and harborage were ideal. If such an island also supported large flightless edible birds, so much the better.

Some wild creatures are considered to be abundant if commonly seen. But some wild creatures are relatively tame, easily seen, and not particularly abundant. Most such cases occur on islands or in remote mainland regions not frequented by humans. On islands particularly, flightless birds evolved in the absence of predatory mammals—birds such as the great auk, the dodo, and the moa. On islands, too, seals breeding and nursing young are protected from the mammalian flesh-eaters of the mainland.

It was only when ships went far to sea on missions of exploration and trade that islands large and small could be reached by humans. For the mariner, large naive birds and mammals invited unrestricted harvest as the rewards of immediate material satisfaction. Most of the extinction of island life caused by Europeans was either through their own predation or the consequences of the animals that they introduced deliberately or accidentally to hitherto mammal-free and snake-free places.

From the seaman's standpoint, ideal islands were those such as the Mascarene group, well out in the Indian Ocean and well located on the route to Indian ports. Here was a temperate climate, abundant wood and fresh water, and large, fat, flightless birds of pigeon ancestry, the dodo and the solitaire, readily clubbed, netted, or shot (the matchlock firearm having recently been developed —the first firearm that could be accurately aimed). Since until then no mammalian predators had existed on these islands, these large flightless birds habitually nested on the ground. Their eggs and young were easy prey for the ship's rats that came ashore, for the domestic swine that were deliberately released to provide a future meat supply, and even for the macaques brought back from India. Meanwhile, other islands along regular sailing routes often were stocked with rabbits, goats, and even cattle, to provide meat for future trips. These herbivorous mammals, particularly the hoofed ones, often had a severe impact on the vegetation that had existed in the complete absence of mammalian foraging. With the weakening of vegetation, the soil became exposed to wind and water erosion. In extreme cases, such as the island of St. Helena, once well-developed forest was destroyed by goats, most of the soil was lost and the island was transformed into a rocky desert. Unique native wildlife dependent upon the original habitat was presumably reduced as its habitat was reduced and in many cases must have become extinct even before recognized and described as part of the world's fauna.

On islands of the Caribbean, primitive mammals existed, presumably rafted out long ago from the South American continent, and as usual on islands, an array of ground-nesting birds. Introduced rats and domestic cats went wild and preyed heavily on the huita (large primitive rodents) and ground-nesting birds, while domestic animals ran wild and damaged native habitat.

An early settlement from England was made on the islands of Bermuda, which lie 570 miles east of present day North Carolina. These islands were discovered by Europeans some time in the 1500s or before; the first recorded visit was in 1515. Some time before 1593, domestic pigs were released on shore so that wild hogs were conveniently abundant when the first 60 English settlers arrived in 1612 under the Third Charter of the Virginia Company.

Among the native birds were petrels which spent most of their year at sea but needed land for breeding. Like others of its kind, the Bermuda petrel constructs a nesting burrow within which to lay and incubate its single egg. Any occupied burrow located within reach of a pig would be quickly found and rooted out, its contents devoured. Pigs, then, eliminated any petrels nesting on the main islands of Bermuda; offshore islets safe from pigs saw the return in early November of large numbers of petrels, called cahow by the settlers. Through January to June, adults, eggs, and fattening young in the nesting colony were a rich food source for the colonists. So during the first hard winter, 1614 to 1615, when other food was scarce, the weakest humans were transported to the most suitable cahow nesting island to sustain themselves on the birds. This was successful in terms of human welfare, but cahow populations were reduced to a point near extinction, at which low level they were kept by rats that made their way to the islets safe from pigs. Acting after the fact, a law was passed in 1621 to 1622 to protect the cahow from humans, but almost no cahows were left to protect. Certainly what had been a rich human resource was almost completely depleted in just a few years. Fortunately, the cahow somehow survived as a species to be rediscovered in recent times, though still barely existing against the tides of predation, competition, disturbance, and chemical contamination of habitat.

Some other species dwelled on or near the mainland and were not so fortunate. Among those now extinct were the giant sea mink, the Labrador duck, and the great auk.

Twice the size of the common mink, the sea mink frequented the North Atlantic coast, the very region visited by European fishermen who traded iron knives and fishhooks for furs from American Indians. This mink disappeared quickly between 1860 and 1880, presumably because of local distribution, high value, and vulnerability. Its former presence is reflected mainly in some vague early accounts and the occurrence of its bones in American Indian shell mounds.

The Labrador duck is thought to have nested on islands along that same North Atlantic coast. It migrated south in the fall and was known to exist in small numbers, to be difficult to attract into shooting range, and to be one of the least desirable ducks to eat. Its rapid decline to extinction about 1875, then, was probably due to a lack of successful reproduction, probably from human predation on eggs and young.

Meanwhile in the North Atlantic, a flightless giant existed, the great auk, called penguin by the French and Newfoundlanders. About a meter tall, this bird nested and rested on rocky islands, safe from the common mainland mammalian predators. In prehistoric times its range extended from Scotland and Scandinavia in an arc of rocky islets extending north, west, and south to Cape Cod. European populations of great auk became extinct in prehistoric times, presumably killed off by humans. Auk populations of the western Atlantic were discovered in 1509. Fishermen found that these birds would stand to be clubbed, or could even be herded into boats as fresh meat during the voyage. For example, on Funk Island, Newfoundland, now an ecological preserve for seabirds, they were killed over a period of 300 years for cod bait, for their feathered skins, and for their fat to be rendered down for oil, until the last one was killed there by 1800. Funk used to mean "evil odor," a name fishermen gave to the island after smelling the odor drifting far offshore from the guano deposited by millions of seabirds over centuries. The great auk became completely extinct in 1844 when fishermen took the last one from Iceland for a Danish skin collector. In 1863 the U.S. consul to Newfoundland was permitted to mine the remains of the great auk on Funk Island. He removed 35 tons of skeletons, sold 5 tons locally at $19 per ton, and shipped the rest to Boston, Baltimore, and Washington to fertilize gardens of wealthy Americans.

Humans love novelty. Humans seem always interested in animals different from those they already know well, particularly if the different ones are large, fierce, or otherwise conspicuous. Medieval rulers presented one another with falcons from Iceland, apes from Africa, peacocks from India, among others. On princely estates, albino deer or other rare creatures were given special attention. Rarity or scarcity makes a thing more valuable in human eyes and thus a prime target for human attention. At the primitive level the hunter brings in the rare or unusual creature as a matter of common interest. A more sophisticated hunter seeks the unusual individual—the trophy. The collector, legal or not, wants the rarity for his collection, alive in his menagerie (in older times) or zoo. All these have contributed to the decline and even extinction of some rare species.

During the early 1500s the Spanish explored their New World possessions and sailed up the western shores of North America. Later, from 1577 to 1580 the English freebooter Francis Drake navigated the Straits of Magellan and sailed northward along the coast to northern California. Even with the imperfect navigation of that day, the western Europeans now had some notion of the tremendous size of the New World and its wealth of resources, including fur.

The maritime nations of western Europe were keen to establish fur-trading ventures in the New World, but that land belonged to Spain by the pope's decree. But the English gradually exerted more and more "unofficial" pressure against the Spanish (Drake and his like looted the towns of New Spain more than once, for example). A major European power in those days, Spain formed an army in Holland, which was under Spanish control, and in 1588 sent a mighty armada to ferry it across the channel to attack England. With fire ships, the English forced the anchored fleet to cut its anchor cables to escape. A providential storm drove the Spanish ships north and west. Handicapped by their inadequate anchors, many were wrecked on rocky shores. For the English, Dutch, and French, this opened access to eastern North America. The Spanish lingered on that coast mainly in Florida.

Furs from the "New World" of North America were eagerly sought by the three most powerful maritime trading nations in Europe. The Dutch established posts such as New Amsterdam that developed into towns. Southward, the English were settled from New Jersey to Georgia, and northward from Connecticut to Newfoundland. The French moved inland on the waters of the St. Lawrence and established a vast fur-trading network through the Great Lakes and along the interior rivers, ultimately from Quebec to the mouth of the Mississippi. In 1670, 6 years after the English had converted the Dutch New Amsterdam into the English New York, the king of England granted a charter to the Hudson's Bay Company for exclusive trade in furs from Hudson's Bay, north of the French influence, and westward.

The Hudson's Bay Company was a monopoly. The legal assumption of the times was that any property discovered by nationals of a European country belonged to the ruler of that country. So the king of England assumed ownership of the Hudson Bay region and all that it contained. In that era, the main product to be sought was fur. By granting a monopoly on the trade in fur to a single firm, the king received payment to the royal treasury. Because the fur monopoly was free of business competition, the king might hope that it would be managed for long-term sustained yield rather than exploited quickly to commercial extinction.

As in any trading monopoly, the first intent of the Hudson's Bay Company was to promote "buying cheap" by being the only buyer, and "selling high" by being the only seller, rather than promoting long-term sustained yield of the fur resource. While theoretically the possibility of maintaining the fur trade indefinitely was not lost on the officers of the company, what was required for this to happen was an understanding of the resource and the absence of any competing organization.

Using England as an example, we can sketch the relationship between a mother country, as it came to be called, and its dependencies, that is, the other parts of the world under its control. Industrialized to some extent, the mother country exported manufactured items in its own ships, and with those same ships brought back raw materials. If it could, it controlled all trade with its dependencies and discouraged any production there of the goods that the mother country manufactured. At first, England manufactured woolen cloth and rum, upon gaining access to Caribbean sugarcane plantations. Importing cotton from its dependencies, it sent back cotton cloth. Having rich deposits of coal and iron ore, it moved quickly into the industrial revolution, manufacturing an ever-expanding variety of metal goods. Through three centuries English control over its dependencies grew ever more efficient, and the extent of those dependencies grew ever greater. The overall economic consequence was that England became increasingly wealthy. Most of this wealth was in the hands of the aristocratic class and those who aspired to enter it.

The aristocratic class was the landowning class, and in England such persons resided to a large extent on their estates. There they continued the ancient aristocratic sports of the field, involving horse, hound, weapon, and game. They also took an interest in the management of their lands, and as wealth and knowledge grew, they made improvements in agricultural productivity and livestock breeding. With ample capitalization, their estates became centers for a system of management that integrated the amenities of life, including game and other wildlife, with economic production.

One consequence of this style of life was a keen interest in the natural world. Enthusiastic, materially comfortable gentlemen collected strange plants and animals from countries dependent on the mother country. They provided financial support for collectors of specimens and for artists who delineated these oddities on the spot. From small beginnings in the 1500s these European collections brought an increasingly rich trove of specimens within reach of specialists who strove to name and classify them. This effort was clarified by Swedish botanist Carl von Linn (1707–1778), who built a system in Latin that provided each organism with a *species* name and grouped similar species together as members of a *genus*, so that the scientific name is the same in all languages.

From this time, Europeans had a reasonably accurate idea of the major groups of warm-blooded animals, as well as those which had been figments of the human imagination, such as mermaids, werewolves, and the like. The 1700s, then, provided the modern starting point from which to reckon the fate of individual known forms of wildlife in a world ever more completely under human domination. For the native inhabitants of North America and their relations to the wild fauna that had so long sustained them, the European invasion brought a tangle of conflicting consequences: new diseases, new tools and weapons, new religious concepts, and a new domestic animal—the horse.

In subsequent decades, beginning about 1565, the Spanish introduced the domesticated horse to North America. By the 1600s the native Indian tribes of the (current) United States were being affected by availability of the horse in the southwest, and European colonists on the eastern shore. But only since about 1720, when the Plains Indians had horses, did the horse have a major impact on American Indian economies and life styles. The horse was used mainly for warfare and hunting bison, and secondarily for burden, allowing American Indians to become more mobile, transporting the collapsible teepee and large amounts of smoked bison meat, as the buffalo herds were followed for a more reliable food source. Yet the horse received only limited use as a beast of burden by Indians, for they had not invented the wheel (although it had been used in Europe since 3500 BC); thus no wheeled carts were used, although the travois was used with dogs and eventually with horses.

On the eastern coast, Europeans brought other new creatures—the organisms responsible for human diseases to which American Indians never before had been exposed, although pre-1492 American Indians were not disease-free, notably from parasites and anemia. Quickly, diseases such as measles, bubonic plague, influenza, tuberculosis, typhus, cholera, malaria, chickenpox, and particularly smallpox killed entire native populations and spread steadily inland to decimate one tribe after another. Even the common cold had been unknown and could be lethal. When European colonists and traders realized the potential of disease to which they had developed immunity, they sometimes deliberately sent measles- or smallpox-contaminated blankets among tribes they wanted to subdue, but this was insignificant compared to the losses caused by accidental transmission. Anthropologists distinguish between microcontact and macrocontact relative to European influences and effects on American Indians. Microcontact occurred face to face. Macrocontact occurred long before most Native Americans ever saw Europeans, from the spread of their trade goods and diseases. For example, when fur traders' boats ascended the Missouri in the 1830s, a smallpox epidemic swept across 5000 miles of the continent, affecting nearly every tribe from the Dakotas to the Pacific Coast, eventually spreading across Alaska and into the Arctic. This particular epidemic ranks among the worst plagues of human history, on a par with the Black Death of medieval Europe that came with merchant ships from the Orient in the 1300s.

Losses to disease created shifts in surviving populations. Whatever stability existed when the continent was fully populated with American Indians was replaced by major population movements to regions different from those which American Indians had long occupied and to which they were culturally oriented by their customary traditions, sacred places, and ancestral spirits. Thus, along with the disruption caused by disease, demands for fur, and warfare with Europeans came a disruption caused by movement.

While the first epidemics were doing their work in North America, European explorers were encountering wildlife abundance of many sorts in many places beyond the ownership or control of any European monarch. They responded expediently with harvest programs designed to yield maximum immediate returns, programs of immediate material gain.

Bibliography

Beazley, C. R. 1964. John and Sebastian Cabot: The discovery of North America. Franklin, New York.
Buchanan, B. J., editor. 1996. Gunpowder: The history of an international technology. Bath University Press, Bath, UK.
Bulliet, R. W. 1990. The camel and the wheel. Columbia University Press, New York.
Claire, C. 1996. Explorers and traders. Time-Life Books, Alexandria, VA.
Crosby, A. W., Jr. 1972. The Columbian exchange: Biological and cultural consequences of 1492. Greenwood, Westport, CN.
Crosby, A. W. 1986. Ecological imperialism: The biological expansion of Europe, 900–1900. Cambridge University Press, New York.
Dahmus, J. H. 1968. Middle Ages: A popular history. Gollancz, London.
Diamond, J. 1997. Guns, germs, and steel: The fates of human societies. Norton, London.
Golder, F. A. 1914. Russian expansion in the Pacific, 1641–1850. Smith, Gloucester, MA.
Hakluyt, R. 1600. The principal navigations, voyages, traffiques, and discoveries of the English nation, etc. Bishop, Newberie, and Barker, London. Reissued in 1965 by Viking Press, New York.
Jennings, F. 1993. The founders of America. Norton, New York.
Metcalf, P. R. 1977. Indians and white diseases. Pages 549–551 *in* H. Lamar, editor. Readers encyclopedia of the American West. Thomas Y. Crowell, New York.
Morgan, W. S. 1989. History of the wheel and alliance and the impending revolution. Rice, Fort Scott, KS.
Morison, S. E. 1971. The European discovery of America: The northern voyages A.D. 500–1600. Oxford University Press, New York.
Morison, S. E. 1974. The European discovery of America: The southern voyages A.D. 1492–1616. Oxford University Press, New York.
Moulton, M. P., and J. Sanderson. 1999. Wildlife issues in a changing world. 2nd edition. CRC Press, Baco Raton, FL.
Roe, F. G. 1955. The Indian and the horse. University of Oklahoma Press, Norman.
Stannard, D. E. 1993. American holocaust: The conquest of the New World. Oxford University Press, New York.
Wahlgren, E. 1986. The Vikings and America. Thames and Hudson, New York.

Chapter 6

EUROPEAN TRADE AND SETTLEMENT

With the discovery of North America by seagoing Europeans, and the growing realization of the abundance of fish in its coastal waters, fishing boats appeared on the cod banks yearly. Those taking their catch ashore for drying could carry the largest cargo homeward, so shore camps provided a source of such wonders as iron knives for local native people. Some offered furs in exchange.

From about 1520 to 1785, European kings laid claim to lands in the New World already claimed and fully occupied by an estimated 2 million to 10 million aboriginals north of the Rio Grande. Familiarity with the Atlantic coast of what was for Europeans the New World generated the prospect for European settlement, particularly after epidemic diseases had weakened the American Indian populations there. By 1540 some 20 European houses existed in St. John's, Newfoundland. In 1565 St. Augustine, Florida, was founded.

Abundant wildlife promised to be a convenient food source and one not protected, as it was in Europe, by a powerful ruling class. So two patterns of human activity—trade, especially the fur trade, and the spread of settlement—had marked consequences for wildlife populations from about 1600.

Both Canada and the United States settled initially from the Atlantic coast and had their most mature commercial establishments there. Attractive mercantile investment opportunities lay in shipping, not only to transport cargo, but also to harvest the commons of the sea. Such ships were not possessed by indigenous people of the New World.

European diseases caused a series of great epidemics that killed half or more of North American aborigines (see chapter 5). These human epidemics recurred from the mid-1500s through the early 1800s, moving westward across the continent, often before any appreciable European penetration. One of the last was the mass mortality of coastal Inuit of Alaska, infected from the whaling fleet in the mid-1800s. In American aboriginal communities, epidemic disease created social disruption.

Maize, as corn is called in the rest of the world, was developed by the native people of the New World into an extraordinary number of varieties for different growing conditions. In fact, American Indian agriculture long sustained some of the world's largest cities. One such city was the Aztec capital Tenochtitlán, located on the site of modern-day Mexico City. Tenochtitlán was larger than Paris, Europe's largest city, until Hernán Cortés found it in 1519 and gunpowder and disease took the Aztec empire apart by 1521. Maize became a success with global implications that led to a population boom in the Old World. Maize transformed agriculture in Africa too, along with peanuts and manioc, about the time when introduced diseases were decimating American Indian societies. The Spanish, Portuguese, and British wanted to exploit American Indians as workers, and were alarmed by their high death rate. With such labor shortages, these Europeans turned to Africa where agricultural advances from maize had caused human populations to increase. That, along with Africa's quarrelsome societies and their Old World immunities to disease epidemics, made the slave trade possible without exhausting the supply.

As early as 1441, the Portuguese had introduced African slaves to Europe, where slavery had been used for thousands of years. In 1493, the year after Columbus "discovered" America, he introduced sugarcane from Europe to the Caribbean, where the Spanish first brought African slaves in 1502 to work the cane fields. American Indian use of nicotine caused curious Europeans to try it too, and in 1619, just 12 years after Jamestown was founded, the Dutch brought the first African slaves to Virginia to work the English tobacco plantations. The slavery system allowed large expanses of landscape to be altered to accommodate monocultures of both tobacco and cotton, exhausting in their demands for soil nutrients. Such a system directly affected wildlife habitats and populations, and human cultures, especially in Southern society. In 1808 the foreign slave trade was abolished. Slavery culminated in the turbulent U.S. Civil War (1861–1865) that reduced the human population in the United States by 600,000, more than all other U.S. wars combined.

The tremendous loss of American Indian lives caused by infection from European contact was followed shortly by a tremendous taking of wildlife by the survivors. The aboriginal restraints on wildlife slaughter—respect for the animal spirit and understanding, on a local scale, of the consequences of overkill—were overcome by a combination of factors including an increasing dependence on trade goods and an increasing acceptance of Christianity and its concept of human dominion over nature. To these must be added the competition between rival humans and human groups for the same resource. This was a far cry from the aboriginal situation, in which tribal members hunted and trapped communally over a large territory for sustained subsistence.

Civilization of western Europe was relatively complex compared to that of American Indians, and well prepared for development of trade between the two. Western Europe enjoyed advanced technology in all fields supporting trade. It produced metal and cloth goods in abundance. It had developed adequate systems of capital investment, accounting, and transport. It could absorb large amounts of raw materials and sell large amounts of finished products. For their part, the Stone Age American Indians, however successful for thousands of years, were avid for such trade goods as iron spearheads, knives, hatchets, and light brass kettles. Western Europe also had three overpowering inventions: the ship, the wheel, and the gun. And it had the horse—and military organization.

The fur trade began as long ago as the 1500s when Jean and Raoul Parmentier brought a cargo of fur to France from Cape Breton in 1520, and the Portuguese seaman Estevan Gomez took the first cargo of beaver skins to Spain from Cape Breton in 1525. But the fur trade began mainly as a sideline of the cod fishery along eastern North America, because the fur industry alone could not cover the overhead costs of transportation then between North America and Europe. Once transportation between the continents was adequate, the fur trade played a major role in the political and economic development of North America. For the first time ever, North America's indigenous people became involved in a global market economy, which, along with the Jesuit fathers, transformed their traditional cultures, economics, and territories. The first transcontinental business enterprise, the North West Company, developed from the fur trade, as did the oldest multinational resource and trading company in North America, the Hudson's Bay Company.

Among the furs traded was that of the beaver. This animal was known to Europeans, for both continents had its own species of beaver, but its numbers in Europe had long been in decline. When it had been more abundant, its heavy underfur (characteristic of many aquatic mammals), in which each hair was barbed, had been valued for the fine felting used to make hats. The decline of European beaver was reflected in the virtual disappearance of beaver felt. But with the possibility of new beaver sources from North America, the potential for a boom in fine-felted hats emerged. In addition, a broad market for furs existed generally in Europe, even in those parts of Russia where furbearers had been trapped to commercial extinction.

The beaver was not the only American furbearer, of course, but it was abundant and vulnerable. Its abundance was the result of the wide availability of its habitat of rivers, lakes, and marshes, and the variety and productivity of the plants on which it fed. Its vulnerability stemmed from the obvious signs of its presence in dams, lodges, and cuttings, and its sedentary colonial life. Its decline was hastened by the availability of the steel trap after 1750 and the trap's mass production in the 1800s.

When the fur trade is mentioned, it is the beaver trade that is really meant. Other furs were taken incidental to beaver. Some, especially the rich sea otter, were far more valuable. But the root and core of the trade was indisputably beaver. A continent was explored, an indigenous race of people was degraded and its culture crushed, and many people died—in part because beaver fur produced better felt than any other fur did. The beaver felt hat, "the beaver," as the hat was called, was fashionable in Europe from about 1550 to 1850. Thus, the felt hat industry, through its need for beaver, became the driving force behind the fur trade and all its ramifications.

Beaver of the northern regions had long been valuable for the American Indians, who made warm robes from several skins sewn together. With continued use, those robes lost the long guard hairs, leaving the soft underfur "wool" in place. It was this wool that the hatters of Europe used in their trade, and so it was these warm, worn robes that were the first object of the trader.

American Indian hunters pursued beaver, which soon had some trade value even if young or in summer coat. Local stocks of beaver declined. As American Indians became more dependent on trade goods, demand for those goods rose.

The three European nations most conveniently located for trade with the New World—Holland, France, and England—were already experienced in manufacture, transport, and trade. Each sought access to the new North American opportunity through safe harbors and convenient water access to the interior, extending its sphere of influence as fast as it could.

Beginning in 1624 the Dutch established trading posts fed by the Hudson River, one of which in time became New York. By 1650 most beaver had been eliminated from the streams on the coastal plain and the lower St. Lawrence Valley between Maine and the Carolinas. Moving up the St. Lawrence in the early 1600s, the French created a fur-trading network that had extended to Quebec and through the Great Lakes by 1659, down the Mississippi to the Gulf of Mexico by 1683, and west to Yellowstone (the Louisiana Territory, after King Louis XIV). This gave them access to the tribes of the temperate interior, with whom they established partnerships of trade for fur. Starting from Hudson's Bay in 1670, the English established trading posts over time as far as the mouth of the Columbia River on the Pacific Coast and westward across present day Canada.

Business considerations often were of equal or lesser importance than political and strategic considerations, for American Indian suppliers of fur also were important as potential military allies or enemies. Each of the European trading nations attempted to make firm alliances with American Indian tribes to maintain the flow of furs. Some tribes, in turn, formed for the first time confederacies to promote mutual support, even though traditionally hostile to each other over disputed territory. The iron weapons that could be bought with furs were hatchets and knives at first, and ultimately firearms, all eagerly sought by every warrior. Until the end of the War of 1812, Europeans and, after 1776, Americans competed for American Indian allies, which meant supplying them with the goods they demanded through gifts and trade. The French were no longer involved in the competition for American Indian allies in the colonies of North America with their defeat there by the British in 1763 in the Seven Years War.

The fur trade was not the only trade, but for three centuries, from 1550 to 1850, it was the trade that, through aggressive competition, shaped the political maps of North America. Beaver flourished wherever there was water and willow (or certain other deciduous trees, especially aspen) all across the country. The animals were easy to find and catch, and beaver robes had warmed American Indian bodies for thousands of years. The wetlands supporting beaver were not appreciably altered by American Indians, so beaver occurred in a continental population of an estimated 10 million, of which 2.5 million could have been harvested annually in perpetuity with prudent habitat and harvest management. But conditions of the time left no scope for prudent management. The trade for furs created greed and competition between trappers, between tribes, soon between English and French, and ultimately between the fur companies. Locally, beaver were often far more abundant than traditional American Indian needs required.

Despite indigenous losses to European diseases, many tribesmen survived to take part in the competitive take of beaver for trade. Competition existed between one hunter and another, the more successful one obtaining more of the trader's goods. Competition existed between one tribe or tribal confederation or another for the same goal. And, as trading posts were established ever more deeply across the continent, competition between posts increased. The total flow of furs rose steeply.

This whole era was marked by trade-related tribal aggression. The Iroquois (the Five Nations Confederacy) sought a middleman position through a monopoly of their fur trade with the Dutch, and by 1700 were able to force the Chippewa (Ojibwa) eastward into present day Minnesota, northern Wisconsin, and upper Michigan. That brought the Ojibwa into conflict with the Sioux, who were driven westward into conflict with still other tribes.

Access to trade goods, particularly firearms, was often the key to success in war. On the northern Great Plains, for example, the Blackfoot tribe obtained firearms from the Hudson Bay traders to the north before their competing tribes in "buffalo country" were as well armed. Consequently, the Blackfoot expanded the hunting territory they largely controlled at the expense of other tribes which hunted buffalo and trapped beaver. Beaver were easily located and trapped, and thus most likely to be trapped out of regions where their skins could reach the market. That caused trappers, especially white trappers, to expand their search for beaver and encroach on more American Indian land, producing conflict and bloodshed because American Indian trappers were competing, but mostly in the United States. Less trapping conflict occurred in Canada because trading posts there used American Indians as trappers more often than trading posts did in the United States. Nonetheless, the quest for beaver was a driving force in the exploration and settlement of North America by Europeans. The city of St. Louis, for example, had its humble origin at the confluence of the Mississippi and Missouri rivers, buying furs from and supplying trappers who used these water courses and their tributaries to gain access to trapping grounds as far away as Yellowstone. Even today, St. Louis has one of the few major fur auction houses in North America.

Newly established trading posts in the interior had a ripple effect also on local American Indian economies. These Indians increased their demand for European goods, and increased their hunting and trapping pressures on local wildlife populations, often compounded by competition from European settlers. Due to the resulting depletion of fur and game within their customary territories, trading post Indians often compensated by charging trespassing fees to distant native tribes wanting to sell their furs to other trading posts, setting themselves up as middlemen. That increased the cost of furs to the European traders, encouraging further territorial expansion by Europeans seeking cheaper furs.

For the American Indian hunter, whose traditional technology was that of stone and bone, the fur trade offered access to steel knives and hatchets, warm wool blankets, firearms, metal pots, pretty beads, and alcohol. Some came to spend their whole productive time in trapping, obtaining all things, including food, from the trading post, and began to lose their traditional subsistence lore.

In 1821 the two dominant fur-trading organizations in the north merged: the North West Company, which had taken over the ancient French fur trade, and the Hudson's Bay Company from England. Unbridled competition for immediate material satisfaction caused resource depletion, which was recognized. Having a monopoly and so large a measure of control over the fur market, the merged company, i.e., Hudson's Bay Company, began to institute measures of economy and conservation in lands too far north for conventional agriculture. Uneconomical trading posts were closed, to the detriment of local native populations that had become dependent upon trade goods. In much of the country still suitable for trapping, the competitive exploitation characteristic of the early 1800s was replaced over the next century to more exclusive control of each trapping area by a single small group. This was different from the aboriginal situation. Social organization and proprietorship for many Algonkian Indian bands in Canada changed from large groups of families that hunted and trapped communally held areas to small groups of families that hunted and trapped discrete, exclusive territories within the tribal boundaries. In temperate parts of North America quite a different pattern was emerging. Still using Stone Age technology and weakened by disease, the aboriginal inhabitants were being replaced by westward-moving, technologically advanced settlers of European stock.

Through the first half of the 1700s the population of the English colonies grew, but expansion westward beyond the Alleghenies was blocked by presence of the French and their Indian allies. This impediment was removed with defeat of the French by English forces in 1763, thus ending the Seven Years War (French and Indian War) that gave England a new colony—Canada. No longer threatened from the west, hence no longer dependent on English military protection, U.S. colonists eventually broke away from the mother country in 1776. As a consequence of the American Revolution (1776 to 1784), each of the original 13 colonies became an independent nation before their eventual confederation into the United States of America in 1789. When each state became an independent nation, the citizens of each such nation assumed the legal prerogatives of the king of England, including ownership of wildlife. In a way, this legitimized what every armed person was already doing—taking wildlife anywhere at any time.

With removal of the French block to westward settlement (1763) and with United States independence (1776), all lands west of the eastern seaboard states to the Mississippi River became U.S. territory. Lands west of the Mississippi had been claimed by Spain according to the rules of those days, then passed by treaty to ownership by France. In 1803 President Thomas Jefferson bought these lands from a needy France for $10,000,000 (Louisiana Purchase), thus doubling the size of the United States. He sent Meriwether Lewis and William Clark on a reconnaissance across these lands to the Pacific coast. In 1806 they returned and their published report described some of the wealth in wildlife to be found there —the bison of the plains, the beaver of the mountains, and the sea otter of the coast, among other things. Fur company trappers and traders quickly followed up, first concentrating on beaver in a "beaver rush" to the Rocky Mountains and, beyond that, largely extirpated beaver by mid-century.

By the 1840s the silk hat began to replace the felt hat, so beaver prices dropped sharply. Declining beaver prices, depletion of beaver from overtrapping, and reduced beaver habitat from forest clearance and expansion of farming changed the fur industry. Still important economically, it was less so, and raccoon then became the dominant furbearer in the fur trade until the end of the U.S. Civil War (1865), although muskrat was more important in numbers traded.

Ownership and use among American Indians is considered communal in their tribal territory. But personal ownership among American Indians is individual; each hunter personally owns his clothing, ornaments, and equipment. Trade goods then were personal possessions of individuals, of individual value and use. In their quest for furs to trade for personal possessions, individuals competed directly with other individuals with the same goal. In any particular locality, the result was the decline of vulnerable, valuable wildlife. In the northern regions of most valuable beaver, the time came when wool blankets rather than the beaver robes of old warmed the American Indians. By about the mid-1800s beaver in much of North America were commercially extinct. The beaver had affected the landscape by damming streams and creating ponds that benefited many other species of wildlife. That came to an end in many regions.

In North America north of Mexico, the fur trade did not drive any furbearer to extinction, but it did play a leading role in the decline of American Indian populations and cultures. Before the European fur traders, American Indian tribes filled the continent in densities reflecting the natural productivity of their particular territories. Constant rivalry over territory preserved less frequented areas between tribes within which game could recover the numbers lost to hunters. Wars were carried out between tribes having similar weapons. When some tribes obtained the better European weapons, groups of tribes formed confederations, eliminating the wildlife refuges in the no-man's-land between those tribes, and providing centrally directed military operations.

The resulting cultural impact was compounded by replacement of traditional religious beliefs of American Indians with those of white men. In its various forms, Christianity drew from the Bible the assurance that humans had a soul and other creatures did not, that humans were superior to animals and had dominion over them, and that humans could freely use animals as desired. This was substantially different from the American Indian belief that both humans and other animals had life in the supernatural world and that it behooved humans to treat other animals with respect even as humans subsisted on them, or suffer retribution. The new religious teachings (common to both Catholic and Protestant faiths) fitted well with the immediate material satisfaction of unlimited fur harvest among American Indian tribes, and also the immediate material satisfaction of European settlers who were increasing along the Atlantic coast. Firm in their belief of dominion over plants and animals, traders, colonists, and even missionaries left for a later day the interpretation of responsible stewardship of earth's natural resources, without concern for spiritual consequence. Many a wildlife population felt the impact.

The trapper could travel light and fast and bring back his light but valuable catch by boat or horse. He was followed by the settler. Settlement involved clearing land for establishing subsistence farms; settlement was the governmental aim of both Canada and the United States. The United States essentially completed its expansion by its attack of Mexico, which was forced to cede much of the present day Southwest to the United States in 1848, and with its purchase of Alaska from Russia in 1867 ("Seward's Folly"). Also in 1867, Canada officially became a separate nation, its expansion less sanguinary than that of the United States, after England's experience with Canada's southern neighbor.

For generations before European settlement, the original forests of the Atlantic coast had been kept partially open by fires deliberately set each November by American Indians. With frequent fires, wildlife of the forest edge and openings gained habitat. Wild game adapted for grass and shrublands were abundant: white-tailed deer, wild turkey, bobwhite quail, cottontail rabbit, ruffed grouse, and even that eastern form of the presently threatened pinnated grouse (or prairie chicken) called the heath hen, now extinct. Even elk and bison were found on the eastern seaboard. These fires that kept the forest open decreased with the increase of European farmers, but more forest was cleared outright for agriculture.

Hardwood forests of the eastern half of the continent grew on farmable soils. The settler need only clear the encumbering trees and plant his crops. But clearing the forest by hand was a slow process. During the early years, while the first fields were being tediously cleared, the frontier family lived on wild foods—fish, game, and the fruits and nuts of the forest. One frontier son reported that the white meat of the wild turkey was called "bread," and only the darker flesh of deer or bear called "meat." Mammals bearing valuable furs were eagerly pursued, one family competing with another, and species easy to locate, like beaver, were often cleaned out altogether. Hunted year-round for meat and skins, hoofed game and black bears soon became scarce as the country became settled. When extra-heavy snows piled up confining bands of elk, local settlers made a killing.

During the early 1700s the eastern slope of the Appalachians was being inhabited by pioneers from older colonial settlements. From such beginnings came a breed of colonists facing not outward toward the sea, but inward toward the land, and increasingly well adapted to exploring and exploiting the land. Remote settlements were largely self-sufficient, with the trades of woodworking and blacksmithing adequate to the need. Among colonial inventions was that of an improved firearm. It was a small-bore rifle firing a lead sphere wrapped in leather or cloth, which imparted a spin to the projectile. It was at once much easier to load (hence, could be fired more rapidly), less prone to fouling from the black powder of the day, and more accurate and with much greater range than had been known before. This was used with effect by such as Daniel Boone, exploring out into the "new lands" of Kentucky, and was called the Kentucky rifle.

Backwoodsmen armed with such weapons were impossible to control by governmental edicts, as shown by the struggles of the colonial government of North Carolina. The land in south Atlantic colonies such as this was parceled out by the English king to wealthy Englishmen, who naturally tried to carry on as their right the privileged hunting regime of their homeland. Their aims are reflected in the second game law of North Carolina, enacted in 1745, which linked the hunting right to a certain measure of residence or land ownership and therefore wealth. Such discrimination against nonresidents and those not owning property was found quite unenforceable. An armed population simply ignored any law designed to control the take of wildlife, and government was not strong enough to enforce compliance. Any wild creature that was of use, dead, to humans, could be taken without restraint. Among the American colonies, local extirpation was the order of the day. Under continuous hunting pressure, the larger game—which originally included moose, elk, and bison as well as white-tailed deer, wild turkey, and beaver—dwindled and disappeared from settled regions.

Ownership of wildlife was a state prerogative in the United States and a provincial prerogative in Canada, though in each case the federal government came to develop wildlife interests. Ownership of land was handled differently. In the United States all lands that were not privately owned at the time of its Independence declared in 1776 (i.e., the former Crown lands or King's Waste) became the property of the states in which they occurred. They were then ceded to the federal government which then disposed of much of them to private ownership of one sort or another. In Canada such lands remained in federal ownership as Crown lands, except that Crown lands became the responsibility of the province in which they occurred. Crown lands in the territories remained federal.

Land was dirt cheap; once established, ownership was virtually absolute. The federal government promoted settlement. Immigration soared. For the common person of western Europe, born and raised in a system that equated land ownership with wealth and social stature, the prospect of owning land was a powerful inducement to emigrate to the New World. The American Indians, who owned the land in the first place, became less of a problem in the land-taking after the infamous Indian Removal Act of 1830 and treaties during 1853–1856 and 1866 forced them to move to reservations. At the same time, the farmer colonists were producing many children who grew up well skilled in the subsistence agriculture and necessary handicrafts of the frontier.

With the way westward open, hunters and trappers explored new lands and settlers followed. It was the pioneer's aim to claim and cultivate a farm as subsistence for himself and his family. In his view, the eastern deciduous forest encumbered the land.

As in previous days of agricultural expansion in the Near East or western Europe, continual fragmentation of North American hardwood forests changed wildlife vulnerability, wildlife habitat, and even wildlife species. With expanding European settlement, the ancient forest was seen as an impediment that had to be removed before cultivation could begin. The settler was an ax man; mature trees were chopped down or killed by girdling and felled by repeated fires at their bases. The trunks, limbed, were moved out of the way on community logrolling days. As most of today's game and many nongame species are associated with forest edge, forest fragmentation increased their numbers at the expense of interior wildlife species and those requiring large undisturbed territories. Human predation and human-caused changes in the landscape affected different species in different ways. Larger mammals became more easily found as cover decreased and more and more people and dogs were keen to find them. In settlement days, swampy lands provided something of a sanctuary, since it was largely beyond the power of frontier technology to dike and drain. As the mature forest was fragmented, forest edges and weedy farm fields and pastures expanded. Around the clearings, forest-edge and forest-opening wildlife flourished. Wild turkeys, ruffed grouse, bobwhite quail, gray squirrels, fox squirrels, and cottontail rabbits were abundant farm game and, with their high reproductive rates, long a staple source of meat among forest farms.

The more suitable agricultural soils were deep and fertile, had gentle slopes, and had reliable rains during the growing season. There the forest and its wildlife dwindled rapidly as agriculture spread and mobile new seed-eating species came in from more open regions. In regions less suitable for agriculture, such as in the hills or on thin soils, fields were scattered through a residual forest that provided habitat for wild turkey, squirrels, ruffed grouse, and a few black bears and white-tailed deer if hunting pressure was not too intense.

For subsistence farmers, presence of wildlife was a mixed blessing. Wildlife was obviously a natural resource to be used to the fullest extent possible, but wildlife could damage crops. When farmers planted seed, some seed-eating bird or rodent might find and devour it. When the seed sprouted, the succulent green shoot was choice food for all sorts of grazers from geese and rabbits to deer and elk. Ripening grain or fruit attracted flocking birds of many species. The Carolina parakeet was strongly attracted to fruit orchards. Stored grain was eaten and soiled by house mice and rats. Fruit trees could be girdled by meadow mice or porcupines and browsed in winter by deer or elk. The more prosperous farmer became less dependent on wild meat and began to consider much wildlife as pests to be controlled. But his sons and their sons still trapped muskrats and skunks and hunted squirrels and rabbits. Though their success yielded immediate material satisfaction, their major satisfactions were those beyond the material.

Nonmaterial satisfactions are a complex that includes all elements of the chase, the re-enactment of older, supposedly less trammeled times, the enjoyment of nature in all its times and seasons, and the approbation of the family and community. A father might say "It's in their blood" and indeed it had been "in the blood" of their ancestors of thousands of years back. It was such hard-to-define attraction of nonmaterial satisfactions that eventually began to exert a controlling influence over the rampant drive for immediate material satisfaction that characterized the 1800s in North America, when making a living was still very difficult for most folks.

Meanwhile, as settlement expanded westward, the more conspicuous birds and mammals tended to decline in the face of unrestricted hunting. Over the course of the 1800s, two birds made vulnerable by their particular habits were killed to extinction.

The passenger pigeon was probably, aboriginally the most abundant single bird species in North America, numbering into the billions, as well as we can now estimate. Yet archeologists do not find many bones of passenger pigeons in pre-Columbian strata of Indian middens, even though pigeons were good to eat and readily caught. This indicates that the mass of birds in the history books was an irruption symptomatic of a disrupted ecosystem. The pigeon passed seasonally over the hardwood forests of North America, eating beechnuts, acorns, wild fruits, and the like, moving in large flocks and nesting colonially south of the Great Lakes. As in other pigeons, only one or two young were hatched, but these were exceptionally well nourished by pigeon milk secreted from the parent's crop. Before they had ever flown, these squabs were extremely large and fat, choice human prey. Therefore, human predation focused on the nesting grounds. As late as 1871 one of the largest nesting aggregations of the passenger pigeon gathered in the sandy scrub-oak barrens of south-central Wisconsin. It was estimated to total some 136 million birds. Its presence and magnitude were welcome news to hunters who by this time had access to city markets for sale of game. The newly invented telegraph spread the word far and wide. Thousands of market hunters arrived and millions of birds were shipped out at 2 cents apiece. Similar heavy predation at nesting sites, continued clearing of the hardwood trees on which the pigeons fed, and continued decline of pigeon populations went on together. A victim of overharvest and habitat destruction, passenger pigeons needed extensive climax oak forest and critical mass of breeding birds, i.e., they apparently needed some minimum number as a catalyst for breeding. As their populations decreased, so too did the social efficiency of their colonial breeding. Humans are a species best adapted to successional rather than climax communities. Many human activities associated with land use, such as forestry and agriculture, continually retard succession of plant communities, with marked effect on climax species such as passenger pigeons. The last remaining flocks of passenger pigeons occurred in the Lake States. The Chicago Fire of October 8, 1871 indirectly expedited their ultimate demise when trees were cut throughout the Lake States to rebuild Chicago, but not from the area surrounding Green Bay, Wisconsin. The Great Peshtigo Fire, the most devastating forest fire in U.S. history coincidentally occurring the exact same date as the Chicago Fire, burned 1.25 million acres in six counties and killed over 1200 people, while altering wildlife habitat extensively to either the benefit or detriment of various wildlife species. (The Chicago Fire killed 300 people and got all the press.) The last passenger pigeon died in 1914 in the Cincinnati Zoo.

The habits fatal to the Carolina parakeet were its roosting aggregations in hollow trees, the return of a flock to the bodies of those shot, and particularly the apparently purposeless damage to the farmer's fruit. Apples, oranges, and peaches were patiently cultivated in hopes of profitable crops, but were cut by parakeets and dropped to the ground, uneaten. The orchardist shot at flocks, which flew back over their dead to be themselves shot. And when he could, the farmer found roosts in which the birds were at his mercy. Parakeets declined as settlement spread through the broad-leaved nut-producing forests that originally covered the southern half of the present United States from the Atlantic coast to beyond the Mississippi River. Like the passenger pigeon, their decline toward extinction was due to inadequate habitat to form large social groups for breeding, and continued human predation, not only by orchardists, but also professional live-bird catchers, plumage hunters, and by casual hunters, since parakeets were conspicuously colored. Like the passenger pigeon, the last Carolina parakeet died in 1914 in the Cincinnati Zoo.

During the 1800s the aggressive United States expanded across the continent to the Pacific shore, seized and purchased land from Mexico, acquired Alaska from the Russians, and appeared to the Canadians to have invasion in mind. Canada, which had remained a British colony known as British North America, long consisted of Upper Canada (Ontario), Lower Canada (Quebec), and Territories. From 1867 due to the putative United States threat after its Civil War, the various provinces expedited their previous plan to confederate into a formal country. Talk of union in Canada began around 1790 and serious efforts began in 1850. Discussions of a union of the Maritime Provinces in 1864 precipitated action. Still, that it occurred shortly after the U.S. Civil War ended in 1865 was no coincidence, for the United States was no longer preoccupied with war and was able to conduct its expansion of Manifest Destiny westward and northward (like Canada), as it did before the Civil War with its Mexican War in 1848, and after the Civil War with its purchase of Alaska from Russia in 1867.

Profit from wildlife required a market. As cities grew, wildlife products could be sold, but first they had to be transported. The three available sorts of transport in the early 1800s were foot, horse, and boat, all slow, hence suitable mainly for nonperishable skins and feathers.

The flow of perishable wild meat to growing city markets required dependable transportation. Beginning in the mid-1800s this requirement was met by the railroad. By 1850 railroads linked the states east of the Mississippi and tied into the steamboat lines on the Mississippi and its major tributaries. With help from the telegraph, hunters with their netting equipment could travel within striking distance of a colony of passenger pigeons and barrels of squabs could be sent off in railroad ice cars to city markets. It became easier to move the winter harvest of ducks and geese from ice-free bays of the south Atlantic states to urban outlets farther north. With no constraint on this harvest of the common property in wildlife, anyone who liked to hunt could now market his kill. A revealing recollection comes from one John Hutchins, who began his career as a market hunter and trapper about 1816 and kept at it for half a century in upstate New York; his recollected life wildlife harvest totaled some 100 moose, 1000 white-tailed deer, 10 caribou, and 100 black bears. With this increasing commercial pressure, the large game animals were soon extirpated from accessible regions, and with the advance of every railroad track, new regions became accessible.

Meanwhile, with liberal federal support through grants of public land, U.S. railroads were being pushed westward to California, across the range of bison.

The railroad workers provided a good market for commercial hunters. And when trains were running, wildlife products could be shipped east to the centers of wealth and industry. Improvements in firearms had paralleled improvement in transportation. In the 1820s the percussion cap began to replace the flintlock (often on the same weapons), preventing misfires in wet weather. But a greater jump in efficiency came with perfection of the center-fire cartridge about 1860, followed by the repeating firearm within that same decade. Now the hunter had an accurate, rapid-fire weapon, reliable even in rain. Better yet, large-scale manufacture of identical parts had brought the costs down. Practically anyone could afford to be armed, and many were.

When humans eliminated the last great auk from the face of the earth in 1844, it was noted, if at all, as an isolated and remote case, causing no concern. But as the commercial kill of wildlife grew rapidly for prosperous northern markets during the 1860s, prominent sportsmen became concerned.

Commercial use of bison did not start with railroad and buffalo gun. American Indians had used and traded buffalo robes for generations. Early white hunters did the same whenever they could find a way of getting the heavy hides to market. When St. Louis had established transportation links to eastern markets via steamboat to New Orleans, the buffalo robe trade picked up. As early as 1832 over 40,000 buffalo hides, taken largely by native hunters, were shipped from but one of many western trading posts to St. Louis.

After disease killed off the American Indians, the population of bison more than sextupled, with a vast expansion of range. Archeological digs in middens indicate that also occurred to elk and mule deer.

Bison were widespread throughout the central and eastern grasslands of North America, with greatest densities in the Great Plains. By the time the railroad had been pushed west of the Mississippi, virtually all bison in the eastern forest glades were long gone, but millions still roamed the Great Plains. These were the resource that supported the native tribes that were becoming increasingly hostile to the white invasion. So the commercial kill of bison was not only allowable business practice of whites for that time, but also a help in promoting white settlement by weakening the American Indian ability to resist, in addition to the western "Indian Wars" that killed an estimated 50,000 Indians.

The slaughter of bison had more to it than commercial gain or "management of the Indian question." It was a particular example of a general mentality, namely, wholesale killing in the name of sport.

Two basic types of human hunter might be termed the common hunter and the aristocratic hunter. The common hunter was essentially a harvester, taking game by any expedient means for material gain, social status, and with agriculture and trade, profit as a market hunter. His success in business was affected by the amount of game he could harvest. His status was affected by his skill in taking game. The aristocratic hunter sought challenge, the sort that would develop his skills as a soldier, including skill with weapons, with social status as reward.

The two types of hunter, different in many ways, both believed that killing large numbers of game was not only permissible, but actually admirable. And the presence of buffalo in the millions certainly provided opportunity to kill large numbers of game.

When the perceived needs of the northern forces in the U.S. Civil War had pushed the railroads across the southern prairies in the 1860s, the stage was set for a quantum jump in the slaughter of bison. In the 1870s, with the Civil War over, new advances in firearms, and a national economic slump, many people became hide hunters. The first 3 years after railroad transportation became available eastward from Dodge City, Kansas, in the midst of buffalo country, a qualified observer estimated that some 4,000,000 were killed and most of their hides shipped east. This was consistent with the policy of the U.S. Army to slaughter the herds to reduce the food supply of the Plains Indians, thus starving them into submission. Despite political opposition to this process, bison were doomed. The question was settled on military grounds, although in 1874 a bill was passed by the U.S. Congress "to prevent the useless slaughter of the buffaloes within the territories of the United States." General Sherman, of Civil War fame, advised against it and President (and former General) Grant vetoed it.

In 1875 the Texas herds became available following military pacification of the American Indians, followed in 1876 by arrival of a railroad line to Ft. Worth, Texas. By the end of that decade, Texas bison had been hunted to extirpation. The northern herds which had been hunted commercially for decades, with the hides freighted down the Missouri River, were made more accessible by arrival of the railroad to mid-Montana in 1881. By 1883 commercial hunters could find nothing left to hunt. The bison in Canada fared no better; 256 remained by 1889. By then, the "Indian question" had been resolved.

New workers (shooters, skinners, camp cooks), driving their wagons toward the bison killing fields, experienced varying sensations of sight, scent, and sound. At first approach the landscape was dotted with bison skeletons. From a distance, the view from the wagons was of an expanse of skinned, dried, relatively odor-free carcasses. As the workers approached nearer, the pervasive buzzing and presence of flies and the stench of the massive array of rotting carcasses were all but unbearable. The foul odor gradually waned, as the wagons approached the edge of the killing fields where the many carcasses were still fresh, lying next to their skins stretched, staked, and fleshed. In the end, bone collectors loaded wagons with bison skeletons to be shipped East by railroad and ground into fertilizer or used in refining sugar, until these entrepreneurs too were put out of work by the lack of bison bones. Between 1868 and 1881 alone, an estimated $2,500,000 was paid for bones. With 100 skeletons to the ton and an average price of $8.00 per ton, that comes to 31,250,000 bison. Once the most numerous large mammals that ever roamed the earth, bison, estimated at 30,000,000 to 60,000,000 about 1860, were reduced to 1091 in 1889 in North America. It took just 30 years.

The dramatic slaughter of bison in particular made a significant impact upon American and Canadian consciousness, since it was thoroughly reported in the newspapers and magazines of the day. Over and over the particular point was made that all these thousands of animals had been killed *and the meat wasted*.

For the average American and Canadian reader, that was the most reprehensible part of the whole affair, since, in the popular consciousness, a major material value of game was as human food.

Bison were soon replaced by herds of domestic livestock: horses, sheep, and cattle. The former predators of the bison, principally wolves and to some extent grizzly bears, turned to this new abundant prey. For the emergent ranching culture, war on predators seemed a basic necessity. If possible, wolves, grizzlies, and cougars were to be eliminated from the grassy plains and adjacent forest habitat. And so they were.

Studded by innumerable potholes left by retreating glaciers, the prairie provinces of Canada were producing countless waterfowl. This heartland of North American waterfowl production—the so-called duck factory of the prairie provinces—was thrown open to virtually unrestricted shooting, as in the 1870s Canadians pushed their own rail line across the Great Plains of Manitoba, Saskatchewan, and Alberta. Market hunters and affluent sportsmen from Europe, Canada, and the United States flocked by train to the region each spring and autumn for spectacular shooting at the massed flocks. This spring gunning pressure was devastating because it was concentrated on the nesting ducks of the Canadian prairie pothole region—the main production base of the continental waterfowl resource, where most of the continent's ducks are produced. Over time, the spread of agriculture into the prairie pothole region first produced grain, encouraging some waterfowl species, and then, by filling and draining wetlands, reduced waterfowl nesting habitat drastically.

The expanding agricultural frontier did not immediately destroy the fur trade, as is commonly thought. Though beaver were gone early, skunks, muskrats, raccoons, and mink were abundant enough in the highly agriculturally developed Midwest for local harvest. In Canada, less affected by agriculture, the beaver of the rivers and lakes and the pine marten of the forest continued to be the trapper's principal objects.

Rapid expansion of white man's agriculture over the more fertile and level lands of the continent was accompanied by forcing remnant American Indian tribes onto reservations. The native people of lands too far north for agriculture were more fortunate. Their contacts with the invading culture were often painful, but their populations recovered and their cultures survived to a greater or lesser extent.

Bibliography

Berry, D. 1961. A majority of scoundrels: An informal history of the Rocky Mountain Fur Company. Harper, New York.

Bieder, R. E. 1995. Native American communities in Wisconsin 1600–1960: A study of tradition and change. University of Wisconsin Press, Madison.

Bolen, E. G., and W. L. Robinson. 1999. Wildlife ecology and management. 4th edition. Prentice Hall, Upper Saddle River, NJ.

Borland, H. 1975. The history of wildlife in America. Arch Cape Press, New York.

Borland, H., editor. 1965. Our natural world: The land and wildlife of America as seen and described by writers since the country's discovery. Doubleday, Garden City, NY.

Champagne, D., editor. 1994. The native North American almanac: A reference work on native North Americans in the United States and Canada. Gale Research, Detroit.

Cook, J. 1967-74. The journals of Captain James Cook on his voyages of discovery. Edited by J. C. Beaglehole and R. A. Skelton. Cambridge University Press, Cambridge, England.

Cook, J. 1971. The exploration of Captain James Cook in the Pacific, as told by selections of his own journals, 1768-1779. Edited by A. G. Price. Dover, New York.

Cronan, W. 1983. Changes in the land: Indians, colonists, and the ecology of New England. Hill and Wang, New York.

Crosby, A. W., Jr. 1972. The Columbian exchange: Biological and cultural consequences of 1492. Greenwood, Westport, CN.

Dagg, A. I. 1974. Canadian wildlife and man. McClelland and Stewart, Toronto.

Estes, J. A., M. T. Tinker, T. M. Williams, and D. F. Doak. 1998. Killer whale predation on sea otters linking oceanic and nearshore ecosystems. Science 282:473-476.

Foster, J. 1978. Working for wildlife: The beginning of preservation in Canada. University of Toronto Press, Toronto.

Foster, J. E., D. Harrison, and I. S. MacLaren, editors. 1992. Buffalo. University of Alberta Press, Edmonton.

Gard, W. 1959. The great buffalo hunt. Knopf, New York.

Gerstell, R. 1985. The steel trap in North America. Stackpole Books, Harrisburg, PA.

Graham, E. H. 1947. The land and wildlife. Oxford University Press, New York.

Greenway, J. C., Jr. 1967. Extinct and vanishing birds of the world. Dover, New York.

Guggisberg, C. A. W. 1970. Man and wildlife. Arco, New York.

Hardin, G. 1968. The tragedy of the commons. Science 162:1243-1248.

Hawley, A. W. L. 1993. Commercialization and wildlife management: Dancing with the devil. Krieger, Malabar, FL.

Hewitt, C. G. 1921. The conservation of the wild life of Canada. Scribner, New York.

Innis, H. A. 1970. The fur trade in Canada: An introduction to Canadian economic history. University of Toronto Press, Toronto.

Irmscher, J. 1999. John James Audubon: Writings and drawings. The Library of America, Penguin Putnam, New York.

Jennings, F. 1993. The founders of America. Norton, New York.

Krech, S., III, editor. 1981. Indians, animals, and the fur trade: A critique of "Keepers of the Game." University of Georgia Press, Athens.

Krech, S., III. 1999. The ecological Indian: Myth and history. Norton, New York.

Lanctot, G. 1960. Histoire du Canada. Library Beauchemin, Montreal.
Mann, C. C. 2002. 1491. Atlantic Monthly 289(3):41–53.
Martin, C. 1978. Keepers of the game: Indian-animal relations and the fur trade. University of California Press, Berkeley.
Matthiessen, P. 1987. Wildlife in America. Viking Press, New York.
McHugh, T. 1972. The time of the buffalo. University of Nebraska Press, Lincoln.
Metcalf, D. R. 1977. Indians and white diseases. Pages 549–551 *in* H. Lamar, editor. Reader's encyclopedia of the American West. Crowell, New York.
Morison, S. E. 1971. The European discovery of America: The northern voyages A.D. 500–1600. Oxford University Press, New York.
Moulton, M. P., and J. Sanderson. 1999. Wildlife issues in a changing world. 2nd edition. CRC Press, Boca Raton, FL.
Newhouse, S., et al. 1894. The trappers guide. Forest and Stream, New York.
Ogden, A. 1941. The California sea otter trade: 1784–1848. University of California Press, Berkeley.
Palmer, T. S. 1912. Chronology and index of the more important events in American game protection, 1776–1911. U.S. Department of Agriculture Biological Survey Bulletin 41.
Phillips, P. C. 1961. The fur trade. University of Oklahoma Press, Norman.
Ray, A. J. 1987. The fur trade in North America: An overview from a historical geographical perspective. Pages 21–30 *in* M. Novak, H. A. Baker, M. E. Obbard, and B. Malloch, editors. Wild furbearer management and conservation in North America. Ontario Ministry of Natural Resources, Toronto.
Roe, F. G. 1955. The Indian and the horse. University of Oklahoma Press, Norman.
Roe, F. G. 1978. The North American buffalo: a critical study of the species in its wild state. University of Toronto Press, Toronto.
Schorger, A. W. 1973. The passenger pigeon: Its natural history and extinction. University of Oklahoma Press, Norman.
Tober, J. A. 1981. Who owns the wildlife? The political economy of conservation in nineteenth century America. Greenwood Press, Westport, CN.
Trefethen, J. B. 1975. An American crusade for wildlife. Winchester Press, New York.
Wilson, A. 1808–1814. American ornithology; or the natural history of the birds of the United States. 9 volumes. Bradford and Inskeep, Philadelphia.

Chapter 7

WILDLIFE CONSERVATION IN THE COLONIAL MOTHER COUNTRY

Except for the province of Quebec, the settlement of the United States and Canada proceeded to a large degree from English colonies along the Atlantic coast. During the Colonial period, from 1600, the common language formed a bond between the former mother country and most of the New World. Privileged persons from each visited and became familiar with conditions on the opposite side of the Atlantic. This exchange grew over time and by the end of the 1800s, when steamships had made ocean travel fast and comfortable, most well-educated, politically influential Americans were well acquainted with the abundant wildlife in the English countryside. This abundance of wildlife was typical of most western European countries, but how it could be reconciled with expanding development of industry and trade was a question for Americans to ponder as they saw wildlife in their own country rapidly becoming extinct under a regime of uncontrolled common use and habitat loss.

The steps by which the legal hunting rights of the English commoner were gradually reduced to nothing have been described (see chapter 4). The class that benefited was that of the landowners. In medieval days, rulers granted control of specified lands to their henchmen in return for military duty. The land-controlling aristocrat, in turn, had to have the military support of the commoners under his protection. In the Renaissance when trade grew again, the land-controlling classes became the land-owning classes. Various aristocrat-serving statutes of the 1200s strengthened the legal foundation for the absorption of common lands into the landlord's ownership. In addition, the Black Death of the 1300s carried off whole families without leaving heirs, their lands then passing to the local nobleman by escheat. During the Tudor era of the 1500s and beyond, many surviving common fields were converted more or less by force to private use, to encourage the national prosperity through wool. Local magnates passed common lands to rich landowners through enclosure, i.e., legalized fencing, which continued in subsequent centuries, justified as necessary for more efficient agriculture. These trends increased the economic power associated with land ownership. Political power also was involved; with emergence of the British House of Commons as the principal legislative body, the local landowner more or less automatically chose, or was, the local representative in that House.

The term "new men," used in the 1500s, referred to common men who had risen to positions of wealth or authority. The Tudors recognized, rewarded, and

The Colonial Mother Country

employed many new men in their successful attempt to elevate the Crown over the hereditary nobles, to concentrate the national power at the center. Many a new man arose by the fortunes of an increasingly mercantile England. With wealth, he sought power and social position. The road to the aristocratic stratum was through land ownership. Estates, then, slipped from the grasp of a hereditary nobility into that of the upwardly mobile entrepreneurs. These and their descendants could live like other gentlemen upon the income from their investments. The investment in land yielded a return from the rents paid by tenants who actually cultivated the farms of the estate. In its ideal form, the estate as a whole consisted of the farms and a stately home for the landlord, his guests, and the servants of the house, and a village housing the workers of the estate. Usually the manor house was set in a large walled park, often stocked with deer. During the full development of country estates, in the 18th and 19th centuries, landscape architecture on a large scale flourished and many a lake or grove were created to perfect the ideal vista. The pervading model was that of classic times when the beauties of nature were extolled over the works of humans.

Typically, estates were entailed, passing wholly to the oldest son. Younger sons could look for heiresses, opportunities in military or colonial administration, or the law. With long-term integrity of the estate guaranteed by entailment, long-term plans for improving the estate could be developed and carried out. The twin aims of these were first to improve the estate as a suitable environment for the landlord and his family, who lived there much of the year, and the many visitors of their social class; and second to improve the estate as a source of economic return.

Wildlife, particularly game, was an important element of the estate environment, for hunting (the chase of game with dogs, followed on horseback) and shooting were widely pursued by the landlord class. After the extinction of wolves and wild boars, the favorite huntable game came to be the red fox, which often provided a long run, challenging for foxhound and horseman. The hedgerows separating farm fields were dense enough to hold livestock but low enough to be jumped by fox-hunting horsemen. It became the usual fence on English estates, providing shelter and nest sites for a host of small birds, mammals, and other creatures, and travel routes for larger species.

With development of light, well-designed shotguns late in the 1600s, shooting became popular. Thereafter, a gentleman could "shoot flying" and often employ dogs especially bred to locate, point, and retrieve game birds. The principal game birds desired came to be the English (originally the Mediterranean) pheasant and the gray (Hungarian) partridge. These were provided with suitable habitat for a free-living existence, of which an important element in farmland was thick residual grass from the previous growing season to provide early spring nesting cover. These game birds, particularly the pheasant, also were raised with the gamekeeper's help, the eggs produced by wild hens being hatched out under bantam hens, and the chicks fed until adulthood. Heavy stocks of game birds were a prime attraction for potential predators, so gamekeepers waged a constant war on all threats to eggs, chicks, and adults, namely, a variety of wildlife that included rats, weasels, stoats, house cats, badgers, crows, jays, hawks, and owls. Control of poachers, too, was part of the gamekeeper's task.

Management of farm units of the estate was conducted by tenants in ways consistent with needs of game, as determined by the landlord and his advisors. A typical unit of habitat for pheasants would be a woody copse, with evergreens and undergrowth to break the wind, and a more open warm interior where the birds could feed and roost. On the typical estate, farmland was managed for game by hedge fencing, control of livestock grazing, carefully planned development of woody cover, and rigid control of predators (except foxes). Many small wildlife species not pursued as game benefited from such management.

Agriculture developed rapidly from primitive beginnings on the English estate. It included cropping systems, animal husbandry, and ultimately fertilization, drainage, and plant selection. The impetus was the desire of the landlord to derive more income, backed up by his ability to invest capital in promising improvements. The landlord class, then, had an interest in how the land and its products were managed. Gentleman travelers observed improvements abroad and tried them out at home.

The traditional cropping pattern on a farm field was a bread grain (wheat or rye) one year, followed by spring-sown barley, oats, beans, or peas, followed by a year of fallow. With little or no fertilization, productivity was low. As an improvement from Flanders in the mid-1600s, crop rotation was introduced, which included turnips and clover, both livestock foods. With more livestock came more manure for fertilization to increase grain production. This advance was followed by introduction of the seed drill from abroad. With seeds sown in rows, the space between rows could be cultivated, greatly reducing competition from weeds, and again increasing crop production. Thus the leisured class provided leadership in a steady agricultural advance, first by picking up ideas from abroad and then by developing new ones at home.

A pattern prevailed of more stock, more manure; more manure, more crops; more crops, more stock. The wealth and security of ownership pattern encouraged improvement of livestock lines for production of meat and milk. Careful control of reproduction in all sorts of domestic livestock, as well as horses and dogs, led to development of many breeds we know today.

Through the 1700s and 1800s agricultural advances irregularly continued. English royalty further legitimized such rural interests by their pursuit of field sports and improvement of their own estates. In 1784, while the American Revolution was concluding and the era of North American wildlife exploitation was beginning, a new periodical appeared in England, the *Annals of Agriculture*. The king of England (under a suitable pseudonym) contributed. By the 1840s the Royal Agricultural Society had been formed in England and the discoveries of Justus von Liebig on plant chemical needs applied to crop fertilization, while the last of the beaver were being scoured from the Rocky Mountains, the southern fur seal and California sea otter were commercially extinct, and thousands of bison hides were being floated down to St. Louis. British production of bread grains was three times what it had been in olden times, and by the 1860s English agriculture attracted world attention.

In the later 1800s, as cheap grain began to flow into England from North America and Australia, the English estate became less economically important for crop production. But it remained a focal point for aristocratic pursuits. By the end of the century it was easier to see a deer in an English park than in the North American forest. The abundance of a few intensively managed game species on European estates that also produced farm and forest crops impressed American visitors. How could it be that the spread of European settlers in North America was marked by widespread wildlife exploitation to the point of actual or virtual extinction of valuable wildlife species over whole regions, while much denser human populations, practicing much more intensive land management, could at the same time maintain an abundance of game?

From our modern perspective, it is clear that while wildlife was abundant on the English estate, it was not diverse. Many species had been hunted to extinction in earlier centuries. Species that were extirpated there before the year 1200 include beaver, bison, brown bear, moose, reindeer, and wolf. Unlike North America, Great Britain does not have wide-ranging herbivores and carnivores, except for red deer (elk). Through agriculture, forestry, and habitat fragmentation and deterioration in Britain, birds such as bustards, ringed plovers, and red-backed shrikes have disappeared while species such as stone curlews, woodlarks, and wheatears have declined severely.

But it was game in the motherland that focused the attention of European settlers in North America, not wildlife diversity. The fact that intensive land management in Europe had been accompanied by the loss of many wildlife species was not as striking, at this time, as the abundance of the few game species that had been successfully integrated with European agriculture. So when the time came for Americans to seek counsel on wildlife conservation, they turned to western Europe for advice.

Meanwhile, since they harbored the families of the upper social class, estates of the colonial mother countries, notably England, France, and Holland, produced each new generation of military officers and colonial administrators. Most of these young men grew up in the country, learning early to ride and shoot, to fish, to pursue an interest in horses and dogs, to become familiar with agriculture and animal husbandry, and to develop some degree of interest in the natural world. Those who went abroad were enthusiastic hunters, often undertaking pursuit of large dangerous predators that threatened their colonial charges. Some wrote about wildlife in their colonial haunts. Retiring home again, they brought the trophies of the chase.

As colonial empires grew and prospered, exotic plants and animals were shipped to the mother countries, where zoological gardens, arboreta, and gardens of exotic plants developed. Specimens went to mother country museums, where specialists were employed to work out the proper classification of the colonial biota.

Wild animals from foreign places were kept as captives by wealthy persons, often rulers, long before the days of Rome. In Europe, zoological gardens often were maintained by wealthy nobles as private menageries; valuable birds and mammals served as princely gifts. English kings had small menageries for their royal pleasure for centuries before the colonial era. But with the flood of new animals from the colonies, the care of zoo animals passed to The Royal Society in 1829. This was the small beginning that grew to the present imposing collection at Regent's Park in London.

The colonial mother countries sent out administrators who, often enough, already had an interest in animals. This interest was encouraged by the interest of the upper social class at home. When wildlife in the colonies became threatened, generally by human population increase and pressure on wildlife habitat (as it had in western Europe in medieval times), colonial administrators set aside some of the best remaining habitats as wildlife sanctuaries (just as their ancestors had done in medieval days). Local inhabitants around each of these wildlife sanctuaries could no longer use those lands legally. Those who did so illegally were termed poachers and controlled by military power. From the time most of the colonial wildlife sanctuaries were established, around the 1930s, to the breakup of the colonial empires, around the 1950s, enough police power was at the disposal of the colonial administrators to control most poaching. With breakup of colonial empires into a multitude of small, often poor, nations, the sanctuaries were generally maintained in principle, but were much more difficult to protect against use by local inhabitants.

The "gentlemanly code" of hunting had prescribed "correct" behavior since medieval times and was firmly ingrained in the minds of the privileged sportsman, who made up the ruling class at home, and the younger-brother officers abroad, who also concerned themselves with game. For them, the English poacher with his snares and the aborigine with his traditional nets and pitfalls were repugnant—the sooner stopped, the better. The notion that one method of taking game was no different from another as far as the game population was concerned was outside their frame of reference. In addition, their homeland persecution of predatory birds and mammals, which they were brought up to accept and applaud, was part of the attitude of gentlemen sent abroad to govern the colonies. Cultural concepts of wildlife conservation came to Canada and the United States principally from England through both upper class immigrants and well-to-do Americans observing the abundant game of English estates firsthand.

Bibliography

Bennett, H. S. 1948. Life on the English manor. Cambridge University Press, Cambridge, England.

Bubenik, A. B. 1976. Evolution of wildlife harvesting systems in Europe. Transactions of the Federal-Provincial Wildlife Conference 40:97–105.

Christian, E. 1817. A treatise on the game laws. Clarke, London.

Dagg, A. I. 1977. Wildlife management in Europe. Otter Press, Waterloo, Ontario.

Hudson, R. J. 1993. Origins of wildlife management in the western world. Pages 5–21 *in* A. W. L. Hawley, editor. Commercialization and wildlife management: Dancing with the devil. Krieger, Malabar, FL.

Leopold, A. 1933. Game management. Scribner, New York.

Lueck, D. L. 1995. The economic organization of wildlife institutions. Pages 1–24 *in* T. L. Anderson and P. J. Hill, editors. Wildlife in the marketplace: The political economy forum. Rowman & Littlefield, Lanham, MD.

Myrberget, S. 1991. Game management in Europe outside of the Soviet Union. Pages 41–53 *in* B. Bobek, K. Perzanowski, and W. Regelin, editors. Global trends in wildlife management. Swiat Press, Krakow, Poland.

Parker, E., editor. No date. The Lonsdale keepers book. Seeley, Service, London.

Strutt, J. 1898. The sports and pastimes of the people of England. Chatto and Winders, London.

Sutherland, W. J. 1995. Introduction and principles of ecological management. Pages 1–21 *in* W. J. Sutherland and D. A. Hill, editors. Managing habitats for conservation. Cambridge University Press, New York.

Taber, R. D. 1961. Wildlife administration and harvest in Poland. Journal of Wildlife Management 25:353–363.

White, T. H. 1936. England have my bones. Putnam, New York.

Wolf, M. L. 1995. An historical perspective on the European system of wildlife management. Pages 254–263 *in* W. F. Sigler, editor. Wildlife law enforcement. 4th edition. Brown, Dubuque, IA.

Chapter 8

WILDLIFE CONSERVATION IN NORTH AMERICA: REGULATION

A principle impediment to interpreting history is that the written record was produced by the small educated class, and so often tends to reflect value judgments held by that class at the time of writing. Thus for England and western Europe around 1600 the written and legal history of human-wildlife relations and values indicates that land ownership should result in wildlife ownership. But the common people often acted as though they should have common ownership and common access to wild creatures. They "poached" game and fish whenever they could; when caught they suffered punishments.

The poacher's motivation appears to be at least threefold. First, the often meat-hungry commoner obtained game for personal consumption. Second, he was attracted by enjoyment of the chase. Third, by taking what was asserted to be the landlord's property, he avenged himself for real or perceived mistreatment by the landlord or his minions. In Europe when war or revolution reduced the probability of catching the poacher, common taking of game increased.

With European colonization of the North American Atlantic seaboard, abundant wildlife provided apparently unlimited opportunities for colonists to take food or furs. From the 1600s well into the 1800s as settlement moved westward, no real probability existed that any laws protecting wildlife (and there were some) would be enforced; the ordinary citizens took wildlife freely for personal use and for sale whenever markets developed.

For example, fed by the railroad system during the 1860s, the public markets of New York, Brooklyn, Boston, and Philadelphia displayed the following species of birds and mammals: 2 species of swans; 4 of geese; 26 of ducks; 6 of grouse, 43 of marsh birds and shorebirds including snipe, rail, crane, gulls, and curlews; also horned grebe, coot, loon, wild turkey, quail, woodcock, passenger pigeon, numerous songbirds, bison, white-tailed deer, mule deer, elk, moose, caribou, antelope, bighorn sheep, mountain goat, hare, rabbit, squirrel, black bear, raccoon, bobcat, opossum, woodchuck, porcupine, skunk, beaver, otter, badger, and muskrat. In 1873, an estimated $500,000 of game was sold in Chicago retail markets: 600,000 prairie chickens (at $3.25/dozen); 300,000 quail (at $1.25/dozen); 60,000 pigeons (at $1.00/dozen); 450,000 pounds of venison (at 8¢/pound); 400,000 pounds of buffalo (at 7¢/pound); 225,000 pounds of antelope (at 10¢/pound); 30,000 pounds of elk (at 5¢/pound); and 10,000 pounds of bear (at 8¢/pound). Cities around the United States and Canada marketed virtually all species of birds and large mammals. And of course there was the plume market for feathered hats. During two separate walks along streets of New York City in 1886, ornithologist Frank Chapman counted 542 of 700 women's hats with feathers or parts of 39 recognizable species of birds. In 1902 at the London Commercial Sales Rooms, 1608 packages of heron plumes were sold. At 30 ounces apiece, that's 48,240 ounces. About four herons produce an ounce of plumes, so the 1608 packages contained the plumes of about 192,960 herons. In 1903 a hunter received $32 per ounce of plumes, which made the plumes worth about twice their weight in gold then. Later the price rose to $80 per ounce.

Wildlife populations in the more densely settled east were declining by 1850, as the pressure of hundreds of local hunters took its toll. But as the railroads connected more remote hunting grounds to city markets, a lively wildlife trade continued.

Just as no social stricture had existed through human history on the sale of game, no social stricture existed on heavy game kills by individuals, except, among prudent tribesmen, an abhorrence of waste. With the advance of civilization, rulers boasted of their bags, the sporting fraternity lauded the daily kills by skillful shooters, calling them "high guns," and Buffalo Bill Cody claimed hero status for his heavy kills.

A preponderance of citizens (and voters) acted as though wildlife should be free for all to take without hindrance. The Report of the Commissioners of Fisheries of Massachusetts stated as early as 1868 that people ignore game laws because we insist on considering wild animals as our remote forefathers did when wildlife was abundant and people were scarce. In the 1800s the mistaken assumption was widespread in Canada and the United States that all natural resources in North America existed in an abundant, ceaseless supply. In 1963 that assumption led former U.S. Secretary of Interior Stewart Udall to term that fallacy the "Myth of Superabundance," i.e., the intoxicating profusion of natural resources of the North American continent which enticed people to think in terms of resource infinity rather than fact.

Under the constitutions of the United States and Canada, any responsibility not specifically assigned to the federal government was automatically to be that of each individual state or province. This was interpreted as giving each state or province responsibility for the common property of wildlife within state or provincial borders.

Given some encouragement toward representative government, North American colonies benefited from a protracted civil war within England (1642 to 1652), which divided and occupied the English ruling class and to an extent diverted their attention from strict control of the American colonies for commercial purposes. By English, and before it, Roman common law, wildlife was the property of none, and thus common property. English law had evolved to the advantage of the rich landowners, but the basic ancient law of common property formed the basis for colonial, and later, state, provincial, and federal American and Canadian law. During the settlement period, English wildlife law was not acceptable due to its unbalanced sense of proportion relative to its allocation of wildlife to the rich and the poor. In the new nations of Canada and the United States, the landowner, far from being the all-powerful person of Europe, was handicapped by deliberately weak laws against trespass; this for long allowed the public to hunt publicly owned game within privately owned habitats. Although wildlife is a public resource, laws against trespass on private land have steadily been strengthened in modern times, so that large landowners have more wildlife benefits than do small or nonlandowners.

The histories of wildlife exploitation and conservation in Canada and the United States have run more or less parallel. But Canada has been spared the extreme loss of animals that the United States has experienced, mainly by virtue of a lower human population and extensive lands unfit for agriculture.

During the treaty period, 1789 to 1871, American Indians surrendered their lands to the U.S government for exclusive rights to smaller tracts, reservations, on which they were expected to live, but did so in squalor. In 1789 Congress appointed the Secretary of War to oversee American Indian affairs. In 1824 the Office of Indian Affairs was established in the War Department, which became the Bureau of Indian Affairs in the Department of Interior in 1947.

By 1900 most American Indians in the United States and Canada lived on reservations or reserves, respectively, and were surrounded by nonnatives. Not until 1924 were U.S. Indians given citizenship and voting rights (U.S. women beat Indians to voting rights by 4 years, blacks beat Indians by 54 years); not until 1960 were Canadian Indians granted the same rights! In 1952 the U.S. Bureau of Indian Affairs decided that American Indians could live anywhere; many continued residing on former reservation lands. Indians have a certain autonomy in managing wildlife resources on their own lands, and in some cases have gone to court and won treaty rights to harvest wildlife off their lands.

Wildlife conservation requires rules (based on biological understanding) to provide adequate wildlife habitat, to control human predation, and some way to enforce those rules. Every forward-looking state, province, and territory eventually passed legislation aimed at wildlife protection. Over time, regulations intended to promote wildlife welfare have become increasingly complex as an ever-increasing mix of human values and behaviors have had to be incorporated.

Historically, wildlife law has had four main goals. Wildlife laws can be written (1) to facilitate removing (hunting) animals from populations managed to produce sustained annual yields in theory and in practice similar to any livestock operation; (2) to regulate human behavior, i.e., to encourage or restrict use of weapons, to license hunters, specify weapons allowed, specify species to be hunted, specify dates for hunting, specify daily bag and possession limits, and limit access to control hunting pressure; (3) to vindicate the alleged rights and desires of wildlife, as today the Endangered Species Act and National Environmental Policy Act accord certain rights to wildlife in the United States; and (4) to favor one socioeconomic class over another with regard to rights to take wildlife.

Ecologists have divided wildlife regulations into restrictions on the take, habitat improvement, and stocking. England used three legislative techniques, eventually handed down to Canada and the United States, to restrict the size of the take: (1) a limited number of people could hunt; (2) during restricted periods; and (3) with controlled methods. Added in the North American colonies was a new regulation banning commercial sale of game. While regulation of hunting is an important tool in wildlife conservation, it is not as important as conserving adequate wildlife habitat.

The history of wildlife management in the United States and Canada can be divided into five approximate categories based on attitudes, condition, and management strategies: (1) era of abundance (1600 to 1849); (2) era of overexploitation (1850 to 1899); (3) era of protection (1900 to 1929); (4) era of game management (1930 to 1965); and (5) era of environmental management (1966 to present). Each major wildlife management effort was aimed at a problem characteristic of an era: (1) local closed seasons were attempted during the era of abundance; (2) bag limits, hunting licenses, and game wardens were introduced during the era of overexploitation; (3) federal protection, migratory bird protection, and game refuges characterized the era of protection; (4) duck stamps, federal aid, multiple use, and wilderness system developed during the era of game management; and (5) endangered species, environmental protection, nongame programs, and protection of Alaskan lands have matured during the current era of environmental management.

In 1896 the authority of the state with respect to wildlife on private land was established by the U.S. Supreme Court, which ruled in Geer vs. Connecticut that game is the property of the state rather than the landowner. From these beginnings developed the system of wildlife conservation practiced in the United States and Canada. Its principal elements are as follows:

1. Since each state wildlife agency is financially supported by the sale of hunting and fishing licenses, it considers the purchasers of those licenses its clients and attempts to increase their numbers.
2. Since wildlife belongs to all state and provincial citizens in common, the charge for hunting and fishing licenses must be low enough to be affordable by all.
3. The state or provincial legislature delegates authority to a wildlife commission or board (United States) or senior civil servant, i.e., deputy minister (DM) (Canada) to make wildlife regulations, but if the board or DM decrees regulations unacceptable to enough voters, the legislature can withdraw that delegated authority.

The United States government is responsible for five general areas of wildlife resources: (1) federal lands; (2) tax-levying authority (e.g., the duck stamp); (3) power to make treaties (e.g., migratory birds); (4) marine mammals and fish; and (5) interstate transport of wildlife (via the Lacey Act of 1900). The states are responsible for all resident game and nongame wildlife and fish, and also have tax-levying authority through issuing various licenses and permits.

In Canada, the federal government has wildlife responsibility for: (1) federal lands; (2) tax-levying authority (e.g., the duck stamp); (3) power to make treaties (e.g., migratory birds); (4) marine mammals; and (5) freshwater and saltwater fish, except that jurisdictional confusion exists between federal and provincial governments with regard to fish. Like the states, the provinces are responsible for all resident game and nongame wildlife, and issue licenses and permits.

Canada and the United States have legislation specifically to protect threatened and endangered species. So do the provinces and states for regional situations.

As wildlife declined, the various states and provinces began to respond, haltingly, to their perceived responsibility for wildlife within their borders. With the obvious threat of wholesale slaughter going on everywhere, their first attention naturally turned to the possibility of controlling human predation. In the early 1800s, for example, Massachusetts outlawed the taking of larks and robins (1818), upper Canada (Ontario) outlawed the taking of deer (1821), Maine outlawed the taking of moose (1830), and Massachusetts outlawed the taking of heath hens (1831).

Passing from province to province and state to state, migratory game such as waterfowl was the property of any particular province or state only when it was within the borders of that province or state. This led to competition between provinces and states to take as much as possible before opportunity was lost. This is reflected in both legislation and its repeal under public pressure. For example, in 1838 New York outlawed use of batteries, i.e., multiple guns, then used to kill large numbers of clustered waterfowl; this law was repealed. In 1846 Rhode Island outlawed shooting of wood duck, black duck, woodcock, and snipe during spring migration to northern breeding grounds; this law was repealed.

These and similar protective laws had little effect on the killing of wildlife because no good way existed to enforce them. Taking the common property of wildlife had always been the right of all members of the community for whom the meat and skins of wild animals were valuable. The ruling class made common use illegal. Whenever such efforts weakened as in the New World (and later during European revolutions), the old common right was reasserted. For the pioneer, hunting and trapping were long important aids toward survival. Even as life became easier, a cultural belief prevailed that game was important family food. This provided justification for continued free access to the commonly owned game.

At the same time, most citizens accepted the protection of nongame species, which they liked to see but did not generally eat. In response to political leadership of the growing, prosperous, urban population, 12 states legislated complete protection of nongame birds between 1851 and 1864. Materially secure bird lovers succeeded in striking a responsive chord in an American public with a strong utilitarian bent; they emphasized the good practical work that small songbirds did to consume weed seeds and insect pests.

The urban population grew in numbers and material prosperity through the 1800s. Major cities of the United States and Canada were in close communication with England. Considering themselves society's leaders, privileged, well-educated individuals became familiar with conditions at home and abroad. The privileged class of North America accepted the wildlife-related values of the English privileged class. If he was a hunter, he took the name of *sportsman*.

Many a sportsman established shooting estates in the English tradition, and sought regulations or closed seasons, hunting methods, bag limits, and sale, storage, and transportation of game. But through much of the 1880s such efforts made little change in the freedom with which the ever-increasing human population took wildlife. They also did little to counter the consequences of overkill throughout the country, consequences that by 1880 were dramatized by the demise of the passenger pigeon and particularly the buffalo.

While many North Americans of European descent took wildlife for food, when opportunity for trade occurred, they seized it. Furs were traded first, but during the second half of the 1800s several rapidly advancing developments favored the commercial game hunter. With growth of industry in the northeastern states, the population and purchasing power of cities grew, strengthening the marketplace for wild game. Transportation by ship and railroad became faster and more extensive so that game on ice could be shipped cityward from greater distances. Communication improved so that word of wildlife concentrations (such as the huge aggregations of nesting passenger pigeons) could spread quickly. Firearms became cheaper and more efficient. Some regulation and enforcement were needed.

Following European precedent, protective laws were passed. Many a legislature made hunting of one species or another illegal. But such laws could not be enforced in the face of public opinion that clung faithfully to the hope that the good old days could go on forever.

It was no secret that hunting in Europe was the prerogative of the privileged class, so it was easy for opponents of protective legislation to brand it as a device to ensure continued sport for the wealthy alone. Commercial hunters, "market hunters" particularly, could argue that they, the common people, should not allow the wealthy to eliminate the common right to take the common wildlife property, as occurred in the old country.

In reality, the age of general wildlife abundance in the more heavily settled eastern states ended around 1850, and that in the U.S. West with the last of the buffalo about 1890. During the interval between these dates, various states and provinces tried to fulfill the responsibility for wildlife custodianship in the name of their citizens, and groped toward effective programs. The first objective that they perceived was somehow to control human predation.

Over the second half of the 1800s, various states and provinces responded haltingly to their perceived responsibility for wildlife within their borders. By 1880 most of the modern game laws were generally in place in the United States: licensing hunters (New Jersey and New York in 1864); bag limit (Iowa in 1878, 25 prairie chickens/day); banned market hunting (Maryland in 1872); and distinguishing resident from nonresident hunter (New Jersey in 1864). In general, the more rural states were slower to attempt to control hunting. Only since 1910 has every state had a wildlife agency. (The federal wildlife agencies in contemporary form did not come into being until 1940 for the U.S. Fish and Wildlife Service and 1947 for the Canadian Wildlife Service.) By about 1900 wildlife conservation concepts had been integrated in most states into a characteristic pattern: to restore and sustain game populations through control of annual harvest; to regulate behavior of hunters through restrictions on weapons, methods, seasons, species, and bag and possession limits; to support enforcement with funds obtained through an annual hunting license, cheaper for state residents and more expensive for nonresidents. But legislation was not enough.

In 1850 New Hampshire and Massachusetts developed the first game warden systems in North America; Maine followed in 1852. In 1865 Massachusetts organized the first state wildlife agency. In states that had not yet done this, wildlife regulation was often the responsibility of county government. But as yet no effective ways of supporting enforcement officers had been developed.

If laws existed, they would be effective only if enforced. The obvious answer to enforcement of laws was to employ enforcement officers. But this required funds and a receptive legal system. Experiments were made with systems that paid enforcement officers a part of the fines levied against the lawbreakers they captured. This was sadly open to corruption and often judicial indifference to the seriousness of the crime, particularly when it was committed by a neighbor. A frequent complaint among early wildlife administrators was that breaking the wildlife law by a member of the community was locally acceptable, but breaking it by some outsider was a punishable crime.

A workable system finally evolved out of accommodation to public opinion. Most people favored some assurance of fair shares for all. This would entail particular control of individuals currently taking "more than their share." Most people considered the highest use of game as food for the hunter's family rather than as a commodity for sale, and most people preferred a maintenance of huntable populations rather than a continued decline.

These opinions bore against commercial or market hunting as taking too much and doing it for money. It was easy for the general public to suppose that commercial (or market) hunters, taking game for profit, were causing the noticeable decline in many game species. This was an oversimplification; commercialization was profitable only where it was cheap to take, process, and transport game relative to its market value. Also contributing to wildlife declines were the less obvious, well-armed, numerous rural populations, motivated by the joy of the hunt and desire for meat, that exerted a steadily mounting continuous pressure on their prey. For the first time in human history, it seems, a serious effort was made to ban commercial sale of game. Ultimately this effort would succeed, with one result being the general conviction that sale of game was immoral.

Providentially, the concept of "fair shares" had popular appeal. It proposed that through open seasons, bag limits, and constraints on methods (weapons, decoys, baiting, etc.), everyone, rich or poor, would have equal access to wild game populations. These measures of control were gradually accepted as part of the developing hunting culture in Europeanized North America, more rapidly in the more prosperous states and provinces and more slowly in the poorer ones. With this acceptance it was feasible to levy a small annual fee (the hunting li-

North America: Regulation

cense) to support a corps of enforcement officers, to ensure that the "other fellow" would behave himself.

With proceeds from license sales, state wardens could be hired to enforce regulations. But since regulations are enforceable only to the extent that they have public acceptance, wildlife regulations had to be tailored to conform with public opinion. Typically the cost of a license was low enough to be generally affordable, the bag limit (per day or year) had to be large enough for individual satisfaction but small enough so that the more successful were not perceived to threaten the opportunity of the less successful, and the weapons and methods of taking were such that the poor as well as the rich could participate.

In modern terms, this arrangement made the state or provincial commission (representing the public good) and the license buyers (each representing the individual good) as stakeholders in comanagement of the wildlife resource. Within this comanagement arrangement, the license buyers were not one group, but many local groups. Each local group acted as though it had some special ownership within its local territory. This behavior appears to be motivated by two human perceptions already discussed: the idea of a degree of communal ownership in the local environment and the custom of mutual support within the local community. Both of these are practically universal among rural communities past and present. One of the consequences of the "local ownership" attitude is that in the early days of wildlife conservation, private landowners had little legal support if they wanted to control trespass by the hunting public.

In carrying out their purpose of protecting and managing wildlife populations, these state commissions were handicapped by shortages of knowledge and funding, and often recalcitrant elements among the public. At the same time, commercial take of marketable game was increasing, and becoming increasingly unpopular with most hunters who were not involved in it. About 1900 the general opinion was that game populations would ultimately disappear as the country was developed, but that meanwhile they could be shared out for a longer time if the yearly take could be controlled. This made the obviously efficient market hunters a logical target. A popular task for legislators was to find some way to constrain commercialization of game. This could not be accomplished through the legislation of any single state, as rapid transit by rail and ship could carry game quickly from state to state. Two remedies were found in U.S. federal legislation: the Lacey Act and the Migratory Bird Treaty.

It was within federal powers to administer interstate commerce. Congressman John Lacey (Iowa) introduced the first federal wildlife regulatory act. In 1900 the Lacey Act made it unlawful to have interstate or foreign commerce in wild products taken, possessed, or sold in violation of state or foreign law. Ducks and geese had long been killed in large numbers along the south Atlantic coast quite legally. But now under the Lacey Act they could no longer be sold in large cities of the north if those northern states made sale illegal. It also meant that the feathers trade could be blocked in the same way. Feathers adorned ladies' hats made by urban milliners, and came largely to northern cities from states on the Gulf Coast. In 1992 Canada passed the Wild Animal and Plant Protection and Regulation of International and Interprovincial Trade Act, which is similar to the Lacey Act.

An even more sweeping application of the federal prerogative in both the United States and Canada was through the treaty power. Little noticed by the general public, the first application of this power was the Fur Seal Treaty of 1910. This was aimed at control of excessive and uncontrolled human predation on fur seals on the open sea, mainly by nationals of the United States, Russia, Japan, and Great Britain (for Canada). It was agreed that a controlled fur seal harvest should take place only on the Pribilof Islands breeding grounds (United States), and the profits shared by the four nations.

A domestic problem of more popular concern was the effective conservation of migratory waterfowl. Since these moved seasonally southward through Canada and the United States in fall, and then made the reverse migration northward in spring, no state or province alone had incentive to control the kill. During 1912 to 1915 repeated efforts were made to establish federal authority over waterfowl, but the only constitutional authority that could be found was the vague directive "to promote the general welfare." This might well suffice for a federal program the various states and provinces wanted, but not for a federal program that lacked broad support. The final effort by the United States government in 1915 sought the broad support by expanding the proposed regulation from "waterfowl" to "migratory birds." Songbirds, particularly, had been widely promoted in the United States and southern Canada for decades, both by associations of bird lovers and by governmental biologists pointing to the weed seeds and insect pests that birds consumed. Villains were found, too, in immigrants from southern Europe, especially Italians, who brought their traditional bird-netting skills to the New World. Still, the proposed protective legislation was threatened as being probably unconstitutional.

In 1916 federal authority was established with certainty in the Migratory Bird Treaty between the United States and Canada, ratified by the U.S. Congress and Canada's Parliament in 1917. In 1936, a similar treaty was signed with Mexico. The treaty is broad. It prohibits shooting during the spring migration and it prohibits commerce. It completely protects most migratory bird species from human predation. For those migratory birds that are deemed huntable, notably waterfowl, snipe, woodcock, doves, and pigeons, it establishes federal regulation. In consonance with the thinking of the time, it did not protect predatory birds.

An advance over the concept that wildlife was a resource to be prudently mined was that, like other living resources, it could be depended upon to produce periodic harvests if husbanded prudently. Given the name of conservation, this concept was ardently promulgated by forester Gifford Pinchot. In the early 1890s, Pinchot studied forest management in western Europe, learning the philosophy of sustained yield management, and noting the cultural difference between the authoritarian German and the democratic Swiss forest-masters. Returning, he quickly became the influential spokesman for the introduction of prudent husbandry to the extensive remaining public forest lands. Sensitive to

American utilitarian public opinion, he emphasized the long-term value of sustained production, namely, its utility in practical economic terms as applied to "the greatest good to the greatest number in the long run." When his friend Theodore Roosevelt (Republican) became President of the United States in 1901, Pinchot gained a powerful proponent of his proposals for resource management for material production. Roosevelt gave national prominence to the concept of conservation, and appointed Pinchot as the first Chief Forester of the new U.S. Forest Service which administrated all national forest land in the United States.

At the same time, a popular exponent of the nonmaterial values in nature, John Muir, saw the Pinchot philosophy as a pernicious reflection of the common American habit of valuing everything in economic terms. Many well-fed citizens sided with Muir, some founded the Sierra Club, and all supported the concept of establishing national parks and protecting them from economic uses. But for the greater part of the United States public domain, and the Crown (public) lands of Canada, the popular conservation concepts were those advocated by Pinchot. In Canada, Robert Campbell became Forestry Superintendent of the Forestry Branch in the Department of the Interior in 1907. Unlike Pinchot in the United States, Campbell had a keen and active interest in game protection and enhancement. But the utilitarian views of the likes of Pinchot prevailed relative to using forestland principally for wood production.

From the late 1800s to 1910 the various states and provinces had integrated wildlife conservation concepts into a characteristic pattern: restore and sustain game populations through control of annual harvest; regulate behavior of hunters through restrictions on weapons, methods, seasons, species, and bag and possession limits; support enforcement with funds obtained through an annual hunting license, cheaper for state residents and more expensive for nonresidents. This last proviso obviously is based upon the perceived ownership of game by residents where it exists. As the advice of Pinchot took effect, wildlife was considered a resource that could actually be increased by some sort of prudent husbandry, aiming at what we would call today sustained material satisfaction.

So that game populations could provide higher harvests in the future, their recovery was the goal not only of state and provincial commissions and sportsmen they served, but also manufacturers of weapons and ammunition needed for hunting. These groups organized sportsmen into clubs and manufacturers into the Sporting Arms and Ammunition Manufacturers Association. Manufacturers had first attempted to collaborate in wildlife restoration with nongovernmental groups, such as the bird-loving Audubon clubs already supporting wildlife protection for nonmaterial satisfactions. But members of bird conservation groups were politically opposed to all hunting in this era, believing it to be the cause of all wildlife decline, and so refused the offer of financial support from the manufacturers' group. Thereupon, the manufacturers' group funded its own foundation, the Sporting Arms and Ammunition Manufacturers Institute.

From 1913 this institute supported and organized annual meetings focusing on ways to increase game populations. These meetings were attended by state, federal, and private individuals and by experts in European methods to whom they could turn for guidance.

From Europe the concepts that gained currency during this era (about 1905 to 1925) were control of poachers and predators (that competed with sportsmen for game), increase of production through artificial means (game farms), and amelioration of habitat loss through artificial means (winter feeding, cultivation of food patches). Appropriate enough for intensive, expensive game management on European estates, two of these managerial practices, artificial propagation and artificial feeding, proved to have little relevance for landscape-scale North American conditions, where the necessary funds were lacking. But they were promoted for the next 2 decades, ultimately to be superceded by habitat management based on an integration of wildlife needs with other goals of land management. Predator control is more complex. Public opinion considered some wild species "good" and other wild species "bad."

A respected American wildlife authority and avid conservationist of the time was William Hornaday, director of the Bronx Zoo, whose writings generally are held in high regard. His writings (in 1914) reflect the concept of "good" and "bad" creatures, and are especially strong with regard to the larger flesh-eaters:

> The wolf: "Wherever found, the proper course with a wild gray wolf is to kill it as quickly as possible."
>
> The coyote: "Every man's hand is against him and he should be killed wherever found in a wild state."
>
> The cougar: "Wherever it is numerous it is fearfully destructive to deer and young elk, and it must be hunted down and destroyed regardless of cost."
>
> Small carnivores: "Every ... mink, skunk, raccoon, opossum and weasel ... is to be regarded as a perpetual enemy of poultry and, unless extenuating circumstances can be found, deserves death. It follows most naturally that a savage little beast which by disposition and weapons is fitted to destroy all kinds of poultry will, in wild regions, be equally destructive to valuable bird life ... "

"For the game of North America, large and small, it has been a fortunate thing that the destruction and disappearance of the fur-bearing animals—game killers nearly all of them—has fully kept pace with the general destruction of game."

> The sharp-shinned hawk: " ... the sharp-shin ... wherever found, old or young ... should be killed without compunction."
>
> Cooper's hawk: " ... the companion in crime of the preceding species, and equally deserving of an early and violent death."
>
> Goshawk: " ... a wholesale destroyer of game-birds, serves no useful purpose, and deserves destruction."
>
> Peregrine falcon: "Each bird of this species deserves treatment with a choke-bore gun. First shoot the male and female, then collect the nest, the young or the eggs. ... They all look best in collections."

North America: Regulation

Hornaday's remarks mirror the general attitude of the time. The Migratory Bird Treaty Act of 1916 to 1918 did not include protection for jays, crows, hawks, or owls, vilified as predators on game birds. Sportsman's clubs held "varmint" shoots and favored bounties for the killing of "bad" species. In absence of any effective opposition, control of mammalian predators large enough to threaten livestock became a federal responsibility.

According to legal concepts of the time, the gray wolf, grizzly bear, coyote, and cougar that were the principal livestock predators in the early 1900s should have come under state and provincial jurisdiction. But the only state and provincial funds for anything connected with wildlife came from license sales to sportsmen, and therefore state and provincial authorities tended to promote goals of sportsmen in their budgeting of funds, leaving little for protection of livestock operators from wild predators. In 1914 with World War I beginning in Europe and North American beef and mutton going to feed the Allies, a U.S. federal program was proposed to control predators of livestock on western rangelands for the support of the war effort. The constitutional support for this was the "welfare" clause (i.e., to promote the general welfare). The western states raised no opposition, so the federal predator control program was created in 1931 when the Animal Damage Control (ADC) Act was passed. (Historically, the "predator control" effort had begun with the first bounty system in the New World as far back as 1630 in Massachusetts Bay Colony, with payment of one penny per wolf.) Additional support for the new federal predator control program came from an expressed concern about rabies in "overabundant" wild carnivores.

By the mid 1920s the gray wolf had been virtually exterminated in the United States, surviving in the Minnesota-Wisconsin-Michigan northlands and northward in Canada. The grizzly bear and cougar were similarly extirpated from most of the west, surviving mainly in the northern Rocky Mountains of the United States and northward. In contrast, the coyote managed to survive through much of the west, often at low population densities, even expanding its range, though diligently pursued in federal programs that succeeded in killing many coyotes and smaller carnivores as well. Range rodent control, too, was part of the federal charge, and burrowing rodents, particularly the colonial prairie dogs, were widely poisoned. A cooperative control program developed among federal agents of the U.S. Biological Survey in the Department of the Interior, ranchers, and state agencies. This cooperative predator and rodent control program generally made a modest annual contribution and persisted for a half century.

In the 1905 to 1935 era, promotion of game production was pursued in part through introduction of species from abroad. Three of the most successful introductions were the ring-necked pheasant (from China), the gray partridge (from Hungary and thence called the Hungarian partridge or "Hun"), and the chukar (from India, Pakistan, and Afghanistan), all from wild-caught stock. To find out how other game birds might fare, many states maintained game farms on which many foreign game birds were raised, with their production placed hopefully in the wild.

At the end of World War I in 1918 when United States and Canadian troops returned to prosperous nations, cheap automobile and railroad transportation gave sportsmen ready access to excellent hunting grounds. Interspersed with marshes and ponds, most farmlands were rich in small game. In forested areas surplus elk were being stocked from Yellowstone National Park, deer populations were recovering because they were protected by the buck law that restricted the kill to adult males, and poaching decreased in prosperous economic times.

With aims of game protection and restoration for the hunter during the 1920s, organizations financed two sorts of field studies for additional information concerning game biology: intensive investigation of the ecology of individual game species (such as bobwhite quail, ruffed grouse, and deer), and extensive study of land use practices on rich soils of the agricultural Midwest. Both of these demonstrated the immense capability of much game to reproduce abundantly under favorable conditions, and the last, conducted by Aldo Leopold, also demonstrated the strong influence of land use patterns on such conditions.

Supported by the Sporting Arms and Ammunition Manufacturers Institute, Leopold's investigations (1928 to 1930) provided insights that led to his book, *Game Management*, in 1933 and to the report of the American Game Policy Committee of the American Game Association, of which he was chairman. The American Game Policy (of 1930) emphasized the need to

1. Extend public land ownership and integrate game with other uses of public land;
2. Protect landowners from damage on private lands and compensate them for game production;
3. Develop fruitful interaction among sportsman, landowner, and public to promote game;
4. Train professionals for game management;
5. Develop an understanding of game biology;
6. Join nonhunters and scientists with sportsmen and landowners in funding and sponsoring game management; and
7. Provide support from general funds to improve all kinds of wildlife, with sportsmen paying for game management, and private funding assisting wildlife education and research.

Obviously another stakeholder existed in the comanagement pattern for game conservation in addition to the state or provincial game department, the licensed hunter, and the sporting arms and ammunition manufacturer, namely, the manager of private land, often the most productive land on the continent. The American Game Policy explicitly stated that the owner of private land should be protected from damage, either from game or hunters presumably, and compensated for game production. But implementation of the policy emphasized only the transfer of land from private to public ownership (with emphasis on waterfowl habitat) and development of a deeper understanding of wildlife biology.

The drought of the 1930s exacerbated the loss of waterfowl habitat that had already occurred through drainage and filling of wetlands caused mainly by agriculture. This crisis in continental waterfowl production was met, in part, by a federal program. In 1934 political cartoonist and enlightened sportsman J. N. "Ding" Darling was appointed as first director of the U.S. Bureau of Biological Survey, forerunner of today's U.S. Fish and Wildlife Service. He originated the idea of the duck stamp (Migratory Bird Hunting and Conservation Stamp), persuaded Congress to pass it, and contributed the artwork for the first stamp in 1934. Required for hunting waterfowl in the United States, the duck stamp is a federal license sold annually to migratory gamebird hunters to raise funds for acquiring and managing wetlands. The parallel Canadian duck stamp (Migratory Bird Hunting Permit) emerged in 1966. Darling also was the driving force behind developing Cooperative Wildlife Research Units, established in 1935 on many land grant university campuses in the United States. Led by a federal biologist, each unit was supported partly by the state wildlife agency, partly by the Wildlife Management Institute (as the sporting arms and ammunition foundation was now called), and partly by the university to conduct research on state wildlife problems and train students to become professional wildlife biologists. (The Ding Darling National Wildlife Refuge on Sanibel Island, Florida, was named in his honor.)

State wildlife departments needed additional funds to investigate the biology of wildlife resources and develop programs of restoration and management, funds that could not be obtained from state legislators in competition with demands for education, highway construction, law enforcement, and the like. This wildlife need was met in 1937 by legislation drafted by Carl Shoemaker, a conservationist from Oregon, and promoted by sportsmen and industry to authorize a tax on the sale of sporting arms and ammunition to aid states in wildlife restoration. He got Senator Key Pittman (Nevada) and Congressman A. Willis Robertson (Virginia) to sponsor it. Robertson added 29 words: " . . . and which shall include a prohibition against the diversion of license fees paid by hunters for any other purpose than the administration of said state fish and game department . . . " With that, the Pittman-Robertson Act was authorized in the United States. As they came to be called, P-R funds provided substantial financial support to state wildlife agencies. They also provided a way for federal authorities to guide state practices. Some state governors and legislators had been in the habit of raiding the state game funds for various worthy purposes unrelated to wildlife conservation. Under the P-R rules, Robertson's 29 words gave state wildlife agencies exclusive use of game funds raised by license sales in order to receive P-R funds as well. Thus the state game agencies now had two channels of assured support from basically the same group—the sportsmen. Compared to other state and provincial agencies, which had to go begging to the legislature every year for funds and hence were in constant competition with each other, state wildlife agencies were in the enviable position of raising and controlling their own budgets. Their loyalty to their sportsmen clientele is understandable, for the ability of administrators to conduct activities under authority of legislation depends on the level and predictability of funding.

State wildlife agencies now were well supported with regard to obtaining information on game populations and developing management programs. But the private landowner was at a disadvantage with regard to wildlife production. Since wildlife on his land was the property of the state or provincial residents in common, he had no more right to it than any other citizen. Even his right to control trespass in that era could be expressed only by his own costly efforts in fencing, signing, and patrol. Meanwhile, wildlife sometimes damaged his crops, and hunters often visited his land uninvited, sometimes damaging fences.

Ease of trespass made the possibility of charging for access impracticable in most cases. So the presence of game on the land of the private landowner, generally a farmer in the more fertile regions, seldom provided income and often added cost. Not surprisingly, farmers were often less than enthusiastic about including wildlife as a desirable crop.

Bibliography

Anderson, S. H. 1999. Managing our wildlife resources. 3rd edition. Prentice Hall, Upper Saddle River, NJ.

Bean, M. J. 1983. The evolution of national wildlife law. Prager, New York.

Belanger, D. O. 1988. Managing American wildlife: A history of the International Association of Fish and Wildlife Agencies. University of Massachusetts Press, Amherst.

Bolen, E. G., and W. L. Robinson. 1999. Wildlife ecology and management. 4th edition. Prentice Hall, Upper Saddle River, NJ.

Bolle, A. W., and R. D. Taber. 1962. Economic aspects of wildlife abundance on private lands. Transactions of the North American Wildlife and Natural Resources Conference 27:255-267.

Borland, H. 1975. The history of wildlife in America. Arch Cape Press, New York.

Committee on Agricultural Land Use and Wildlife Resources, editors. 1970. Land use and wildlife resources. National Academy of Sciences, Washington.

Chapman, F. 1903. The economic value of birds to the State. Lyon, Albany, NY.

Dagg, A. I. 1974. Canadian wildlife and man. McClelland and Stewart, Toronto.

Ehrlich, P. R., D. S. Dobkin, and D. Wheye. 1988. The reader's handbook: A field guide to the natural history of North American birds. Simon & Schuster, New York.

Foster, J. 1978. Working for wildlife: The beginning of preservation in Canada. University of Toronto Press, Toronto.

Gilbert, F. F. 1993. The vision: Wildlife management in North America. Pages 23-33 in A. W. L. Hawley, editor. Commercialization and wildlife management: Dancing with the devil. Krieger, Malabar, FL.

Gilbert F. F., and D. G. Dodds. 2001. The philosophy and practice of wildlife management. 3rd edition. Krieger, Malabar, FL.

Giles, R. H. 1978. Wildlife management. Freeman, San Francisco.

Gray, G. 1995. Wildlife and people; the human dimensions of wildlife ecology. University of Illinois Press, Urbana.

Hornaday, W. T. 1914. Wild life conservation in theory and practice. Reprint 1972. Arno Press, New York.

Irmscher, J. 1999. John James Audubon: writings and drawings. Penguin Books, New York.
Leopold, A. (Chairman). 1930. Report to the American Game Conference on an American game policy. Transactions of the American Game Conference 17:284–309.
Leopold, A. 1933. Game management. Scribner, New York.
Lund, T. A. 1980. American wildlife law. University of California Press, Berkeley.
Lyster, S. 1985. International wildlife law: An analysis of international treaties concerned with the conservation of wildlife. Grotius, Cambridge, England.
Matthiessen, P. 1987. Wildlife in America. Viking Press, New York.
Moulton, M. R., and J. Sanderson. 1999. Wildlife issues in a changing world. 2nd edition. CRC Press, Boca Raton, FL.
Musgrave, R. S., and M. A. Stein. 1993. State wildlife laws handbook. Government Institutes, Rockville, MD.
Musgrave, R. S., J. A. Flynn-O'Brien, P. A. Lambert, A. A. Smith, and Y. D. Marinakis. 1998. Federal wildlife laws handbook with related laws. Government Institutes, Rockville, MD.
Palmer, T. S. 1912. Chronology and index of the more important events in American game protection 1776–1911. U.S. Department of Agriculture Biological Survey Bulletin 41.
Regelin, W. L. 1991. Wildlife management in Canada and the United States. Pages 55–64 *in* B. Bobek, K. Perzanowski, and W. Regelin, editors. Global trends in wildlife management. Volume 1. Swiat Press, Krakow, Poland.
Scalet, C. G., L. D. Flake, and D. W. Willis. 1996. Introduction to wildlife and fisheries: an integrated approach. Freeman, New York.
Shaw, J. H. 1985. Introduction to wildlife management. McGraw-Hill, New York.
Sigler, W. F. 1995. Wildlife law enforcement. Brown, Dubuque, IA.
Smeltzer, J. F. 1985. Wildlife law enforcement: An annotated bibliography. Colorado Division of Wildlife, Fort Collins.
Strom, D. 1986. Birdwatching with American women. Norton, New York.
Tober, J. A. 1981. Who owns the wildlife? The political economy of conservation in nineteenth-century America. Greenwood Press, Westport, CT.
Trefethen, J. B. 1975. An American crusade for wildlife. Winchester Press, New York.
Trombetti, O., and K. W. Cox. 1990. Land, law, and wildlife conservation: The role and use of conservation easements and covenants in Canada. Wildlife Habitat Canada, Ottawa.
Udall, S. 1963. The quiet crisis. Holt, Rinehart, and Winston, New York.
Warren, L. S. 1997. The hunter's game: Poachers and conservationists in twentieth-century America. Yale University Press, New Haven, CT.
Williamson, L. L. 1987. Evolution of a landmark law. Pages 1–17 *in* H. Kallman, C. P. Agee, W. R. Goforth, and J. P. Linduska, editors. Restoring America's wildlife 1937–1987. U.S. Fish and Wildlife Service, Washington.
Wing, L. W. 1951. Practice of wildlife conservation. Wiley, New York.

Chapter 9

WILDLIFE CONSERVATION IN NORTH AMERICA: LAND USE TO 1945

In addition to commercial hunting, the factor that most influenced wildlife populations in North America was land use and its effect on wildlife habitats. American Indians had modified the landscape probably over thousands of years by burning parts of their hunting grounds periodically. This promoted grasslands and open woodlands producing good forage for game. For some centuries before European colonization, American Indians in suitable regions began to clear some natural vegetation and grow domestic crops on a small part of their tribal lands, hunting and gathering over the remainder. They had no concept of individual ownership beyond the clothing, ornaments, weapons, etc., of the individual person. The land that supported them, the tribal territory, was used and defended by the tribal members in common.

Europeans had once had similar customs, but with the rise of kings came a rise in the concept of kingly ownership of his domain and his transfer of portions of it to his retainers. At times he bestowed only surface rights to the land, retaining royal ownership in whatever resources might lie beneath. For centuries the original common lands and the newer private lands were intermingled, but as has been seen, the trend was for a more and more complete land ownership by the ruling class.

European colonists in North America came from nations in which most land was owned by landlords who had not hesitated to evict many small farmers into poverty and keep the rest on as obedient tenants. Leaving the oppressed conditions of the Old World for the New, settlers from Europe were eager to achieve complete ownership of whatever land they could acquire.

In the United States, individual states first owned all land not in private hands, but soon ceded these to the federal government. Land was being surveyed even in colonial days to establish identifiable boundaries. With nationhood, a survey system was instituted for the entire country, constantly extended as new regions were acquired. With permanently marked section lines, an established survey grid set a pattern of mile-square land units (sections) in groups of 36 (townships).

Where this system was in place, each individual section (and smaller portion) could be identified and used for purposes of the federal government when on land still in the public domain. These included grants in payment for services, sales to bring cash into the national treasury, gifts to promote rapid settlement, and reservations for permanent public use. Those lands passing into private hands were ordinarily owned completely, surface and subsurface alike, for whichever use the proprietor desired. Anything less would have been politically untenable. Unlike in Canada generally, in the United States it was long the policy to pass public land into private ownership, a policy unpracticed by and confusing to the indigenous people.

In the early United States, hunters and trappers explored ahead and pioneer settlers followed close behind into the regions more favorable for farming. It was soon seen that a strong westward advance provided a strong claim to regions still contested by European powers. As for the fur trade, before 1900 most furs were exported from North America to European and other markets. By 1900 the United States in particular was importing furs as the fur market in North America expanded. In fact, between 1860 and 1880 mink ranching began in the United States.

Rapid settlement became a national aim. The early vision was of a nation of traditional subsistence farmers, self-reliant in practically all their needs. The common occupation was traditional farming. It encouraged large families, with children in their teens ready to move from the old farm and create another much like it on the widely available additional land.

Traditional farming depends on human and domestic animal power and provides sustenance for farm families and domestic animals. The available time and energy limit the amount of land that a family can farm, and also dictate the variety of crops the farm must produce. The farm is divided into smaller fields to accommodate the diverse crops needed locally by humans and livestock. One major crop is practically always grain (wheat, barley, corn, etc.) for human food and domestic animal supplement. Spreading and increasing with the westward flow of settlement, North American grain production had a major impact on seed-eating wildlife.

Larger seed-eating native game birds such as prairie chickens (including the now extinct heath hen of the seaboard colonies), sharp-tailed grouse, wild turkeys, and the various species of ducks and geese, among others, found cultivated grains an excellent winter food. Waste grain left after harvest (and also grain stored over winter in fields) improved winter living conditions for these, if other habitat elements such as nesting cover and drinking water were adequate. Early agriculture often led to rapid increases in population, once seed-eaters had learned to eat this new food. Prairie chickens, sharp-tailed grouse, and bobwhite quail were relatively large, easily seen, and valued as game. These initially flourished with grain farming and even expanded their ranges.

The relative abundance of these game birds increased as grain farming spread in regions of productive soils. One observer noted that in 1835 a day's hunt on Illinois farmlands for prairie chickens might yield a dozen a day, but in the following era 50 a day was possible. Similar rising levels of game bird abundance with the spread of grain farming were noted widely across the continent.

But in the best regions for farm production, this abundance was followed by a steep decline, continuing through the late 1800s and beyond. The decline was obvious and caused concern, but its cause was not understood.

Popular villains decimating game were supposed to be predatory animals, commercial market hunters, and "game hogs" who took more than their share. These were demonized in three national magazines that appeared in the 1870s: *American Sportsman* (1871), *Forest and Stream* (1873), and *Field and Stream* (1874). These provided evidence against the "enemies of game" along with tales of hunting, fishing, and natural history. Such publications supported the growth of public opinion against the supposed causes of game declines and set the political stage for measures to reduce predators, ban the sale of game, and limit the allowed daily or seasonal "bag" by the more skillful hunters, all of which became parts of the wildlife conservation effort by the early 1900s.

These assumptions about the causes of game decline had some validity for large species with relatively slow reproductive rates, such as elk, deer, and particularly bear. But prairie chickens and sharp-tailed grouse were another matter because their precipitous decline was so dramatic. Their reproductive rates were so high that, as long as habitat was favorable, a large proportion of the fall population could be shot each year, followed by a good hatch and a restored population. Not until the era of population research began in the 1920s was the sequence of events understood that caused the prairie grouse boom and bust in the fertile midwestern states through the mid- and late 1800s.

Field studies of wild populations demonstrated that integration (interspersion) of the critical habitat needs—food, cover, and water—were correlated with success of reproduction and survival of young; most game species did well when these essentials were close to each other and poorly when they were far apart. The daily movement of an undisturbed individual or flock was far shorter than had been supposed. On fertile farmland the introduction of grain provided abundant food. As long as some uncultivated land (nesting and escape cover) and water were near the ever more numerous grain fields, populations of grain-eaters such as prairie grouse increased—the situation Illinois experienced between 1836 and about the 1860s. But as ever more intensive farming continually converted uncultivated to cultivated grainfield, a time came when cover for nesting and resting near available food became critically short.

This sequence occurred whenever high farm productivity encouraged increasingly intensive agriculture. It was quantified for wheatfields of eastern Washington and sharp-tailed grouse. There, grouse populations increased as the proportion of the Palouse prairie converted to wheatfields increased, up to a point; when the proportion of landscape in wheat exceeded 70%, the grouse population abruptly declined to near regional extinction.

In the fertile midwestern states, the proportion of land under intensive cultivation had risen to 75% in Illinois about 1880, in Ohio about 1890, in Iowa shortly after 1900, and continued to rise. Meanwhile the Midwest population of seed-eating prairie grouse, once so abundant, dramatically declined toward zero. The intensity of cultivation continued through the years of World War I (1914 to

1918) and into the early 1920s, as commercial farming became ever more different from the traditional subsistence regime of the North American pioneer and settler.

Traditional farms could well be termed subsistence farms, for they met almost all needs of the farm family and their livestock. With its various fields in different crops separated by weedy, shrubby fence lines, the traditional farm was ecologically diverse. Additional diversity was provided by areas not cultivated: woodlots, marshes, and steep or rocky places. The glaciated regions of the north-central United States and adjacent Canada were characterized by numerous marshes and ponds (potholes) that produced an abundance of waterfowl, muskrats, mink, and many other species.

The Jeffersonian vision of a nation of self-sufficient farmers was shattered by a national need for food for the workers in the burgeoning industrial cities from the mid-1800s. Encouraged by government, railroads were extended from eastern Canada and northeastern United States inland, soon reaching the fertile midwestern states and prairie provinces, and then westward in the United States and Canada, transporting surplus crops to market. Ready access to markets began to shift farm production toward cash crops, starting the transformation of the traditional farm to the commercial farm.

Federal programs that supported agriculture included the U.S. Indian Removal Act (1830), U.S. Morrill Act (1862, 1890), establishing the agricultural (land-grant) colleges, U.S. Homestead Act (1862), opening federal lands for free settlement, and much later Canada's Agriculture Rehabilitation and Development Act (1962). Other early acts that abetted economic land expansion in the United States were the Pacific Railroad Act (1862) and the Timber and Stone Act (1878). The General Mining Law (1872) is still in effect today. It allows title to surface areas of public land as well as underground mineral rights and has caused some of the most desirable public lands to be removed from public ownership.

All wars have some impact on the landscape, thus altering wildlife habitat and populations. The U.S. Civil War was no exception. For example, during the battle of May 5–7, 1864, known as the Wilderness, located in a tangled maze of second-growth woodland and underbrush on the south bank of the Rapidan River in Virginia, the woods caught fire from the shelling. In the process of inadvertently altering wildlife habitat, the fire burned about 200 wounded Union soldiers to death. (About 25,500 men were lost in the bloody 2-day battle.)

The Civil War hastened the shift from traditional to commercial farming through growth of northern industry and transportation. The railroad came first in improving the mobility of people to exploit and settle new regions. Not far behind, in Germany, were Gottlieb Daimler and Karl Benz, who in 1885 independently developed the gasoline automobile, which in 1908 Henry Ford mass produced in the United States as the affordable Model T. With their needs for roads (and fossil fuel), the car and truck dramatically altered the landscape, accessibility to remote regions, human settlement, marketing of agricultural and other products, and impact on wildlife populations from habitat fragmentation and change, hunting, and general human encroachment.

With ready markets and transport, agriculture in the more productive regions quickly progressed from subsistence to commercial management, an adaptation encouraged by establishment of state colleges in the United States for research and extension (i.e., making the results of research available to the public) funded by federal tax dollars. A rich store of agricultural knowledge was already available in England and other older countries, but much new knowledge also had to be acquired for peculiar North American conditions. The focus of effort was always toward practical results that would enhance productivity of the land in agricultural crops, and the most favorable economic benefits to farmers. Wildlife was of interest to the farm community mainly as "good" species that consumed injurious insects or weed seeds, and "bad" species that damaged crops. For this reason much early federal wildlife research focused on food habits.

During the late 1800s to early 1900s several trends in agricultural land use continued to grow stronger in the productive farming regions of fertile soils and adequate rainfall, producing major trends that steadily reduced wildlife habitat diversity:

1. Sale of farm products brought cash that could be used to buy more efficient farm equipment, replacing several men wielding scythes with one— the man with a horse-drawn mower. Shortly after the turn of the century, the horse was being replaced by the tractor, and the mower by the combine. Each step toward more mechanical efficiency increased the amount of work that a man could do in a day. So farms grew larger as more successful farmers bought out their neighbors, and fields became larger as fences between former neighbors were removed.
2. With each increase of cash and power, more changes could be made in the original landscape. Wet fields, marshes, and ultimately ponds could be drained and cultivated; streams could be straightened; gullies could be filled and cultivated; and woodlots, no longer needed for fuel, could be cleared and cultivated.
3. As farm advice from universities improved, each region specialized more in the crop or crops for which it was best suited, leading toward regional monocultures.
4. As higher-yielding crops were introduced, more fertilization was needed to maintain production.

Wetlands not converted to farmland by draining were still affected by agriculture on their watersheds because cultivated lands were subject to water erosion, which carried silt into ponds and streams. Effects of silt include reduction of photosynthesis and hence reduced oxygen production by aquatic plants, smothering of bottom organisms, and increasing dead organic matter which decays and consumes oxygen. Such deleterious effects were compounded by a well-intentioned but disastrous federal program of carp introduction, which ensured that bottom sediments would be well stirred. So wetlands were not only being reduced in area but also in productivity.

The more productive farmlands were the very regions where game had recently been so abundant, but the resulting decline in wild species there continued to disturb the major groups concerned with game abundance: the states and provinces, which were responsible for wildlife and had recently begun to sell hunting licenses to hunters and fishermen; the license-buying sportsmen; and the manufacturers of sporting arms and ammunition. Through the early 1900s these groups collaborated to consider remedies. They favored abolition of market hunting and sale of game, predator control, artificial breeding and feeding of wild game, and introducing game species perhaps better suited to new farmland conditions.

Not until the era of the late 1920s to early 1930s was the need recognized for facts about what was actually controlling game populations. Funds raised to support field investigations focused in two ways: intensive study of individual game species and extensive study of game on productive soils of the Midwest where game had been so abundant and was now so scarce.

It was becoming clear that the landowner and his values and behavior controlled land use and the pattern of land use that controlled wildlife populations in the more productive regions of the continent. But over most of the agricultural land of the United States and Canada, interests of sportsman and landowner diverged. Though landowners in frontier days had been subsistence farmers, they had increasingly become commercial producers, as the national heavy transportation network had developed. As a businessman, each landowner made managerial decisions with considerations of economic investment and return in mind. As noted earlier, wildlife did not figure as an economic asset, since wildlife belonged to the citizens of the state in common, and in any event could not (except for furs) be sold on the open market. Furthermore, weak protection against trespass let hunters roam largely at will across private farms. So the economic value of game to the farmer ranged from neutral to negative, as each made managerial decisions based on crop production and cash income.

In the 1930s while the American Game Policy was being considered by game conservation stakeholders (sportsmen, state game agencies, and sporting arms and ammunition manufacturers), farmers were suffering economically. Drought withered seedling crops and wind carried away finely cultivated topsoil, especially in the Dust Bowl region of the Great Plains in the United States. The depressed economy meant depressed values of those crops that did mature. The drop in farm income often made impossible the payments on mortgages, crop loans, and farm equipment.

While national programs were being considered and devised, impoverished people on the land (and often their jobless cousins from the city) were reverting to the ancient subsistence economy, taking wildlife for food from their local territories, despite whatever protective laws were on the books. Their neighbors in the same fix did the same thing or at least understood and condoned. For enforcement officers, arresting someone seemed futile if he would be dismissed by the court with a warning or, if fined, could not pay and might be jailed at public expense.

The 1930s were a time of economic catastrophe for North America. Severe drought was joined by the Great Depression that made human suffering commonplace. For the United States, the response was to turn toward revival of the economy through public works. (Construction of the mighty Grand Coulee Dam on the Columbia River in Washington state, for example, began in 1933 as a project to make work more so than to make hydroelectricity, even though it caused severe environmental damage from massive flooding and from completely blocking salmon migrating to their spawning grounds in British Columbia 150 miles upstream.) Public works concerning renewable resources called for a measure of professional knowledge. This led to support of professional education in renewable resources. Schools of agriculture and forestry already existed, and had their supporters in state and federal legislatures. Similar separate specializations began to emerge relative to range, water, wildlife, and recreation.

Agricultural stakeholders included farmers, commercial buyers, crop transporters, agricultural colleges and experiment stations, state and provincial agricultural bureaus, departments of agriculture for the United States and Canada, and sympathetic state, provincial, and federal legislators. They looked for public help. Anxious to pull their nations out of the financial depression, the federal governments began to provide assistance. New or enlarged government programs aimed to increase farm production and income: dams to store water for irrigation and produce electricity to pump that water and provide rural electrification; crop research and the means to promulgate the results through farm advisors; cash support for crop values; and other similar programs. Along with more rain and then the demands of World War II, such measures vastly increased the need and ability to produce more commercial farm crops through more intensive management: more complete cultivation of productive soils, greater use of high-producing crop strains, greater application of fertilizer, and a stronger tendency toward monoculture of the crops best suited to each particular region.

As the fertile farmland became more monotonous and homogeneous, it provided less of the environmental diversity that would support a diversity of wild plants and animals. Simple habitats support only a few species, but quite well. The adapted species increase rapidly and are pests to be controlled if they damage the crops. As chemical insecticides were developed and could be afforded, they were used more, with new crop strains and chemical formulations compensating the tendency of pest insects to develop resistance.

To the sportsman, widespread introduction of the alien ring-necked pheasant and the gray partridge somewhat remedied the continued loss of habitat adequate to maintain substantial populations of native game birds, such as the three species of prairie grouse (sharptail, greater prairie chicken, lesser prairie chicken). Both aliens managed to reproduce and spread even as cultivation became more intense, up to a point. The pheasant was also easy to raise in captivity; well-advertised production and release by state game agencies promoted favorable public relations.

The onset of World War II, 1939 (Canada) to 1941 (United States), slowed and often reversed the pressures of commercial crop production on wildlife habitats on fertile soils. The crops were still in high demand, but diversion of industry to the materiel of war made it increasingly difficult to keep farm machinery in repair, gasoline was less available, and many farm sons went into the service. Often this reduced the amount of land under cultivation. Abandoned farm fields soon were producing volunteer plant cover; some wildlife species flourished in these restored habitats. But following World War II the intensity of cultivation, environmental simplification, and use of chemical pesticides soon exceeded earlier levels.

During European settlement particularly in the United States, national policies favored passing land from public to private ownership; the regions most suitable for commercial agriculture became more and more intensively cultivated, as we have seen. By the period 1880 to 1900 highly productive commercial farmlands were so intensively cultivated that resident native game birds had dwindled away.

In this same era the vast regions unsuited for intensive agriculture—for example, forested mountains and dry grasslands—remained largely in public ownership but were used locally and commercially without government control or supervision. New public values and uses for these less productive lands began to emerge.

The concept of devoting units of landscape to human pleasure and recreation was no new thing. The rich and powerful had created such parks and paradises for themselves for centuries past. Even in the new United States and Canada, wealthy persons had large estates for their own pleasure, on the European model. But wildland public parks were not commonly owned and open to common use anywhere until 1872, when Yellowstone National Park was marked off from the rest of the United States public domain (federal lands) for retention in public ownership as the first extensive wildland national park in the world. (Nevertheless, despite park regulations, park employees and political appointees continued to slaughter wildlife for fun and profit for another 22 years.) An earlier national park, the small Arkansas Hot Springs National Reserve, had been set aside 40 years earlier in 1832, and provided the model for public lands reserved for protection and public enjoyment.

Canada received its first national park in 1887, Rocky Mountains Park, which was to become Banff National Park. In both nations, other national parks were carved out of scenic, though thought to be materially unproductive, parts of public domain, particularly in the mountainous arid west. Typically on each, wildlife was protected from hunting, at least in theory. For local legislators, this was acceptable because the actual areas involved were relatively small or remote and remaining public lands extensive. Then, too, the rapidly increasing access by train promised local economic profit from tourism.

Ever since the mid-1800s prospectors searched the western mountains for precious minerals in the extensive remaining public domain. When they could, these prospectors often burned off the encumbering vegetation to reveal characteristics of the surface, and at other times cut timber for mine props and lumber. The advancing railroads needed railroad ties (sleepers) cut from the forest, and soon provided transport of lumber to the market. Accidental fires were common. The public forests, in short, were being consumed by local material needs.

Concern for these publicly owned forests grew, and as early as 1864 George Marsh's book, *Man and Nature*, documented many mountain forest abuses in the ancient Mediterranean lands, abuses that had turned flourishing forested regions into stony deserts, with the strong implication that the same pattern was clear in North America. Public forests were reserved from private ownership and protected as valuable watershed cover. That concept grew. By 1891 in the United States the first forest reserves were withdrawn by presidential proclamation from the public lands that were slated for disposal; in Canada the first forest reserves were authorized in 1906 by the Forest Reserves Act. The main establishment of forest reserves was between 1891 and 1910, and at first the forests, like the parks, were proposed to be wholly protected wildlife refuges. But they were so extensive that this proposed reduction in hunting opportunity was completely unacceptable to the local political communities. The idea of national forests as wildlife refuges was quickly dropped.

Under Gifford Pinchot, in 1910 the U.S. Forest Service was formed to administer the forest reserves, and Pinchot, politically astute, arranged to have this service placed in the powerful federal U.S. Department of Agriculture, thus separating the administrations of the federal land and wildlife agencies: forests under USDA, and parks, rangelands, and federal responsibilities for fish and wildlife under the comparatively low-budgeted U.S. Department of Interior. This separation established a continuing weakness in the U.S. federal ability to function as an effective stakeholder in coordinating local natural resource programs that included lands under separate jurisdictions of the U.S. Department of Agriculture and U.S. Department of Interior.

Pinchot promoted the concept of economic utilitarian conservation, the integrated production of many goods and services from the same public lands, a philosophy at odds with that of John Muir, the nature apostle, then deeply involved in establishing Yosemite National Park and the Sierra Club. Unlike Pinchot, Muir believed in preserving large undisturbed tracts of land for natural and esthetic purposes largely nonmaterial. Pinchot's view prevailed in the extensive national forests, while Muir's prevailed in the much less extensive national parks.

A similar split in administration occurred in Canada between the Forestry Branch (public forests) and the Parks Branch (public parks), each responsible for wildlife affairs in its own domain. The Forestry Branch does not directly manage the public forestlands, but collaborates with each province, which is the direct manager of the public forests within its boundaries. The states also manage forestlands. These are lands, two sections in each township, that were universally reserved for the support of public education, and which are often forested. In summary, then, most public forests are provincially managed in Canada and federally managed in the United States, while a much smaller area in the United States is managed by each state and even some counties.

About the same time period, Gordon Hewitt and James Harkin stand out as Canada's great wildlife crusaders for their varied, tireless, and peerless contributions to Canadian wildlife: Harkin as commissioner of Canada's national parks during their development and expansion years, when protection for wildlife in Canada was nil; Hewitt as entomologist for the Canada Department of Agriculture. Harkin shared the philosophy and passion of John Muir, but disagreed with Canada Forestry Superintendent Robert Campbell who wanted all wildlife matters, including those in the national parks, handled by his Forestry Branch. In 1917 wildlife protection in Canada's national parks was to remain within the Parks Branch rather than the Forestry Branch. Hewitt was largely responsible for Canada's entry into agreement with the United States regarding the Migratory Bird Treaty. Hewitt and Harkin were ably supported by Prime Minister Wilfred Laurier and his minister of the Department of Interior and chairman of the Commission on Conservation, Clifford Sifton. Because commissions on conservation cooperated closely on both sides of the border, the United States and Canada emerged with almost identical policies to conserve wildlife (see chapter 8).

About this same time period, various landmark books led the way toward establishing a reliable factual basis for future development of conservation programs. In 1909 Canadian biologist Ernest Thompson Seton began publishing his comprehensive four-volume *Lives of Game Animals*, crammed with facts of the lives and deaths of the game and furbearing mammals of North America. American preservationist William Hornaday published *Our Vanishing Wild Life* in 1913 and *Wild Life Conservation in Theory and Practice* in 1914, Canadian entomologist Gordon Hewitt published *The Conservation of the Wild Life of Canada* in 1921, and American wildlife professor Aldo Leopold published *Game Management* in 1933.

An early task of the U.S. Forest Service was to control forest fires. Another was to regulate the harvest of sawlogs. Forest rangers also kept records of game abundance and collaborated with the new state wildlife agencies in attempting to control excessive killing of game by wild or human predation. In Canada such tasks fell initially to provincial forest rangers, since most forested lands were Crown lands administered by the provinces, and ultimately to newly established provincial wildlife agencies except for fire control and logging.

As the state wildlife agencies became stronger, the U.S. Forest Service gradually left wildlife affairs to them and confined itself to managing trees on national forest land for production of lumber. Through the early 1900s fires and logging on both public and private forestlands in the West rapidly increased the amount of shrubby regenerating forest. In the same era, extensive marginal farmlands in the East were abandoned as uneconomical, and there too the shrubby regenerating forest crept back. Wildlife of the subclimax forest increased as its habitat increased, a gain noticed principally in the form of conspicuous game species such as mule deer, white-tailed deer, and ruffed grouse. In regions where hunting was effectively regulated, deer particularly became more abundant. By the 1920s deer were so abundant in some localities that they were overusing their more nutritious forage and perishing in winter snows. The first reaction of wildlife agencies and their sportsmen clientele was to provide supplemental winter food. This practice was customary in the intensively managed conifer forests of Europe, but it was impractical over most of the huge stretches of North American forests.

In the same 1920s era the biological observations of Herb Stoddard, Aldo Leopold, and other American investigators demonstrated that the natural rate of increase in the common game species was much higher than had commonly been thought. In 1933 Leopold brought together his thoughts on game biology and production in the book *Game Management*, and spoke of *biotic potential*, the unimpeded rate of reproduction. He realized that population growth at such a rate would soon fill any available habitat, and that competition then would occur between one individual and another for the scarcer necessities of life. Deer winter-kills (through starvation) that began to occur here and there demonstrated the validity of this concept. The task of the hunter was to make a sharp reduction in the deer population in autumn, following which the survivors would be at a comfortably lower population density and have an easier time through the adverse winter season. Paul Errington in 1945 developed the concept further by finding that muskrat populations of relatively lower winter levels showed a proportionally high reproductive gain the following year, while dense winter populations showed a lower reproductive gain the following year, a relationship he termed *inversity*. These constructs provided a basis for game management that supported the aims of state and provincial wildlife agencies and manufacturers of sporting arms and ammunition.

While the public forests in the United States were first being regulated by the U.S. Forest Service from 1910 to the mid-1930s, extensive semidesert public lands were not yet under professional federal management. The U.S. range livestock industry acquired its own federal agency, first with the Taylor Grazing Act of 1934 and then with the U.S. Bureau of Land Management in 1946. This federal agency was given charge of those parts of the public domain not already assigned to some other agency—the driest parts used mainly for seasonal grazing, plus scattered units here and there—making the U.S. Bureau of Land Management the largest public landowner in the United States, with almost twice the land area as the U.S. Forest Service. But unlike the U.S. Forest Service and the U.S. Natural Resources Conservation Service (the former U.S. Soil Conservation Service) in the well-funded U.S. Department of Agriculture, the U.S. Bureau of Land Management was placed within the relatively low-budgeted U.S. Department of the Interior along with the U.S. National Park Service and the U.S. Fish and Wildlife Service.

The situation in Canada has been somewhat similar to that in the United States. Wildlife management in Canada began at the federal level with the Commission of Conservation constituted by Wilfred Laurier under the Conservation Act of 1909. With passage of the Dominion Forest Reserves and Parks Act of 1911, Canada became the first country in the world to have a government organization devoted solely to management of national parks. (The national parks system in the United States began in 1916.) Parks Canada now is within the Department of Canadian Heritage. Like the U.S. Fish and Wildlife Service in the U.S. Department of Interior, the Canadian Wildlife Service was in the Canada Department of Interior, but as a division of the National Parks Branch and did not begin until 1947. The U.S. Fish and Wildlife Service began as the U.S. Biological Survey in 1885; the name changed in 1940. The Canadian Forest Service began in 1911, but unlike its counterpart in the United States which began in 1898, it administers no national forest system because the provinces administer all their own forestlands. Canada has no counterpart to the U.S. Bureau of Land Management or the U.S. Natural Resources Conservation Service.

In the 1930s and 1940s governmental involvement in land use took additional forms. In the United States, federal funds became available for the purchase of private lands suitable as public waterfowl refuges. These were administered from 1940 by the newly established U.S. Fish and Wildlife Service, which also became responsible for older programs such as predator control and marine mammal conservation, and in later years would be given responsibility for endangered species.

The consequences of the drought in the 1930s raised concern for soil erosion and other deleterious effects of private farmland management. That concern was expressed in 1935 in the establishment of the U.S. Soil Conservation Service. The farm-planning experts of this agency included wildlife habitat considerations. But for the farmer, wildlife values were of a nonmaterial sort that were of scant relevance to his efforts to rise beyond immediate material satisfaction (survival) to sustained material satisfaction (pay the mortgage and raise the kids), since so much of the farmer's capital was tied up in land, buildings, machinery, and livestock.

The emphasis on economic return from land management was operative not only on farmland but on forestland and rangeland, too. Like private lands, the federal forests, state and provincial forests, and Bureau of Land Management lands were managed to produce wood, grass, or agricultural crops, and the benefits to wildlife, if any, were incidental. The trend toward monoculture, landscape homogenization, and resultant loss of wildlife diversity was emerging in the 1930s and became continually stronger in subsequent decades, encouraged by availability of credit and development of cheap, effective agricultural chemicals: pesticides and fertilizers.

Two additional U.S. federal agencies, the Bureau of Reclamation and the Army Corps of Engineers, were engaged in making arid lands more productive by damming streams and diverting the stored water into irrigation canals. This had a major consequence for arid land wildlife, since in its natural state a stream through an otherwise dry landscape is a linear oasis of highly productive riparian habitat, used at least seasonally by a diversity of wild species. Damming the stream floods the formerly fruitful shore, and drawdown during the growing season reveals bare banks of low productivity. But this was of little concern at the time, when the major national need was providing employment and general economic recovery from the Great Depression of the 1930s.

Establishment and growth of private, state/provincial, and federal entities responsible for renewable natural resources was paralleled by the inception and growth of programs of professional education in colleges and universities.

Through the 1930s enrollment in the various renewable resource curricula rose, and the degree of specialization within these curricula increased, fueled by the growth of knowledge. These developments in universities corresponded to patterns in governmental circles, where no single comprehensive land use agency existed, but rather an increasing number of separate agencies responsible for private farmland, national forests, state forests, national parks, national rangelands, national water development, and the like, each staffed by professionals differently prepared to deal with different resources.

Further, each renewable resource had as stakeholders not only educators and practitioners, but friends in state and federal legislators, users of the resource, manufacturers of specialized equipment, and often public support through nongovernmental organizations. Over time, then, each different renewable resource on each landscape type under each agency's mandates had its own different group of adhering stakeholders. These stakeholders shared concepts, support, and personnel. The scope of each resource group was both statewide/provincewide and national, and its internal uniformity and cohesion were continually maintained by professional and personal communication.

Given the ancient continuing human tendency toward tribalism, particularly among young men, each different natural resource came to be the focus of a different group of adherents. In the case of the wildlife resource through the first half of the 1900s, a dominant wildlife group focused on game species. Its stakeholders were state and provincial game departments; licensed hunters and their sportsmen's clubs; the national grouping of state clubs in the National Wildlife Federation (a nongovernmental group); university wildlife professors, Cooperative Wildlife Research Units in the United States, and associated students; Association of Sporting Arms and Ammunition Companies (which funded the influential Wildlife Management Institute); the federal U.S. Department of Interior Bureau of Sport Fisheries and Wildlife (which houses the U.S. Fish and Wildlife Service); and the federal Canadian Wildlife Service in the Canada Environmental Conservation Service within the Department of Canadian Heritage. The U.S. Fish and Wildlife Service dealt with game through responsibility for waterfowl, including dispersal of duck stamp receipts, and through overseeing funds raised by Pittman-Robertson taxes on sporting arms and ammunition (and later, in 1950, Dingle-Johnson taxes on sport fishing tackle). Communication within the game community was maintained by the Wildlife Management Institute's annual North American Wildlife Conference (1936), The Wildlife Society's *Journal of Wildlife Management* (1937), several popular magazines devoted mainly to hunting and fishing, and the like. This game community was highly successful in restoring game numbers through regulation of hunting, particularly on public lands, and adding to public lands through acquisition particularly of wetlands vital to breeding, migrating, and wintering waterfowl.

Despite urgings of the American Game Policy, through the 1930s landowners had received only modest recognition by the game community. When bothered by game damage to crops, farmers often were urged by the state game agency to open land to hunters. If the landowner preferred not to open land, the trespass protection law was minimal; most state law (presumably influenced by game interests) required posting against trespass and diligence by the owner to detect and warn trespassers, expensive in money, effort, and time.

As early as 1930 the American Game Policy recognized that landowners controlled the regions of best soils that had produced the heaviest game populations in the early days of settlement, and that the landowner would have to be made an active participant if game was to be restored on these productive lands. Nonetheless, even with recovery from the drought and the Depression, little progress was made toward incorporating the landowner in the wildlife restoration effort. The farmland owner focused on cash crops, the commercial forestland owner focused on saleable timber, the rangeland owner focused on livestock forage. Public lands such as those administered by the U.S. Forest Service and U.S. Bureau of Land Management focused on the same timber and grassland as their private neighbors.

The intensity of management was proportional to the productivity of the land. The most productive lands would best repay managerial investment; these lands were the fertile farmlands which were changed the most from the state of nature. Forestlands and rangelands were less naturally productive and so management was economically constrained from as much change. But economically affordable new managerial aids were coming—delayed for a time by World War II of 1939 to 1945—but ready then to change most wildlife habitats for the worse.

Bibliography

Allen, D. L. 1954. Our wildlife legacy. Funk and Wagnalls, New York.

Anderson, T. L., and P. H. Hill, editors. 1995. Wildlife in the marketplace. Roman & Littlefield, Lanham, MD.

Belanger, D. O. 1988. Managing American wildlife: A history of the International Fish and Wildlife Agencies. University of Massachusetts Press, Amherst.

Bolle, A. W., and R. D. Taber. 1962. Economic aspects of wildlife abundance on private lands. Transactions of the North American Wildlife and Natural Resources Conference 27:255–267.

Borland, H. 1975. The history of wildlife in America. Arch Cape Press, New York.

Brokaw, H. P., editor. 1978. Wildlife and America. U.S. Fish and Wildlife Service, U.S. Forest Service, and National Oceanic and Atmospheric Administration, Washington.

Buss, I. O., and E. S. Dziedzic. 1955. Relation of cultivation to disappearance of sharp-tailed grouse from southeastern Washington. Condor 57:185–187.

Clark, C. H. D. 1976. Evolution of wildlife harvesting systems in Canada. Transactions of the Federal-Provincial Wildlife Conference 40:122–139.

Committee on Agricultural Land Use and Wildlife Resources, editors. 1970. Land use and wildlife resources. National Academy of Sciences, Washington.

Cox, K. W., editor. 1987. Wildlife conservation on private lands. Wildlife Habitat Canada, Ottawa.

Dagg, A. I. 1974. Canadian wildlife and man. McClelland and Stewart, Toronto.
Dudly, J. P., J. R. Ginsberg, A. J. Plumptre, J. A. Hart, and L. C. Campes. 2002. Effects of war and civil strife on wildlife and wildlife habitats. Conservation Biology 16:319–329.
Dunlap, T. R. 1988. Saving America's wildlife. Princeton University Press, Princeton, NJ.
Errington, P. L. 1945. Some contributions of a 15-year study of the northern bobwhite to a knowledge of population phenomena. Ecological Monographs 15:1–34.
Errington, P. L. 1956. Factors limiting higher vertebrate populations. Science 124:304–307.
Foster, J. 1978. Working for wildlife: The beginning of preservation in Canada. University of Toronto Press, Toronto.
Geist, V. 1993. Great achievements, great expectations: Successes of North American wildlife management. Pages 47–72 *in* A. W. L. Hawley, editor. Commercialization and wildlife management: Dancing with the devil. Krieger, Malabar, FL.
Gray, G. G. 1995. Wildlife and people: The human dimensions of wildlife ecology. University of Illinois Press, Urbana.
Hewitt, C. G. 1921. The conservation of the wild life of Canada. Scribner, New York.
Hornaday, W. T. 1913. Our vanishing wild life: Its extermination and preservation. New York Zoological Society, New York.
Hornaday, W. T. 1914. Wild life conservation in theory and practice. Reprint 1972. Arno Press, New York.
Hylander, C. J. 1966. Wildlife communities: From the tundra to the Tropics in North America. Houghton Mifflin, Boston.
Judd, S. D. 1905. The grouse and wild turkeys of the United States, and their economic value. Bulletin 24, U.S. Bureau of Biological Survey, Washington.
Kallman, H., C. P. Agee, W. R. Goforth, and J. P. Linduska, editors. 1987. Restoring America's wildlife, 1937–1987. U.S. Fish and Wildlife Service, Washington.
Leopold, A. (Chairman). 1930. Report to the American Game Conference on an American game policy. Transactions of the American Game Conference 17:284–309.
Leopold, A. 1931. Report on game survey of the north central states. Sporting Arms and Ammunition Manufacturers Institute, Madison, WI.
Leopold, A. 1933. Game management. Scribner, New York.
Marsh, G. P. 1864. Man and nature; or physical geography as modified by human action. Scribner, New York.
Matthiessen, P. 1987. Wildlife in America. Viking, New York.
Morrison, M. L., B. G. Marcot, and R. W. Mannan. 1992. Wildlife-habitat relationships: Concepts and applications. University of Wisconsin Press, Madison.
Moulton, M. R., and J. Sanderson. 1999. Wildlife issues in a changing world. 2nd edition. CRC Press, Boca Raton, FL.

Organization for Economic Cooperation and Development. 1989. Agriculture and environmental policies: Opportunities for integration. Organization for Economic Cooperation and Development, Washington.

Palmer, T. S. 1912. Chronology and index of the more important events in American game protection 1776–1911. U.S. Department of Agriculture Biological Survey Bulletin 41.

Regelin, W. L. 1991. Wildlife management in Canada and the United States. Pages 55–64 *in* B. Bobek, K. Perzanowski, and W. Regelin, editors. Global trends in wildlife management. Volume 1. Swiat Press, Krakow, Poland.

Reiger, J. F. 1986. American sportsmen and the origins of conservation. University of Oklahoma Press, Norman.

Sealet, C. G., L. D. Flake, and D. W. Willis. 1996. Introduction to wildlife and fisheries: An integrated approach. Freeman, New York.

Seton, E. T. 1909–1928. Lives of game animals. 4 volumes. Doubleday and Page, New York. Reprinted in 1953 by Branford, Boston.

Stoddard, H. 1931. The bobwhite quail: Its habits, preservation, and increase. Scribner, New York.

Tober, J. A. 1981. Who owns the wildlife? The political economy of conservation in nineteenth century America. Greenwood Press, Westport, CT.

Trefethen, J. B. 1975. An American crusade for wildlife. Winchester Press, New York.

Trombetti, O., and K. W. Cox. 1990. Land, law, and wildlife conservation: The role and use of conservation easements and covenants in Canada. Wildlife Habitat Canada, Ottawa.

Wing, L. W. 1951. Practice of wildlife conservation. Wiley, New York.

Chapter 10

WILDLIFE CONSERVATION IN NORTH AMERICA: 1945–1970

World War II (1939 to 1945) saw a heavy need for agricultural production. Ready markets existed for all that could be produced. But in the course of the war, shortages of fuel, machine parts, and labor left many pieces of uncultivated fertile land scattered through agricultural regions. Soon thickly grown with weedy vegetation, these provided cover; farm game became abundant. On forestland and rangeland, the big game of the subclimax forest and shrubland continued to increase. When the war ended, state and provincial wildlife agencies were in the happy position of having large numbers of game species available and large numbers of sportsmen to buy their licenses.

State and provincial wildlife programs continued to emphasize enforcement and control of legal harvest, but particularly in the mountainous West a new objective also was to increase hunting pressure to control certain big game populations relative to their available food. Deer and elk moved down from the often publicly owned mountains in response to heavy snow, and wintered in traditional areas now often on private land at lower elevations, consuming livestock forage or damaging orchards. Some mountainous national parks spilled their protected herds onto neighboring private lowland cattle ranches in winter. So big game wintering on private lands often caused economic loss to landowners. Two remedies were popular: focus hunting pressure by sportsmen to reduce the offending populations and to a lesser extent buy up the most critical "problem" ranges. State and provincial wildlife agencies became steadily more experienced and competent in directing and controlling recreational big game hunting pressure for three objectives:

1. To provide relief from excessive wildlife damage to the landowner;
2. To keep big game populations in balance with their supply of plant food; and
3. To maximize hunting opportunity and hence the sale of licenses and agency income.

States and provinces successfully managed the increasing big game populations on public lands in the immediate postwar years through manipulation of seasons and bag limits. But the state approach to farmland game such as bobwhite quail and cottontail rabbits was less effective. Typical service programs included habitat improvement such as shrub plantings, zoning cooperating farms to protect the farmstead from invading sportsmen, and artificially producing large numbers of male ring-necked pheasants for release just before the season opened. The length of the open season varied with the balance of political power between farmers and sportsmen. Where farmers were particularly strong, as in Utah, the pheasant season was reduced to a single weekend. But in most states it extended over 1 or more months. A long open season discouraged attempts to establish private shooting estates, for that meant a long expensive time of patrol to control trespass. The political consequences of a long open season, then, were to benefit most license buyers and reduce the tendency of the rich to reserve hunting opportunities for themselves, and to benefit the landowner with financial profit from game production.

On the whole, the postwar situation was favorable for average hunters. Their income and leisure were adequate for the modest costs of license and travel. The whole state or province was open to their hunting trips. For greater but still reasonable costs, they could hunt in other states or provinces. Big game was still increasing and was being more heavily harvested. By lucky drawings or buying additional permits, hunters in some states and provinces could take an annual harvest of several deer per year.

Public rangelands had been heavily grazed during the days of settlement and early exploitation, and during the drought of the 1930s. At the same time, cutting and fires affected much forestland. In each case, the result was an increase in shrubby vegetation. Wildlife adapted to benefit from this change included deer (white-tailed and mule). With a measure of protection from human predation, deer increased to fill their expanded habitat. For the most part, the state agencies responded to this increasing abundance of deer—also elk and pronghorn antelope—by increasing hunting opportunity. The kill of those game species rose steadily from 1945 to 1965.

Waterfowl hunting was best for the member of the privately owned and managed duck club, but the hunter willing to devote some time and energy could find the birds, particularly since new waterfowl refuges now often had attached lands for public shooting. The average hunter found most farmlands accessible, for trespass protection was still weak. The amount of game produced on farmland tended to vary with the amount of uncultivated land that provided cover; but uncultivated land declined steadily until 1970, when little was left, basically. Conversion of small farms into large farms continued, with a further increase of large uniform fields, monoculture, and efficient mechanization, all accompanied by intensive clearing of wooded areas and removal of windbreaks and extension of cultivation to all possible corners. This drastic reduction in habitat diversity steadily reduced the diversity of wildlife on farmlands.

Having enjoyed good wartime markets for crops, the United States and Canada went on to provide food and fiber for the recovery of Europe at the end of the war. Industry turned to production of farm machinery, ever more powerful and efficient in cultivating, harvesting, ditching, leveling, and the like. Chemical fertilizers derived from cheap petroleum, and to some extent replaced nutrients lost to high-yield crops and soil erosion. And two new sorts of chemical aids became available: herbicides and fungicides to control weeds, and insecticides to control insects, often grouped under a single label—pesticides.

By creating large expanses of single crops, commercial agriculture reduces variety of animal habitats and diversity of animal species. But remaining species, often insects, adapt to the new environment and can become extremely abundant. If they damage the crop, they are objects of control through application of insecticides. Insecticides applied against target pests kill nontarget invertebrates as well in both terrestrial and aquatic environments. Juvenile birds—chicks and nestlings—require high-protein invertebrate bodies as food, but go without and starve when this food vanishes under insecticide spray. Even industrial contaminants can harm wildlife habitats both on site and many miles downwind. At a lower level, insecticide residues are taken up in nontoxic amounts by herbivores (invertebrates and vertebrates alike) and stored in their fat, and then are accumulated by predators and interfere with their ability to reproduce. Similarly, weeds in cropland are subject to control by herbicides; this reduces cover for nesting and concealment. In addition, aerial drift and rain and snow runoff can damage plants and animals in nontarget areas, along with damage to any desirable wildlife directly on the target area, including honeybees and other pollinators.

The black duck population in the eastern United States has declined from acid rain from sulfur dioxide and nitrogen oxides released from smokestacks of smelters, power plants, and other industrial installations, mainly in the heavily industrialized northeastern United States and southeastern Canada. Acid rain has acidified ponds and killed aquatic invertebrates nesting hens and ducklings eat.

When European farms came into full production again after World War II, less need existed for massive U.S. and Canadian crop production. Surpluses piled up. Grain was sold to needy nations that paid in their own currency. Means to reduce U.S. crop productivity without financial loss to farmers were sought. The *Soil Bank* and *Conservation Reserve Program* took land out of crop production for 1 or more years; if moist and fertile, such lands immediately produced wildlife cover, and farm wildlife responded. But even with federal subsidies, or *incentive payments*, for these practices, growing nonsurplus crops or channeling crop surpluses into new markets often was more profitable. For example, surplus grain could go into livestock fattening.

In addition, as industry grew more innovative and productive in Europe and Asia, the U.S. balance of trade shifted. More money flowed out of the country to foreign markets than flowed into U.S. markets. (In 1973 when the cost of imported oil trebled and lines of cars developed at gas stations, the balance of trade became less favorable yet). Sold abroad, U.S. and Canadian farm crops could help meet resulting deficits in the balance of payments. Full farm production again became national policy. The trend continued toward a larger scale that became the more heavily mechanized and chemically dependent agriculture. As a result of these developments and heavy grazing on uncultivated land, the diversity of wildlife and production of game on U.S. and Canadian farmlands continued to decline. For the average sportsman, if access to private farmlands might still be available, much less game was to be found there. The amount of farm game harvested per sportsman per year was much lower than it had been immediately post-World War II. Some sportsmen still habitually hunted, but they had to be content with less and less shooting. The number of younger sportsmen recruited each year declined, partly because the U.S. population was becoming increasingly urbanized, and partly because not enough farm game was to be found. Demographically, small game hunters became an aging population; state agencies faced an era of declining license sales and declining P-R funds and therefore a declining income. (By 1996 only 7% of adult Americans hunted [appendix A].)

The emphasis on crop production that was making U.S. farmland a sort of ecological desert in the period from 1945 to 1965 was also common among managers of rangelands and forestlands. But the inherent low economic productivity of these lands limited the amount of investment in managerial measures, so the impact of management on the natural biotic communities of lands managed for range and forest production was less dramatic than the impact of management on productive farmlands. Also, rangelands and forestlands were not all managed for economic production. This was, and is, especially true of the forested lands of the United States. About half the forested area in the United States is in small ownership and not managed for economic production (see chapter 9).

Federally managed public forestlands also exist in mountainous regions. Unfortunately, early federal enthusiasm for railroad expansion was expressed in the United States by a gift of federal land to encourage progress. Along the line of projected rail expansion in the western forested mountains, a railroad corporation was given title to alternate sections for 20 miles on each side of the track. However this served its intended purpose, it left posterity with an administrative puzzle of alternate public/private forested sections throughout western mountains. On the public sections, administered by the U.S. Forest Service and U.S. Bureau of Land Management, wildlife conservation is one of the stated, though minor, goals of management. On the private sections, administered by the timber industry where the goal is maximized income, wildlife conservation is not a managerial concern.

Canada's forests are 50% more extensive than those in the United States, but are generally less productive due to the colder climate. Private forestlands, like private lands generally, tend to be more productive than public lands, and make up just over half of the landscape in the temperate United States and southern Canada. These private lands have only partially realized much potential for wildlife habitat quality. Agricultural land alone provides some habitat to 75% of the wildlife species in the United States. But restoration of wildlife habitat on private lands remains largely potential; in contrast, public lands have been subject to much more public concern.

During much of the 1945 to 1970s era, all the major public and private forest management agencies in the United States and Canada largely left wildlife conservation matters to state and provincial departments. In their role as managers of big game populations, the states and provinces enjoyed substantial and dependable budgets continually strengthened as wildlife herds increased on cut-over forest blocks, and proliferating forest road systems made mountain lands more accessible. Inconsistent as it might seem, states and provinces played no substantial role in either public or private forestlands programs intended to maximize timber production, which influences wildlife production.

The lumber industry in the United States and to some extent in Canada developed through exploitation of original old-growth forest, largely on private land. But by 1945 it was clear that future wood supplies would come from access to remote stands of federally owned old growth and from second growth on private lands, already logged; management of production forests, public and private, became more intensively focused on timber harvest. New roads took loggers (and sportsmen) deeper into the mountains. Block plantings followed timber harvest, usually monocultures of the single species promising the best economic return, e.g., Douglas-fir. The managerial aim was to produce a valuable, uniform product, readily accessible. The age of the second-growth tree at harvest (rotation age) was judged to be 30 to 120 years, depending on species, product, and site productivity.

Maximizing wood production had such ecological consequences as proliferating roads, creating disturbance, increasing soil movement and siltation of spawning streams especially in mountains, and reducing the abundance of the old and dead trees that furnish food and habitat for many creatures. About one-third of wildlife species depend on standing or down dead wood, either partially or completely, including woodpeckers, which excavate the nesting cavities necessary for many nonexcavating birds and mammals. Loss of older trees, too, means loss of strong limbs capable of supporting nests of large birds such as eagles.

An industrializing society impacts wildlife habitat in two major ways: by making formerly remote regions more accessible to human activities, and by changing the original habitat in many ways. If habitat has not been eliminated entirely, it has been fragmented so severely that edge species of wildlife profit while interior species (i.e., those demanding extensive contiguous habitat away from edges) do not. Most large-scale habitat alteration has resulted from wetlands draining and filling, expanding cities and their associated landfills (the old city dumps), farming, cattle grazing, forestry, mining (metal, coal, gravel, oil), flood control and hydroelectric power, and rights-of-way for roads, railroads, powerlines, and pipelines. Agriculture and forestry have been the most influential.

As an agricultural society becomes an industrial society, accessibility is expanded by development of railroad and paved road systems. In North America, expansion of the railroad system made possible the exploitation and rapid, cheap transport of wildlife products to centers of manufacture and consumption. This led to rapid decline in wild populations, in the absence of harvest regulation. This then was followed by a proliferation of roads through settled regions which, in turn, was followed by penetration and proliferation of roads in the mountains to facilitate timber and mineral extraction, all leading to further decimation of wildlife populations, and worse, fragmentation and destruction of their habitats so that any recovery of wildlife populations was obstructed, or indeed, impossible.

Forests as well as farmlands have been profoundly changed during the process of industrialization. Industrialization provides transportation and creates new markets. For example, forests once covered 95% of western and central Europe and 70% of China; now 20% remains in Europe and 5% in China. Little time was needed to clear 75% of the forests in North America.

An early example is found in the nations of western Europe when they were in the early stages of modern industrialization. During the 1800s, demand for hardwoods fell and demand for softwoods rose, as industrial needs for softwoods in building, papermaking, etc., rapidly increased. Consequently the broadleaf forests of western Europe, and later North America, were deliberately replaced by plantations of softwood conifers. Hardwoods produce better wildlife habitat than softwoods do, but grow more slowly. Nuts and fruits that had been a staple of boar, deer, and forest rodents, among others, were no longer produced in abundance. Arboreal holes characteristic of ancient hardwoods were no longer available for birds and hole-dwelling mammals such as tree squirrels, some bats, and such predators as marten. The foods of various predators declined. Replacement of natural hardwood forests typical of well-watered temperate regions by softwood monocultures affected the understory plants which provide shelter and food for many forest-dwelling wildlife species. With replacement of deciduous hardwoods by evergreen conifers, closely spaced for efficient production, the understory plants were largely shaded out and otherwise unable to grow because shed needles render the soil too acidic.

In western Europe, where large game mammals of the forest were, and are, highly valued, these changes from natural hardwoods to a monoculture of conifers resulted in a serious shortage of winter forage for deer and wild boar. Artificial winter food was provided to maintain populations in such new coniferous plantations. Consequently, education of European foresters has long included instruction concerning winter feeding. Such measures are possible only where they are heavily subsidized and mitigate the population losses of only the favored large game mammals, doing nothing significant to reverse the loss of many other wildlife species.

Compared to centuries-old natural forest, new production forest was simpler in structure. Half of North American forests during pre-European settlement probably contained old growth, and the other half would have been in various stages of forest succession due to natural disturbances such as fire, wind, floods, landslides, insects, and disease. The natural old-growth forest has forest-floor depressions where roots of falling trees have been torn out of the soil, fallen timber, canopy gaps, thickets of shrubs in openings, standing dead trees (snags) and fallen trunks (logs) of different sizes, ages, species, and states of deterioration. Second-growth forest under even-aged management has little fallen timber, little understory when mature, and trees all of one species, size, and age. Viewed vertically, old-growth forest has trees of many different species and growth forms, as well as different ages, so that the canopy is uneven, and the forest multilayered with developed shrub and ground layers in canopy gaps left by dead trees. In contrast, second-growth forest under even-aged management has a uniform canopy of a uniform age and is single-layered when mature, with sparsely developed shrub and ground layers.

With this reduction in vertical structure, the forest managed for rapid wood production supports less diversity of wildlife than does more mature forest. But a few species such as some defoliating insects are able to flourish in second-growth forest and can become periodically abundant. Like farm managers, forest managers countered insect outbreaks in both coniferous and deciduous forests with insecticides.

The cheap and effective insecticides and herbicides were widely viewed as useful new tools for the land managers, and were quickly integrated with their administrative programs. They were put to work for the benefit of farm, forest, and range crop production, without apparent concern for possible side effects or undesirable consequences.

But side effects and undesirable consequences there were. A major problem was that the most effective insecticides, DDT for a prominent example, were fat-soluble, that is, an animal taking in sublethal amounts would store them in its fat. When its fat was mobilized for a seasonal need such as reproduction, that same animal had the insecticide toxins carried in its fatty-acid hormones which went about their physiological business, often with deleterious effects, such as alteration of behavior and reproduction.

In addition, that same animal could be eaten by another creature. This predator would ingest the fat of its victim, with its stored toxins, and receive them into its own fat store. Since a predator's principal employment is catching and eating prey, the predator would eat not one, but a great many contaminated prey individuals and so gain an ever greater amount of fat-stored toxins.

A real possibility existed, then, that through bio-accumulation, insecticides could damage not only the manager's target species, but other species as well. It not only happened, but its happening was reported so clearly that it eventually influenced public perceptions and policies.

In *Silent Spring*, biologist Rachel Carson in 1962 described how insecticide was deposited on leaves when deciduous trees were sprayed to combat gypsy moths. When these leaves were shed and fell to the ground, they disintegrated and were incorporated into the soil by earthworms. Earthworms accumulated insecticides in their tissues, and robins, feeding on earthworms, were poisoned and died, no more a vocal harbinger of spring. (Hence the title.) Attention began to be focused on the side effects of spraying in national forests to combat such defoliators as the hemlock looper, tussock moth, spruce budworm, and gypsy moth. Side effects could include the poisoning of insect-eating forest wildlife such as bats, warblers, or grouse chicks, or the poisoning of trout, ducklings, and other creatures that ate poisoned stream invertebrates when insecticides drifted or were washed into streams. A common example is the river otter with its diet of fish. Measurable concentrations of heavy metal and/or insecticide residues have been found in otters from many places including Great Britain, Denmark, Finland, and the United States.

Given the tendency for bio-magnification up the food chain, as smaller creatures were eaten by larger which in turn were eaten by larger yet, biologists would expect that predators at the top of their food chains would be most affected by the toxic accumulation. A likely candidate for investigation was the duck hawk, or peregrine falcon. Vilified not too long ago as an evil creature, it was now considered as valuable as any other member of the natural fauna, and it was obviously declining. What was found was that contemporary eggshells were thinner than those collected in the prepesticide era, and cracked during incubation.

With the production forest being ever more intensively managed for wood products and the rangelands for grass, wildlife of forest and range was in the same incidental and often precarious position as it was on farmlands. On private and public rangelands, which include all lands unsuitable for farming and forestry except wetlands, invading shrubs that improved deer habitat were viewed by professional range managers as competitors with grass and hence range cattle. Herbicides, fire, and mechanical means cleared sagebrush, shinnery oak, mesquite, etc., wholesale. Exotic grasses, notably crested wheatgrass, replaced native species. Wild herbivores, from grasshoppers to pocket gophers, were poisoned. A new poison, "1080" (sodium fluoroacetate), was found particularly lethal to the dog family, of which the coyote is a member. Over much of the West, "1080" stations were maintained in a widespread pattern, one to a township (36 square miles). At least on public lands, potential for wildlife improvement existed, for wildlife was one of a host of goods and services that managers of these lands were authorized and directed to provide, under a directive called *multiple use,* which sounded fine, but in practice meant fiber first and wildlife last.

The focus on production that dominated the post-World War II years was exhibited too by the professional wildlife conservationist, for little official interest existed in any but principal game species. For these, the aim was to take the biggest annual harvest that could be maintained—the *maximum sustained yield.* Developed in fisheries management, this concept led big game managers to develop systems of harvest that stimulated productivity. Success in managing abundant wild ungulates in the United States was recognized abroad; the 1950s and 1960s saw U.S. experts abroad advising on the ranching of wild ungulates for sustained meat production. Management of whales followed the same philosophy. Established in 1947, the International Whaling Commission attempted to take a maximum sustained harvest of the various whale species, none of them, unfortunately, biologically as well understood as were the terrestrial game species. One fact that emphasized the need for caution is that whales, like other huge creatures, have low reproductive rates.

This emphasis on production by both private business and governmental agencies faithfully reflected the preponderant post-World War II attitude in the United States. But with the 1960s, and the questioning of traditional values aggravated by war in Vietnam (1965–1973), a substantial thrust of public opinion moved away from the prevailing managerial philosophy. One might speculate that in such an extended economic boom, a generation was born and grew up without personal experience of material deprivation—a privileged generation.

Assuming itself to be materially secure, a privileged group can turn its attention to nonmaterial interests.

At the same time, the cadres managing the various renewable natural resources had inevitably been becoming more and more inner-directed, i.e., out of touch with these new cultural changes. Each managerial group was recruited from students attracted to the appropriate professional curriculum by predisposition. In each curriculum, the student was indoctrinated with the traditional philosophy of that particular resource by instructors who had a similar education and had often served in the industry or agency dealing with that resource. Each renewable resource, then, had its adherents: students, instructors, researchers, agencies, industries, and particular user-groups, supporting and served by sympathetic elected legislators. Such a cadre focused on a particular resource and became more and more internally coherent over time, producing accepted terms and philosophies of management, with members meeting one another periodically to reinforce the mutual vision of how *their* resource should best be managed. Eventually, as the whole society developed new perspectives, these traditional professional resource groups began to lose public trust and esteem. Perceived as a threat to the prevailing professional philosophy, new public views tended to draw each resource cadre together in a defensive posture.

In the United States and Canada, such professional resource management cadres were first established for an excellent reason—to rectify damage being inflicted by exploitation. During much of the 19th century, the few government agents responsible for administering natural resources were generally appointed for political service, without much consideration for competence. The U.S. Civil Service Act of 1883 strove to remedy this by developing government agencies within which trained professionals could develop specific programs under broad legislative policies. But trained professionals were few and progress was slow.

Promoted by such as Gifford Pinchot and Theodore Roosevelt in the United States and Gordon Hewitt in Canada, the perceived need for the conservation of natural resources began to stimulate development of professional curricula in some universities shortly after 1900. By the time of the drought and depression of the 1930s, natural resources agencies were gaining professional staff. By the 1945 to 1970s era the professional was ubiquitous, helped in classroom and field in 1960 by Henry Mosby's landmark book, *Manual of Game Investigational Techniques,* commonly called the techniques manual, now into its fifth edition.

During this same postwar era it became increasingly clear that the average professional was constrained by training and interest to focus closely on customary problems of game species, without adequate concern about nongame species, ecosystems, or environmental degradation. During the 1945 to 1965 period, then, growing public dissatisfaction with bureaucratic natural resource administration by both state/provincial and federal agencies increased in the United States and Canada, stimulated in part by publication in 1949 of Aldo Leopold's futuristic book, *A Sand County Almanac*, which helped awaken many people to the benefits of nature and effects of environmental degradation. One resulting political thrust has been called the *Environmental Movement;* it focused first on human environmental quality, and then on the natural environment as a vital component of the human environment. This dissatisfaction was largely felt among the urban population—now much more numerous, financially secure, and better educated than the dwindling human population of the rural regions. The more active urban proponents of the environmental political movement leaned much more strongly toward the John Muir philosophy of "leave nature alone" than to that of Gifford Pinchot, which was "manage nature for tangible products." But their government and its natural resource agencies seemed mostly in the Pinchot camp. The Muir philosophy, never dead, now began to be reasserted via two related paths—international and national.

Bibliography

Allen, D. L. 1954. Our wildlife legacy. Funk and Wagnalls, New York.
Batie, S. S., and D. B. Taylor. 1990. Cropland and soil sustainability. Pages 56–77 *in* R. N. Sampson and D. Hair, editors. Natural resources for the twenty-first century. Island Press, Covelo, CA.
Belanger, D. O. 1988. Managing American wildlife: A history of the International Fish and Wildlife Agencies. University of Massachusetts Press, Amherst.
Bookhout, T. A., editor. 1994. Research and management techniques for wildlife and habitats. 5th edition. Wildlife Society, Bethesda, MD.
Borland, H. 1975. The history of wildlife in America. Arch Cape Press, New York.
Brokaw, H. P., editor. 1978. Wildlife and America. U.S. Fish and Wildlife Service, U.S. Forest Service, and National Oceanic and Atmospheric Administration, Washington.
Canadian Forest Service. 1995. The state of Canada's forests: A balancing act. Natural Resources Canada, Ottawa.
Carson, R. 1962. Silent spring. Houghton Mifflin, Boston.
Clark, C. H. D. 1976. Evolution of wildlife harvesting systems in Canada. Transactions of the Federal-Provincial Wildlife Conference 40:122–139.
Committee on Agricultural Land Use and Wildlife Resources, editors. 1970. Land use and wildlife resources. National Academy of Sciences, Washington.
Cook, P. S., and T. T. Cable. 1992. Developing policy for public access to private land: A case study. Pages 76–93 *in* W. R. Mangun, editor. American fish and wildlife policy: The human dimensions. Southern Illinois University Press, Carbondale.
Dagg, A. I. 1974. Canadian wildlife and man. McClelland and Stewart, Toronto.
Dunlap, T. R. 1988. Saving America's wildlife. Princeton University Press, Princeton, NJ.
Fairfax, S., and L. Burton. 1984. A decade of NEPA: Milestone or millstone. Renewable Resources Journal 2:22–27.
Foster, J. 1978. Working for wildlife: The beginning of preservation in Canada. University of Toronto Press, Toronto.
Gilbert, F. F. 1993. The vision: Wildlife management in North America. Pages 23–

33 *in* A. W. L. Hawley, editor. Commercialization and wildlife management: Dancing with the devil. Krieger, Malabar, FL.

Gilbert, F. F., and D. G. Dodds. 2001. The philosophy and practice of wildlife management. 3rd edition. Krieger, Malabar, FL.

Giles, W. L., D. L. Leedy, and E. L. Pinnell. 1970. New patterns on land and water. Pages 55–91 *in* Committee on Agricultural Land Use and Wildlife Resources, editors. Land use and wildlife resources. National Academy of Science, Washington.

Hagenstein, P. 1990. Forests. Pages 78–100 *in* R. N. Sampson and D. Hair, editors. Natural resources for the twenty-first century. Island Press, Covelo, CA.

Hylander, C. J. 1966. Wildlife communities: From the tundra to the tropics in North America. Houghton Mifflin, Boston.

Kallman, H., C. P. Agee, W. R. Goforth, and J. P. Linduska, editors. 1987. Restoring America's wildlife, 1937–1987. U.S. Fish and Wildlife Service, Washington.

Kaufman, H. 1956. Emerging conflicts in the doctrines of public administration. American Political Science Review 50:1057–1073.

Leopold, A. 1949. A sand county almanac and sketches here and there. Oxford University Press, New York.

Matthiessen, P. 1987. Wildlife in America. Viking Press, New York.

Morrison, M. L., B. G. Marcot, and R. W. Mannan. 1992. Wildlife-habitat relationships: Concepts and applications. University of Wisconsin Press, Madison.

Mosby, H. S., editor. 1960. Manual of game investigational techniques. Wildlife Society, Virginia Cooperative Wildlife Research Unit, Blacksburg.

Moulton, M. R., and J. Sanderson. 1999. Wildlife issues in a changing world. 2nd edition. CRC Press, Boca Raton, FL.

Regelin, W. L. 1991. Wildlife management in Canada and the United States. Pages 55–64 *in* B. Bobek, K. Perzanowski, and W. Regelin, editors. Global trends in wildlife management. Volume 1. Swiat Press, Krakow, Poland.

Society of American Foresters. 1991. Task force report on biological diversity in forest ecosystems. Society of American Foresters, Bethesda, MD.

Thomas, J. W. 1979. Wildlife habitats in managed forests: The Blue Mountains of Oregon and Washington. U.S. Forest Service Agricultural Handbook 553, Portland, OR.

Trefethen, J. B. 1975. An American crusade for wildlife. Winchester Press, New York.

Chapter 11

INTERNATIONAL WILDLIFE CONSERVATION

Episodes in international wildlife conservation concerning North America have been mentioned, notably the Fur Seal Treaty and the Migratory Bird Treaty. The Fur Seal Treaty aimed at restoration and controlled cropping at a higher level of a valuable wildlife product. The Migratory Bird Treaty combined prudent conservation of waterfowl (game) populations for optimum future use, and blanket protection for the small birds known in the English tradition as "songbirds," valued enhancements of human environments. But it did not provide protection for predatory birds such as hawks, owls, and crows.

European nations had colonies mostly in or near the Tropics and were not concerned about wildlife conservation at home; abundance (though not diversity) was well cared for by wealthy landowners. But wildlife conservation in the colonies was of more concern, which ultimately led to international agreements that came to include the United States and Canada.

The rate of exploitation of valuable and vulnerable wildlife was perceived to be increasing in the European-managed tropical colonies. To control wildlife exploitation, colonial administrators had several advantages. Some areas were already protected (particularly in Asia) as hunting grounds of local rulers. Further protective laws could be enforced by the military power of colonial administrators, so additional protected areas were designated even though they had long been within the "ownership territory" of local people. Official designation as "refuge," "reserve," or "park" removed an area from the ownership territory of local people. The inclination toward protection of wildlife populations that was widespread among the European upper class led to the policies of national and international organizations, particularly among colonial nations.

In 1900 during pre-World War I concern with conservation, six colonial powers produced a convention on the Preservation of the African Fauna. By 1902 several European nations agreed to an international treaty "for protection of birds useful to agriculture." In 1903 this was followed by amalgamation of several English organizations into the Society for the Preservation of the Fauna of the Empire. In 1909 an International Congress for the Protection of Nature developed an Act of Foundation of a Consultative Commission for the International Protection of Nature, signed by 17 national delegates in 1913.

In 1922 in England, the International Commission for Bird Protection was established. Currently called International Council for Bird Preservation (ICBP), this organization has remained to this day the leading international organization for bird conservation. A prime mover in establishing ICBP was T. Gilbert Pearson, U.S. wildlife conservationist and secretary of the U.S. National Audubon Society.

In 1925 Dutch conservationist P. G. van Tienhoven established a Netherlands Committee for International Nature Protection, with associated national committees. Shortly thereafter a French Committee for Protection of Colonial Fauna was established. As with the older English Society for the Preservation of the Fauna of the Empire, these European developments arose from increasing concern on the part of colonial mother countries for the faunas of the colonies.

In 1930 the U.S. Boone and Crockett Club organized the American Committee on International Wildlife Protection, with members representing the major nongovernmental conservation organizations in the United States. The American Committee quickly arranged support for preparing books bringing together all available information on extinct and vanishing birds and mammals of the world.

In 1933 the European nations holding colonies in Africa revisited the Convention (of 1900) on the Preservation of African Fauna, and produced a more far-ranging agreement. This emphasized the importance of habitat, and stimulated establishment of protected wildlife sanctuaries, but it suffered from lack of a permanent secretariat to keep things moving. It did not review the status of species in danger of extinction and did not address the question of native hunting rights.

By 1934 van Tienhoven of the Netherlands had pressed the case for international nature protection with the International Union of Biological Sciences, which responded by appointing him to establish an International Office for Documentation and Coordination in the Protection of Nature. Funded by the Dutch government, this office emerged as the International Office of Nature Protection, to gather facts and distribute information. In this era, financial support for nature came largely from the personal contributions of well-to-do individuals, and was neither as substantial nor as dependable as the agency funding of the present day; conservation efforts and productions were accordingly small.

Soon after, works supported by the American Committee from personal funds reached print: Glover Allen's *Extinct and Vanishing Mammals of the Western Hemisphere* in 1942; Francis Harper's *Extinct and Vanishing Mammals of the Old World* in 1945; and James Greenway's *Extinct and Vanishing Birds of the World* in 1958. During the difficult years of World War II (1939 to 1945), the American Committee contributed to the financial support of the International Office of Nature Protection, still in the Netherlands.

When World War II ended and Europe began to recover, interest in international conservation revived. The European colonies were moving toward independence (India led the way and became the two new nations of India and Pakistan in 1947) and the fate of rich tropical fauna was of deepening concern. Colonial nations of Europe had considered themselves custodians of that fauna in Asia and Africa for many years, had built up vast stores of information, scientific specimens, expertise, and living captive animals and plants, and had established and protected wildlife sanctuaries in aboriginal habitats. Now as the colonies began to break into a multitude of new nations, European concern for tropical fauna could no longer be expressed through colonial authorities. But concern was strong and persistent and found new ways to influence events.

Establishment of the United Nations in 1946 and its funding by governments of member nations had profound consequences for wildlife conservation. Four United Nations agencies can be involved with wildlife or related concerns: the United Nations Educational, Scientific and Cultural Organization (UNESCO) in Paris; the Food and Agriculture Organization of the United Nations (FAO) in Rome; the United Nations Development Program (UNDP) in New York; and the United Nations Environmental Program (UNEP) in Nairobi. Julian Huxley, a prominent English zoologist, was the first Director General of UNESCO, resulting in the inclusion of nature conservation within the UNESCO scope of interest. The world's largest source of multilateral grants, UNDP funds a wide variety of projects with environmental consequences as well as projects designed to aid conservation. The World Bank in Washington also provides loans and grants to less developed countries for such things as roads, dams, electrical systems, etc., and recently is trying to ameliorate environmental criticism of past deeds by initiating conservation projects and withholding support from environmentally destructive projects. Formed in 1972, UNEP has less direct involvement with wildlife than FAO and UNESCO; UNEP tends to have human-environmental nature concerns, but it cooperates with other agencies, and has wildlife experts for advice.

Relatively wealthy industrialized nations interact with less developed nations in various ways. These include purely economic arrangement through multinational corporations; national governmental and nongovernmental aid, including aid in economic development; and aid through the support of United Nations organizations, which then provide assistance in agriculture, health, etc. Of these, national governmental and nongovernmental aid programs reflect most closely the prevailing climate of political opinion within an industrialized nation, particularly those with open societies. In the United States, for example, the Agency for International Development (USAID) has for decades been involved in massive engineering works in less developed nations, works aimed toward the advance of economic development, often through the construction of hydropower/irrigation water dams. With the rise of environmental consciousness and political pressure in the 1970s and later, it was not long before federally financed USAID programs came under the sorts of constraints imposed by endangered species and environmental policy legislation. That is, USAID projects had to be examined in light of their probable impact on the values of nature conservation. This led to the preparation of the Environmental Profile by USAID of each nation within which it had a program. Further, it led to serious consideration by USAID of the World Conservation Strategy of integrating economic development with nature conservation. Now it is normal for USAID to provide support for biodiversity as part of a country's portfolio of programs.

Emerging UN agencies might well be constrained by the national policies of their members, so nongovernmental conservation organizations conceived of a new international nongovernmental organization (NGO) to conduct a global wildlife conservation mandate broader and more action-oriented than the existing International Office of Nature Protection. World wildlife conservation leaders agreed that a new international organization should not be a subsidiary of any extant international body, and that its membership should not be restricted to governments. So in 1948 the International Union for the Protection of Nature (IUPN) was created; UNESCO immediately gave it the task of planning a meeting at Lake Success, New York, where a UNESCO conservation program was hammered out in detail, aimed at accomplishing the mission of preserving the entire biotic community on earth, including renewable natural resources on which rests the foundation of human civilization and the very health of human society.

IUPN's objectives were broad. In Article I the objective is to "encourage and facilitate co-operation between governments and national and international organizations," with particular reference to disseminating public knowledge, education, and scientific research as well as to draft international agreements and to develop a worldwide convention for the protection of nature.

International agreements concerning wildlife conservation had already proved successful in the North American examples of the Fur Seal Treaty and the Migratory Bird Treaty, as well as the European international agreements mentioned early in the chapter. To expedite progress, IUPN was designed to move beyond or around strictly government-to-government agreements by building in the participation of NGOs that represented active segments of public opinion, recognizing that aroused and directed public opinion influenced government actions. Its name, International Union for the Protection of Nature, was changed after a few years to International Union for the Conservation of Nature and Natural Resources or, more familiarly, IUCN.

IUCN is a hybrid organization of some 600 member organizations (mainly federal government natural resource agencies, NGOs, and research institutions) that promotes sustainable use and protection of living resources. With a small permanent staff, it drew much strength from volunteer advisors and cooperating organizations and depended on the well-established International Council on Bird Preservation (ICBP) for work related strictly to bird conservation. It early adapted a device perfected by ICBP by creating specialist groups, each consisting of experts on a particular endangered form or group of related forms. Such a group was particularly effective when provided with a permanent IUCN secretary, but funding usually constrained the size of IUCN permanent staff. In 1970, for example, the salaried staff of IUCN jumped from 5 to 18. (By the 1990s the staff neared 400!) For IUCN, some financial support has come from United Nations organizations such as UNESCO and, more recently, the UN Environmental Program, from money originally paid as UN dues by member nations. Resignation of the United States from UNESCO will weaken this source of IUCN support.

Multiple objectives of IUCN include maintaining scientific legitimacy (i.e., being a trustworthy source of counsel), influencing governmental policies and actions for the benefit of nature conservation, and obtaining enough financing to function effectively. Over time, progress has been made in all three areas. Though IUCN has now changed its official name to World Conservation Union (WCU), it is still widely known by its former initials.

Important functions of IUCN in early years included establishment of the Survival Service Commission (SSC), under which the specialist groups fall, and which had the responsibility of providing current reliable information on animals and plants with particular regard to their hazardous existence in the modern world. With initial focus on declining species of mammals and birds, about which most was known, the SSC of the IUCN developed categorizations to describe the degree to which each was threatened.

Classification of individual species included the following: (1) Extinct—species definitely not located in the wild during the past 50 years; (2) Endangered—taxa in danger of extinction if present conditions continue; (3) Vulnerable—taxa likely to become endangered if present conditions continue; (4) Rare—taxa with small worldwide populations that are at risk; (5) Indeterminate—taxa known to be endangered, vulnerable, or rare, but not enough information exists to be conclusive; (6) Out of Danger—taxa formerly endangered, vulnerable, rare, or indeterminate, but now relatively secure; (7) Insufficiently Known—taxa suspected but not definitely known to be in any of the above categories, for lack of knowledge; (8) Threatened—a general term for species endangered, vulnerable, rare, indeterminate, or insufficiently known, used for species with varying categories of subspecies (substituted for Vulnerable by U.S. Fish and Wildlife Service, Canadian Wildlife Service, and many state and provincial agencies); and (9) Commercially Threatened—taxa threatened as a sustainable commercial resource unless regulated, but not threatened with extinction.

Such categorizations focused attention on what needed to be found out to categorize taxa correctly. They also required judgment on just which taxon (i.e., family, genus, species, subspecies) was meant by a listing. The taxon "subspecies," i.e., race, or identifiable regionally adapted interbreeding population, was included because a particular species, say *Canis lupus* (the gray wolf), is comprised of several subspecies (races), some of which are currently secure, others extinct, and still others endangered or vulnerable. This categorization has been obscured by use of the term *endangered species* for every endangered form listed, whether a species or a subspecies, which confuses conservation groups at times.

The Survival Service Commission incorporated earlier and current findings in the Red Data Books. The first two of these covered mammals and birds (prepared by ICBP) and appeared in 1966; one on reptiles and amphibians and another on angiosperm (flowering) plants appeared in 1970. Others followed and revisions are constant. Each page of a Red Data Book is devoted to a single endangered form, and contains available information on its status, apparent reasons for its decline, its current existence in captivity, and principal references concerning it. Currently, the World Conservation Monitoring Centre (WCMC) regularly publishes the Red Data Books. Located in Cambridge, UK, the WCMC is a joint venture of the WCU (old IUCN), UNEP, and the World Wide Fund for Nature (WWF, formerly the World Wildlife Fund—a name still used only in the United States). The WCMC was established to provide a central repository for information on the world's biological diversity, and is the main clearinghouse for data on species and ecosystems.

International wildlife conservation strategies have been unsteadily evolving, and vehicles for pursuing them have become more effective over the past century. Their ultimate success lies in the self-regulated behavior of the many independent nations of the world, since there is no formal enforcement mechanism for making a nation behave in conformance with some international design. But political pressures can be generated and directed in such a way as to cause a nation to reexamine and perhaps modify its position. For example, the U.S.S.R. completely protected its polar bears in 1956 and 1961 when IUCN dropped the polar bear from the Endangered list. That move by IUCN correctly pointed toward lack of scientific justification for complete protection of polar bears by the U.S.S.R., except that it is best to err on the side of caution if biological knowledge is incomplete. With Alaska considering polar bear hunting an important income generator, the United States wanted hunting to continue. A series of moves to develop a more adequate international polar bear conservation program followed, and in 1976 an international polar bear agreement came into force, based on a mass of biological information while recognizing the special right of native peoples.

A similar sequence of events occurred in whale conservation affairs. International congresses have afforded opponents of whaling an opportunity to show that information on whales is insufficient for proper harvest management and that some species seem near extinction. Whaling nations are thus under international pressure to cooperate in developing a more reliable information base. Conservation opinion within each whaling nation questions continuation of the whaling industry in its country. Nonwhaling nations can then add economic pressure by sanctions that put additional pressure on the whaling nation's economy with the aim of forcing that nation to stop whaling. Such nations and adjustments of individual nations are parts of the evolving pattern of international wildlife conservation.

Japan persists in pursuit of whales listed as endangered, as do Norway and Iceland, in defiance of a moratorium on commercial whaling by the International Whaling Commission (IWC) since 1986. In 1992 Iceland quit the IWC, and in 1993 Norway refused to abide by the IWC moratorium by beginning commercial whaling of minke whales. Japan has resumed whaling in the name of "research," a loophole in the moratorium. In 1997 the 39-nation IWC met in Monaco where a compromise was sought to allow Norway and Japan to harvest nonthreatened species of whales, for a collapse of the IWC was feared. But antiwhaling nations, including the United States and Australia, fear other countries, such as Iceland and South Korea, also would demand commercial quotas. It is argued, as in the case of the polar bear, that the biological information adequate for a rational program of whale management does not exist. The attention of Japan to this question can be obtained by threat of expulsion of the Japanese fishing fleet from U.S. territorial waters (i.e., much of the North Pacific and Bering Sea) and, if deemed necessary, a boycott on the importation of Japanese sea products into the United States. While mercantile pressures of this sort often have been applied by nations to one another for centuries, it is only relatively recently that they have been employed in an attempt to reduce human predatory pressures on wildlife.

The IUCN and allied groups recognized from the first that wildlife did not exist in a vacuum; adequate habitat was necessary for its survival. But the entire habitat in the world would not be enough to protect all wildlife from unbridled human predation and habitat degradation. So habitat protection and regulation of human predation were ultimate wildlife conservation goals.

Habitat protection was one of the functions of the national parks of the United States and Canada. Habitat protection was also a function of the wildlife sanctuaries established and guarded by colonial authorities. As colonial empires were breaking up and new nations were emerging in the 1950s and 1960s, the IUCN seized on the national park concept, promoting parks as part of every nation's wealth and heritage and as a valuable source of national income from tourism. It recommended that national parks protect at least 10% to 15% of the total area of each ecosystem occurring in a nation. Wildlife sanctuaries of East Africa, and the foreign exchange generated by the tourism they supported, provided a persuasive example for poor new nations. Arguments promoting new national parks were presented in a series of congresses staged by IUCN and cooperators through what was coming to be called the less developed nations of the world (where the rich tropical biotas were located). Such arguments had the desired result. Old colonial wildlife sanctuaries, royal hunting preserves, and remote, lightly settled, often mountainous areas became new national parks. Today Costa Rica reigns as the nation with the highest percentage of its area in national parks or other protected areas (12% compared to 3% in the United States). There, ecotourism is the main industry; but even with that as incentive, enforcement against squatters and poachers, including loggers, is lax.

The ability of any nation to protect wildlife (or vegetation for that matter) in a national park varies widely. According to the European view, if a national park were to preserve the natural biota, some way of controlling the incursions of local humans for grazing, wood, game, and other products would be necessary. These incursions were labeled as "poaching."

With UN sponsorship in 1962, IUCN completed a catalogue of the world's national parks and equivalent reserves, entitled "The Last Refuges of the World." This catalogue was published and is revised regularly.

Led by Edward Graham of the U.S. Soil Conservation Service, conservation-minded ecologists worked in IUCN's Commission on Ecology toward conserving specific biotic communities, first focusing on arid lands then on wetlands. The wetlands concern was shared by the International Council on Bird Preservation, among others, and led to development in 1962 of a wetland classification scheme and in 1971 to the Ramsar (Iran) Convention (international agreement) on Wetlands of International Importance. Thus emerged a clearer concept that the worldwide scheme of natural wildlife habitat preservation should include all the major different sorts of biotic communities. It was soon apparent that some biotic communities were not yet included within national parks or protected areas, a demonstrable fact that helped stimulate creation of additional national parks.

In serving two broad nongovernmental communities (the internationally minded conservationists and the inhabitants of less developed nations), the IUCN and its cooperators soon found that a simple focus on habitats ultimately did not satisfy either one. Providing much of the funding, nongovernmental conservationists responded more strongly to concerns for charismatic endangered animals than for complex habitats. Citizens of less developed nations that supported most of the world's endangered fauna within their borders found that creating new parks within traditional territories of their rural citizens looked better on paper than on the ground.

Part of the wildlife conservation problem in newly independent colonies was that the new indigenous leaders were educated by former mother countries, generally in Europe. Educated in English, French, Dutch, etc., they naturally absorbed much of the culture of the mother country. That culture, urban-centered, assumed that the way to protect property was to employ police power. So when local people entered new national parks for their traditional subsistence uses of grazing, fuel, game, etc., the response of the new government was to attempt to use force to put a stop to it. This was seldom effective; unless it is a ruthless military dictatorship, no new government can long apply coercive pressure on its citizens. Furthermore, not everyone in a new nation subscribed to the concept that emanated from the privileged urbanites of Europe, that all the world's flora and fauna should be protected forevermore. On the contrary, many an entrepreneur was eager to cash in on any natural resource that could be exploited. So, valuable vulnerable wildlife was subject to predation not only by local inhabitants, but also by mobile poaching gangs prepared to outgun local enforcement.

During the 1960s many new nations, former colonies, joined IUCN. Their representatives brought new perspectives to the traditional European-centered ways of thinking that had long dominated international wildlife conservation. Simple legal protection of national parks and their plants and animals could not always be enforced effectively on the ground.

Ample money was available from industrialized nations to be invested here and there in the world, but almost certainly in "development." And many sorts of development, hydropower dams, commercial farms, mines, to name a few, could have deleterious consequences for wild nature. Yet new poor nations often welcomed investment and development for their immediate economic benefit.

These realities led some within the international conservation community to work toward ways of integrating conservation with development. In 1965 the FAO of the UN set up a wildlife management unit with emphasis on wildlife as a usable, economically valuable, renewable resource. This was quite a different tack than that taken by traditional preservers of nature, including most supporters of the national park idea. Traditional supporters of national parks as biological reserves had difficulty with the new international situation and ignored the fact that national parks in rich industrial nations, with which they were familiar, could easily be protected, whereas new national parks in poor agricultural nations could not. This misconception still lingers; many leading citizens in former colonial areas still feel that allowing considerations of utility to enter nature conservation is a betrayal, of sorts, of the park ideal.

Often national authorities propose that local people can benefit from protected resources by being hired as guards, guides, research assistants, and the like. An example from Guyana illustrates that this approach might be useful, but is not adequate for effective conservation of the resource.

In this case the resource is the population of sea turtles that nests on beaches within an Amerindian territory. Internationally funded research found the sea turtles declining due to overuse. Three local people were hired to patrol the beach, collect scientific data, and protect nesting turtles from human use. The slaughter of sea turtles on the protected beach resumed when the guards were absent from the beach. Resolution leading to sea turtle conservation and ultimately sustainable use—the international goal—required much more than a few beach guards. The course of comanagement came to include advances in communication, education, and identifying practical alternative production of meat for human needs, a constellation of remedies that went far beyond sea turtle population biology, to become part of local human culture. All eight species of sea turtle in the world are endangered due to nesting habitat loss, ocean pollution, and egg collection, especially in countries in Central America and South America where macho cultures and misinformation cause men to collect and eat turtle eggs as a bogus aphrodisiac. This example serves also to show that fully protected natural areas, while necessary for many purposes, do not encompass all the habitats within which endangered wildlife exists. In fact, many endangered species are found only in habitats fully shared by humans and far from any protected natural area. For full plant and animal sustainability, then, we must often operate within human communities.

Practicalities of wildlife conservation and growth of ecological knowledge led to the realization that national parks could not endure as museum pieces. They needed to be integrated with adjacent human cultures as well as national and international aspirations, and they needed to be integrated within the broader landscapes required for the viability of all their biological species. This was easier said than done. The biological objectives were clear: no less than the sustained maintenance of all the extant wild plants and animals of the globe. But roads toward this goal still had to be developed.

To develop effective solutions, the international conservation groups had to deal with several impeding cultural phenomena. Much of the financial support of international conservation comes either directly from NGOs or governmental bodies strongly influenced by nongovernmental organizations. The NGOs had to raise funds from their members. They soon found that an emotional appeal was more effective than a rational appeal, and that a simple message was more effective than a complex message. In fund-raising, the attraction of emotional appeals was also expedient because, unlike rational appeals, emotional appeals did not require much detailed knowledge, either by the fund-raiser or the contributors. The principal contributors to NGOs are those with the principal funds, overwhelmingly city-dwellers. For the city-dweller, animals, pets, or charismatic zoo captives are valued as individuals. For the city-dweller, the police protect valued possessions. So in international affairs, there was an almost overwhelming thrust of financial support toward protection of favored wild species (elephants, tigers, and pandas, for example) by armed guards. The nations with the money—the industrial nations, the urban-dominated nations—showed scant regard for the welfare of humans who shared habitats of the diverse and highly valued biota of nations rich in nature but poor in cash.

Governments of wildlife-rich, cash-poor nations had to deal with local people sharing wildlife habitats and also with the need for money, especially foreign exchange, to support and develop their countries. Investors in rich countries were eager to provide money to poor countries for their support and development, in return, of course, for control of mines, timber concessions, oil fields, commercial tourism, etc. This flow of money was to the capitol of each nation and to new economic developments in the countryside. It might be assumed that local people of the countryside would be happy to go to work for invading developers, but some persisted in their ancient ways of life as well as they could: traditional farming, grazing livestock, cutting firewood, and taking wild animals and plants for food and profit. So while concerned protection-minded urbanites contributed funds through their NGOs for the welfare of wildlife everywhere, the list of species extinct or threatened grew ever longer. New initiatives were called for.

New initiatives generally emerge from seeds already planted. By the late 1960s international conservation leaders recognized that development for profit would continue to be part of the world scene and that protected natural areas might never be large enough or effectively protected enough to ensure survival of all the world's plants and animals. What might well be helpful, though, was to guide development so as to minimize damage to nature, and to learn how to move protected areas from isolation toward integration with surrounding regions inhabited by human communities.

Whereas in an earlier time active international conservationists generally had adequate private means to support their work, the increasing scope and complexity of the field during emergence of new nations following World War II required financial support beyond what even the United Nations offices could provide. In 1961 the WWF (World Wildlife Fund, now the World Wide Fund for Nature) was established as an NGO designed to raise money from private contributions and use it to encourage conservation worldwide.

With the engaging but threatened giant panda (the carnivore that evolved into an herbivore) as its logo, WWF quickly grew into a significant fund-raising body, and one more inclined toward wildlife activism and less concerned with scientific conservatism than IUCN. Each of many nations had its own WWF organization (e.g., WWF-US, WWF-India). Each national WWF entity develops its own goals and guidelines. For more effective international coordination, after some early give-and-take, WWF projects came to be screened by IUCN, and continuing WWF projects were passed on to IUCN for administration. The WWF has given substantial and continued financial support to IUCN. The success of the World Wildlife Fund was due to three major phenomena of the 1960s: prosperity of the United States and Canada and recovery of western Europe and Japan from World War II; emergence of the postcolonial nations and international concern for their wildlife; and growth within rapidly changing industrial nations of concern for the quality of the human environment.

Many species of wildlife simply will become extinct unless human overexploitation is effectively regulated along with habitat fragmentation and destruction, and introductions. The pattern of regulation most appropriate depends on the human culture to be regulated. Further, a tangible, affordable advantage must occur to the individual to get him to cooperate with the regulatory program. Currently, the human predation of wildlife ("bushmeat") in less developed countries is aggravated by the prevailing low standard of living. Local humans need other resources besides wildlife, such as additional farmland and wood fuel for cooking for a burgeoning population. Thus, the rising human population expands into habitat needed for both wildlife and human survival, steadily reducing availability of wildlife, and rendering human survival ever more difficult.

Accumulated experience and new financial and political help suggested reforms and advances which were formalized in national legislation that had both national and international purposes. Nationally, for example, the United States passed the National Environmental Policy Act in 1969 that required preparing an environmental impact statement detailing environmental consequences for every major federally funded or licensed development. This permitted public scrutiny, and reaction, before a major undertaking rather than after. Many other nations, including Canada, adopted similar legislation.

In 1966, 1969, and 1973 the United States passed legislation emphasizing protection of endangered species of wildlife nationally, permitting cooperation in an international convention to control trade in endangered species. Other nations passed similar legislation. The international effort led to the Convention on International Trade in Endangered Species of Wild Fauna and Flora (CITES) that came into force in 1975 with 10 signatories. Subsequently, most nations of the world have joined. Administered from Geneva, Switzerland, CITES includes Appendices I, II, and III. Appendix I lists forms endangered by trade. By this agreement, essentially no legal trade is permitted for these or their parts. Appendix II lists forms that are or might become threatened by trade. For these, trade is strictly controlled through the necessity for licensing (under scientific scrutiny) at both the nation of origin and the nation of destination. Appendix III lists forms that a member nation thinks should be subject to regulation within that nation.

Though complex and burdensome for customs officials, CITES has been successful in reducing trade in endangered wildlife. It is firmly based on factual categorizations, kept up to date, and provided with a UN-funded IUCN secretariat to maintain momentum. Another IUCN branch, the Survival Service Commission, formed Trade Records Analysis of Flora and Fauna in Commerce (TRAFFIC) to produce a continuous flow of the most reliable current information on international wildlife trade, augmented by records on trade and related legislation from individual cooperating nations. By pointing the spotlight of publicity into darker corners of wildlife commerce, TRAFFIC can help generate public concern needed for more vigorous enforcement or legislative reform within the nation of wildlife product origin (generally poor) and within the nation of receipt (generally rich).

Success in controlling international trade in threatened species depends upon general agreement on classification of species (endangered, threatened, etc.) and success in controlling illegal trade. Agreement on classification of species is generally satisfactory when enough information is available and individual species can be newly classified or reclassified according to the current status of each. But difficulties often arise when at least one nation prefers to manage trade for one of their species under an Appendix II listing of CITES, whereas other nations prefer total protection from trade under an Appendix I listing.

Control of illegal trade can never wholly succeed where lucrative markets exist, but a measure of success is better than none, and a continuous high level of public support exists for enforcement efforts. But to be effective, enforcement must be coupled with education and incentive.

Designed to reduce local value of exportable wildlife products by making such international traffic illegal and hence more difficult or even impossible, CITES, for this purpose, has proven to be reasonably effective. But CITES exerts no control whatsoever on wildlife harvested for consumption within a less developed nation, whether to be eaten by a local family or trucked to city markets.

International programs encouraged creation of new national parks and then monitored and tried to control international trade in endangered species. Such programs were clearly aimed at recovery and protection of endangered wildlife. Observation on the ground showed time after time that no matter how closely guarded a park might be and local people kept from entering it, mobile wildlife species within the park often moved out of it in seasonal migrations, searches for food, or dispersal of young. Dispersing animals move into regions already occupied by human societies. Amply demonstrated by animals in parks everywhere, this wildlife mobility refocused attention on the local people who inhabit the region around every park. Conservation authorities who had considered poaching within the parks to be the only local problem now had to expand their view to hunting outside park boundaries.

The IUCN's Bali Action Plan of 1982 acknowledged the need for active management of national parks, in contrast to passive "protection," to conserve ecosystems in a worldwide network that will be most successful through integration of nature conservation with economic development. It recognizes a number of the *activities* listed under its various *objectives*. The Bali Action Plan incorporated ideas that nature reserves should be managed so that both nature conservation and economic development benefit, that management of surrounding regions is relevant to management of the reserve proper, and that developmental patterns should be congruent with local human cultures and contribute to the welfare of those human cultures.

The concept that a nature reserve, no matter how large, should be considered as but part of a landscape that includes its surrounding areas is also finding support in purely biological analyses. That is, no reserve, no matter how large, is large enough to sustain a viable population of its more space-demanding species. Diversity of plants and animals within any nature reserve is so large, particularly in the Tropics, that it is impossible to plan for all their needs simultaneously. The concept that has been developed to overcome this difficulty is that if the needs of the most demanding species for space are met, then the rest of the fauna will automatically be provided for. Pursuing this notion, one is soon forced to focus on large animals and predatory animals, since these require the most space. Large predatory animals thus constitute a key group for conservation concern, not the only group but a group whose welfare automatically includes, umbrella-fashion, the welfare of many smaller species. The first major attempt to apply these concepts on a large scale in international wildlife conservation has been *Project Tiger* in India in 1973.

Two illegal sorts of human wildlife harvesters exist in the less developed nations (which have plenty of laws aimed at wildlife conservation): the household poacher and the business poacher. The household poacher is supposed to be controlled by the local enforcement officer. Generally a poor member of the same community, this official must for his own well-being avoid antagonizing other members of that community. If he does arrest an occasional household poacher, and that person is to be punished, fining is not practicable, the householder having no money. In most countries, physical punishment is not today culturally acceptable. The only alternative is jail, which costs the government money. So the government finds it difficult, generally impossible in fact, to control the household poacher who eats what he takes. Where the wildlife product enters the channels of trade, the task of controlling the business poacher is different. First of all, it is more dangerous, since an armed poaching gang generally commands more firepower than the local constabulary and can complete its raid and be gone before reinforcements arrive. In addition, where money exists, so does potential for bribery or, to put it more diplomatically, a sharing of the proceeds toward an unimpeded flow of trade. In a practical sense, then, control of wildlife harvest is possible only with the active cooperation of local human residents.

The United States and Canada are among the rich nations that try to further wildlife conservation abroad as well as at home. They and other rich nations affect less developed nations both positively and negatively with regard to wildlife conservation. Positively, they provide professional assistance and financial support of specific conservation programs. Negatively, they send corporate investment expecting financial return. Between these extremes lie the national and United Nations programs providing assistance in agriculture, health, and economic development; in the past, these have often had negative consequences. Evidently the rich nations have a hand at times in making wildlife conservation in poor countries more rather than less difficult.

The Communal Areas Management Programme for Indigenous Resources (CAMPFIRE) is a program that began in 1986 and involves rural communities more closely in managing wildlife resources on their lands, and returns revenues directly to communities, which promotes the value of wildlife. The region affected by the CAMPFIRE program supports many wild species, some of which can be used in a sustained way that produces income from safari hunting and meat and other products for local use, and also reduces wildlife damage to crops.

From the point of view of the worldwide conservation goal of perpetuating all living plants and animals, the CAMPFIRE program is more relevant than may seem at first glance. Such a program in the area next to a fully protected core, such as a national park, integrates the welfare of local people and the perpetuation of *populations* of mobile mammals through control of *individuals* that both damage crops and provide supplementary food for humans. This helps to reconcile local humans to the continued existence of the protected core and the likelihood that humans will restrain themselves and others from damaging the protected core through efforts to increase their material welfare. The value of perpetuating *all* plants and animals is a worldwide, not a local, value, so the costs cannot long be exacted from the local population; the worldwide population that values perpetuating all plant and animal species must shoulder a part of the maintenance costs. Protected core areas provide a host of *ecological services*, including erosion control, water infiltration, dry season streamflow, wild relatives of domestic plants and animals, medicinal plants known and unknown, etc. These are principally of value to national governments, which therefore have a responsibility to provide appropriate support to the cost of maintenance. From these considerations it is clear that local people provide and obtain benefits relating to the protected area, and that national and international bodies, obtaining benefits, should also provide program support for national and international benefits.

Rich countries generally realize but ignore the fact that the earth's resources are used in quite an uneven way: citizens of poor nations of the world comprise 78% of the world's human population, but annually consume only 12% of the world's resources. These poorer nations are mostly in Africa, Asia, and Latin America, just those tropical regions whose faunas are of most concern for citizens of rich industrialized nations.

The "less developed" label is in some ways a misnomer applied by economists and political scientists of more developed countries. Less developed countries are highly developed culturally, but the label assumes that the best model for all countries is that of Western-style industrialization. Better labels would be "less consumptive" and "more consumptive," since the average citizen in the United States daily consumes 50 times as much as the average citizen in India, and 100 times as much as the average citizen in some less developed countries.

Habitats are most complex and biotas are most diverse in the tropical and subtropical regions of the earth, which are largely within the borders of more or less underdeveloped (i.e., impoverished) nations. Since there is no question of health insurance or retirement support, and infant mortality is high, a husband and wife can best prepare for illness or old age by having a large family to attend to their needs. Because of poverty, children must work and education is minimal. Illiteracy is high. Poverty, too, limits the diet, on the whole, to starch, with resultant deficiencies in development. Knowledge or interest about the world outside the village is low; the government is a remote entity whose local representatives try to collect taxes or conscript sons for the army or keep people from gathering firewood in national parks. Knowledge of public health being rudimentary, infant mortality is high and so is morbidity of the living, due to various infections. Most families are engaged in subsistence agriculture, with food for the coming day the chief objective.

During the 1970s international conservation thinking was beginning to acknowledge that a variety of enforcement measures were not slowing the loss of wildlife species. A host of isolated examples rendered clearer recognition that conservation of wild plants and animals was closely related to behavior of humans living in that locality, and that behavior was closely related to both their culture and their material welfare.

Unfortunately, local people, rural people, tend to be largely ignored by urban-led governments, and tend to be resentful of governmental efforts to control their activities. And although the biology of wildlife decline or recovery is, or can be, fairly well understood with adequate investigation, the human factor has been neglected. As this fact was more widely recognized, international programs began to be modified to include rural people in proposed solutions to the problem of wildlife decline.

Bibliography

Allen, G. M. 1942. Extinct and vanishing mammals of the Western Hemisphere. American Committee for International Wildlife Protection, New York.

Baillie, J., and B. Groombridge, editors. 1996. 1996 IUCN red list of threatened animals. International Union for Conservation of Nature and Natural Resources, Gland, Switzerland.

Boardman, R. 1981. International organization and the conservation of nature. Indiana University Press, Bloomington.

Child, G. 1984. Managing wildlife for people in Zimbabwe. Pages 118–123 *in* J. A. McNeely and K. R. Miller, editors. National parks, conservation, and development: The role of protected areas in sustaining society. Smithsonian Institute Press, Washington.

Cumming, D. H. M. 1989. Commercial and safari hunting in Zimbabwe. Pages 147–169 *in* R. J. Hudson, K. R. Drew, and L. M. Baskins, editors. Wildlife production systems: Economic utilization of wild ungulates. Cambridge University Press, Cambridge, England.

deVos, A. 1995. The economics of wildlife utilization. Pages 308–312 *in* J. A. Bissonette and P. R. Krausman, editors. Integrating people and wildlife for a sustainable future. The Wildlife Society, Washington.

Dinerstein, E., and E. Wilkramanayake. 1993. Beyond "hotspots": How to prioritize investments in biodiversity in the Indo-Pacific region. Conservation Biology 7:53–65.

Emanoil, M. 1994. Encyclopedia of endangered species. Gale Research, Detroit.

Gilbert, F. F., and D. G. Dodds. 2001. The philosophy and practice of wildlife management. 3rd edition. Krieger, Malabar, FL.

Greenway, J. C., Jr. 1958. Extinct and vanishing birds of the world. Special Publication 13. American Committee for International Wildlife Protection, New York.

Harper, F. 1945. Extinct and vanishing mammals of the Old World. American Committee for International Wildlife Protection, New York.

Hemley, G., editor. 1994. International wildlife trade: A CITES Sourcebook. Island Press, Covelo, CA.

IUCN. 1994. IUCN Red List categories. International Union for Conservation of Nature and Natural Resources, Gland, Switzerland.

IUCN, UNEP, WWF. 1980. World conservation strategy. International Union for Conservation of Nature and Natural Resources, Gland, Switzerland.

Leopold, A. 1933. Game management. Scribner, New York.

Lyster, S. 1985. International wildlife law. Grotius Publishing, Cambridge, UK.

McNeely, J. A., K. R. Miller, W. V. Reid, R. A. Mittermeier, and T. B. Werner. 1990. Conserving the world's biological diversity. International Union for Conservation of Nature and Natural Resources, Gland, Switzerland.

Miller, G. T., Jr. 2000. Environmental science: Working with the earth. 8th edition. Thompson, Florence, KY.

Miller, K., and S. M. Lanou. 1995. National biodiversity planning: Guidelines based on early experiences around the world. World Resources Institute in cooperation with United Nations Environmental Programmes, the World Conservation Union, Washington.

Moulton, M. R., and J. Sanderson. 1999. Wildlife issues in a changing world. 2nd edition. CRC Press, Boca Raton, FL.

Primack, R. B. 1998. Essentials of conservation biology. 2nd edition. Sinauer Associates, Sunderland, MA.

Raybourne, J. E. 1995. Communal wildlife utilization in Zimbabwe. Pages 44–48 *in* J. A. Bissonette and P. R. Krausman, editors. Integrating people and wildlife for a sustainable future. The Wildlife Society, Washington.

Robinson, N. A., editor. 1993. Agenda 21: Earth's action plan (annotated). IUCN Environmental Policy and Law Paper 27. Oceana Publications, New York.

Tambiah, C. R. 1995. Integrated conservation: An alternative approach to sustaining wildlife and local people in Guyana. Pages 57–59 *in* J. A. Bissonette and P. R. Krausman, editors. Integrating people and wildlife for a sustainable future. The Wildlife Society, Washington.

World Resources Institute. 1994. World resources, 1994–1995: A guide to the global environment. Oxford University Press, New York.

Chapter 12

BROADENING WILDLIFE AND HABITAT CONSERVATION

Global conservation entities were established in the 1940s: national cooperation through the United Nations agencies and the addition of nongovernmental and governmental agencies supporting the International Union for the Conservation of Nature and Natural Resources (IUCN). For the first time, reliable financial support existed for professional conservation staffs. International conservation advances previously had been largely the work of individuals, often self-supported. A much broader base of competence and planning began to form. Over the next decades, that base produced steady advances in knowledge of the natural world and human effects on it, and ways that nations could be motivated effectively toward nature conservation. Important new national programs were much broader than the traditional focus on game species. They accelerated from mid-century. Some were generated within national governments and some were stimulated by international agreements designed by global conservation agencies.

International conservation organizations and the international agreements that they developed were largely energized by the perceived need to guide tropical nations toward conservation of their biotic riches. Citizens of rich industrialized nations gave financial support to efforts to preserve the jungle and its interesting denizens far away.

The proliferation of international conservation agreements that characterized the post-World War II years occurred without serious political hindrance from citizens of the United States and Canada, who perhaps thought of them as pertaining mainly to the faraway Tropics. In developing new agreements, international thinking was beginning to be influenced by the opinions of the many poor nations that joined the IUCN in the 1960s. For those nations, the conservation mission announced by the United Nations in 1948 was lacking. That mission was to preserve the biotic community of the entire world, but it did not accommodate the economic development believed necessary for the welfare of their nations. In response, the international conservation community adopted the philosophy of accepting economic development but guiding it in ways supporting the needs of sustained nature conservation. Over time this philosophy was broadened to recognize that local rural people, poor in economic and political terms, coexisted with the greatest wildlife diversity, and so were important players for better or worse in wildlife affairs.

The path toward the goal of cooperation between local people and governments in sustained nature conservation was as yet uncharted. One first step was to change local acceptance of governmental directives to cooperative agreement on goals and means to achieve them. It was proposed that the government view local people as "subjects" rather than "objects," a change easier to envision than to attain. The three objectives developed in international conservation thinking were species preservation, integration with economic development, and achieving cooperation of local rural people. These objectives were in principle accepted in international agreements with which the United States and Canada concurred, but were not readily achieved within the United States and Canada.

Wildlife conservationists have wanted to restore and maintain wildlife populations and habitats, but ever more intensive economic development and resource liquidation eroded wildlife populations and habitats at an ever more rapid and obvious rate. These declines were occurring where wildlife diversity was greatest, in the rural parts of these two nations. And it was in these rural areas that human populations were declining in numbers and, often enough, well-being, as economic exploitation became more efficient. The political thrust of conservation was mainly supported in the prosperous cities rather than in the rural regions where the main growing problems occurred.

Environmentally concerned urbanites showed little active concern about the lives of the poor either in their own cities or in the countryside. Their concerns were for the environmental qualities that they personally valued: clean air and water, and a recreational countryside in a healthy state of nature. In this, about 1970, they matched the international conservation thinkers of 1948 with their goal of preserving the entire world's biotic community.

Earth Day was a good example of the fact that activism for environmental quality sprang from the largely urban prosperous. Convinced by boom times that material needs were assured, economically secure young people could focus their concern on the quality of life. A prosperous and increasing segment of the public was much more concerned about nonmaterial than material satisfactions. This concern was given publicity by Earth Day, 22 April 1970. Promoted by U.S. Senator Gaylord Nelson (D-Wis.), Earth Day celebrated the concept of a high-quality human environment, a celebration that took place on university campuses throughout the United States and Canada and gave momentum to what came to be called the Green or Environmental Movement. Earth Day dramatized an increasing public apprehension by materially secure people concerned about uncontrolled material production. Such concern brought important changes in legislation such as more rigorous standards for the quality of air and water.

Public concern naturally focused first on human health. The news that prenatal development in rodents could be strongly affected by low levels of toxins in the mother's bloodstream was not reassuring for humans.

The decades following 1965 saw an ever-increasing sense of urgency toward wildlife conservation, as the information concerning the worsening status of individual species became more clearly understood. This urgency generated increased activity by government agencies and nongovernmental organizations

(NGOs) in providing support for an ever broadening number of studies which in turn have produced an ever increasing number of unending reports.

The 1970s were characterized by conflict between long established traditional concepts buttressed by classical economics, and the strengthening of concern for environmental quality buttressed by an array of values that were not generally considered in economic analyses. Long established traditional concepts also were challenged by the environmental movement but were still embedded in the prevailing managerial culture, both private and public. A wildlife manager must deal with the existence of all species in perpetuity for sustained material and nonmaterial satifaction, whereas the traditional manager has to deal successfully with time on the scale of hours, days, months, and years to survive and prosper for immediate material satisfaction. A manager in industry who does not please the stockholders can be replaced. A manager in a public agency who does not please the traditional agency clientele can be punished in several ways, among them transfer, reduction in budget, no promotion or salary increase, transfer of certain responsibilities, or reassignment.

By 1970 the United States and Canada had experienced 3 decades of unparalleled prosperity. Citizens whose interests led them to support NGOs had the leisure to be concerned and the money to support the organizations pursuing their interests. The various conservation-oriented NGOs were energized by the first Earth Day and the infusion of enthusiastic new energy into the battle for quality over quantity in human affairs. With more dues-paying members, NGOs could become more active in ways that would please their supporters: Greenpeace could impede whalers, Friends of Animals could free experimental animals from captivity, The Nature Conservancy could acquire unique habitats, the National Wildlife Federation could promote wildlife-friendly backyards, the National Resources Defense Council could take bureaucrats to court if they did not implement pro-conservation legislation.

Meanwhile, the fur trade, once so manifestly economically powerful, continued modestly in Canada even as it declined in the United States, partly because Canada's climate favors production of high-quality fur while precluding development of large-scale agriculture. Canada also is larger than the United States, with far fewer people and human encroachment on habitat. But animal rights activists, mainly an increasingly urban population, have managed to get certain countries and certain states in the United States to ban use of the much maligned but ubiquitous steel leghold trap, or importation of fur caught with leghold traps, or trapping altogether, in addition to a public relations program against wearing fur coats. All this has profoundly affected, and reduced, the once flourishing and influential fur trade. Times had changed.

The aroused and active public stimulated legislators to pass new remedial laws. For example, federal legislation began to include elements of environmental protection, with respect to sorts of environments (water, wilderness) and sorts of threats (waste disposal, pesticides). Use of DDT was severely restricted in 1972, and, encouragingly, in a few years populations of bald eagles, the United States national symbol, began to recover from the problem of thinning and broken eggshells that had been devastating, ultimately to be withdrawn in 1999 from endangered species status. In another reflection of changed public attitudes, the revised Migratory Bird Treaty now extended protection to predatory birds. In fact, the role of predators in the world of nature was more and more widely accepted by the public. Federal activities in predatory animal control had eliminated wolves from the western United States and continued to kill both target and incidental species, but was now subject to increasingly hostile public pressure. Meanwhile, states which had long paid bounties to encourage pressure on cougars, which killed deer, phased out their bounty programs. Urbanized western states such as California and Washington protected cougars altogether.

In more rural U.S. states, widespread tolerance existed toward not only cougars, but remnant populations of grizzly bears. Even a program to reintroduce wolves, extinct in the U.S. West since the 1920s, was widely accepted.

A major legislative advance in 1969 was the U.S. National Environmental Policy Act (NEPA), which reflected the same shift in public opinion that made predators respectable. This Act included both policies and practices. Policy is clearly stated as follows: NEPA Title 1 declares: "It is the continuing policy of the Federal Government, in cooperation with state and local governments, and other concerned public and private organizations, to use all practicable means and measures, including financial and technical assistance, in a manner calculated to foster and promote the general welfare, to create and maintain conditions under which man and nature can exist in productive harmony, and fulfill the social, economic, and other requirements of present and future generations of Americans."

NEPA says that it is the "... continuing responsibility of the Federal Government to use all practicable means, consistent with other essential considerations of national policy, to improve and coordinate Federal plans, functions, programs, and resources [note the directive that enemy agencies peacefully cooperate] so that the United States may

1. Fulfill the responsibilities of each generation as trustee of the environment for future generations;
2. Assure for all Americans safe, healthful, productive, and aesthetically and culturally pleasing environments;
3. Attain the widest range of beneficial uses of the environment without degradation, risk to health or safety, or other undesirable or unintended consequences;
4. Preserve important historic, cultural, and natural aspects of our national heritage, and maintain, whenever possible, an environment which supports diversity and variety of individual choice;
5. Achieve a balance between population and resource use which will permit high standards of living and a wide sharing of life's amenities;
6. Enhance the quality of renewable resources and approach the maximum attainable recycling of depletable resources."

These policy statements invoke the need to *fulfill, assure, attain, preserve, achieve,* and *enhance* social and environmental values implicit in conservation of renewable resources, and are potentially strong or weak depending upon how they are interpreted and carried out by the process that results from the policy. The U.S. National Council on Environmental Quality was established to oversee the process; briefly, this requires that all proposed federal agency actions and actions of federally licensed entities provide an environmental impact statement with values derived from the six-point policy above, showing the expected results of alternative proposed actions, so that the public can be made aware of what is proposed. This is a big change from the earlier situation in which the public usually became aware of federal actions only after they had already occurred.

The concept of NEPA was reflected in state legislation and also had broad international appeal. Many other nations, including Canada, established their own versions, with similar goals.

The intent of NEPA was to force federal agencies to predict the environmental consequences of their actions, and as far as possible to avoid incidental damage to environmental values that their managerial decisions might cause. Application to actual cases was generally successful.

By trying to integrate economic development with environmental quality, NEPA mirrored international conservation objectives. A number of impediments existed to full implementation. Among these was the inadequacy of knowledge needed to accurately predict environmental consequences of alternate actions. (Land management agencies hurried to discover just what flora and fauna existed on lands that they had long managed for timber, grass, flood control, military ranges, etc.) And, when environmental alternatives had to be balanced against economic considerations, some common ground for decision making was needed. Economists worked to quantify values that were largely quality values (aesthetics, nature appreciation, recreation, hunting, fishing, photography, research and education opportunities, etc.). (See appendix A.) But it was soon found that some environmental values, quite real, often could not be quantified in economic terms.

The intent of NEPA also was blunted by agency reluctance or inability to adapt to new directives and to competition between agencies for NEPA-generated funds and tasks. The oversight duties of the Council on Environmental Quality were constrained by the limited budget allowed by Congress. Despite legal pressures from conservation-oriented NGOs, improvement was slow because in an atmosphere of relative ignorance of environmental facts and agency duties, it was difficult to assign blame or require specific action through litigation. Still, the NEPA legislation, which still stands, contains remedies for these impediments that could be applied through strong enough governmental insistence augmented by NGO action—in other words by aroused widespread public pressure.

Arousing widespread public pressure is a proper role for NGOs in any democracy, since government tends to respond eventually to strong enough public pressure. Public pressure can be aroused if the strong but vague unarticulated feelings of individuals can be focused by articulate communicators. During the 1970s environmental quality in the sense of clean air and clean water had public support and governmental response. When enforced, clean water legislation affected wetland wildlife favorably, for example. But something more comprehensive was needed. Thinking of wild plant and animal welfare in terms of their own gardens and pets, the public did not always rally to the population welfare concepts of ecosystem conservation like it did to the thought of whole species endangerment or extinction.

Before the Endangered Species Act (ESA), the various states and provinces had exercised custodial responsibility for all resident wild creatures within their borders. As a practical matter, they paid most attention to game species, since those were the species of interest to their license-buying sportsman clientele. Game species made up only a small proportion of all wild species, so most species were of interest mainly to bird lovers, schoolchildren, and obscure specialists, none of whom contributed funds to state or provincial wildlife agencies. Now, it appeared, some of those wild species were endangered or threatened with extinction and were therefore under federal, not state or provincial, jurisdiction. Just which species would become a federal responsibility remained to be discovered.

Looking ahead, the U.S. Fish and Wildlife Service had recognized the emerging federal interest and ultimate responsibility for endangered species by bringing together the 1964 Redbook, "Rare and Endangered Fish and Wildlife of the United States—Preliminary Draft." Shortly thereafter, in 1966, the U.S. ESA was passed and then, in subsequent years, strengthened. The tasks assigned to the relevant federal agencies under this act were to assess the degree of endangerment of every native biological species in the nation, to list those in danger of extinction, and then to conserve the listed species, to avoid jeopardizing them, to avoid taking them, and to avoid destroying critical habitat. Not until 1995 was the Canadian Environment Act of 1993 enacted, which established a more rigorous, detailed, and complex review process than used before with other legislative support.

Listing threatened species also implies delisting them if and when the species has been restored to a viable population or found already to exist in a viable population but mistakenly listed. Restoration requires adequate habitat as a major factor. The responsible federal agency is required to develop a recovery plan for each listed species and as part of that plan to identify critical habitat. Habitat deemed critical for survival and recovery is protected from habitat modification or degradation that actually kills or injures wildlife by impairing essential behavioral patterns such as reproducing or obtaining food, water, or shelter. This protection is required not only from governmental agencies on public land but from all persons on private land too. In addition, federal agencies cannot authorize, fund, or issue permits or engage in other actions likely to jeopardize the existence of any endangered or threatened species or destroy or adversely modify critical habitat.

Investigators soon found that many wild species of plants and animals within the United States and Canada were indeed threatened or endangered. For each, the law required a recovery plan and guarantee that no governmental action would detract from its survival, and that critical habitat must be identified and protected. Given this general introduction to the complex problem or complexity of problems that characterize the topic of endangered species, it is relevant to examine the actual legislation intended to encourage progress toward solutions.

The federal agencies responsible for implementing the Endangered Species Act in the United States are the U.S. Fish and Wildlife Service in the U.S. Department of the Interior and the National Marine Fisheries Service in the U.S. Department of Commerce. The listing process (as Endangered, Threatened, etc.) can be initiated by either of the two responsible government services or with a petition from another entity.

The appropriate service considers each petition and determines if the listing is (Category 1) warranted, (Category 2) unwarranted although likely but inadequate information exists, or (Category 3) unwarranted because the species is no longer endangered or it is extinct or its taxonomy has been revised. In making its listing determinations, the service must consider overuse, predation, disease, threats to habitat, inadequacy of current protections, and any other factors affecting existence of the petitioned species. The services must not consider the economic impact of their listing decisions.

Given the large number of species already recognized as endangered in the United States, the research still needed to provide required data on each one, and the funding limitations, the federal effort often will be forced to invoke Category 2 and simply postpone consideration of many species possibly facing extinction. Further difficulties exist. The legislation intended to be protective requires that conforming adjustments be made in all federal programs of land and water management. Agency programs must not engage in any action (including authorization, funding, and permit issuance) likely to jeopardize the existence of any endangered or threatened species or result in destroying or adversely modifying its critical habitat.

One can scarcely overestimate the consternation these constraints generated among federal agencies; their traditional programs might be jeopardized by the putative welfare of some obscure species completely outside their frames of reference. And the threat was real. For example, the Tellico Dam in Tennessee was stopped in midconstruction because of threat to the existence of the snail darter, a tiny fish. In fact, the dam was built because a so-called "God Squad" was appointed with authority to determine if overriding human interests were involved, thus weakening the ESA (see p. 170).

To avoid such conflict, prior consultation between federal agencies has become customary. In each case the service (U.S. Fish and Wildlife or Marine Fisheries) is required to prepare a biological opinion of the consequences of a proposed managerial action. If this opinion does not state that the proposed action will jeopardize any creature that has been listed or proposed for listing, the proposed action can proceed.

It is obvious that either service can seldom make a persuasive "jeopardy opinion" because each service is faced with the need to assess the possible consequences of numerous potential agency actions for a huge number of species whose needs are as yet little known. This situation points up a chronic weakness in making environmental decisions in courts of law: when enough factual information exists about an environmental situation, the solution of problems ordinarily can be seen; but it is unusual to have enough factual information. If a controversy occurs, each side tries to demand the burden of proof from the other. If one side accepts the responsibility for burden of proof, and factual information is inadequate, that side will inevitably lose the argument. To demand a jeopardy opinion from the U.S. Fish and Wildlife Service concerning some projected federal land management is to place the burden of proof on the U.S. Fish and Wildlife Service. Therefore it is not surprising that jeopardy opinions are not only uncommon, but they rarely stop a proposed action anyway.

From earlier chapters it can be seen that efforts to preserve and protect natural ecosystems have a long history in the United States and Canada, a much longer history than the ESA. Natural ecosystems allow natural increases and decreases and ecological interactions of all wild plants and animals within their borders, in conjunction with adjacent or other ecosystems that provide habitat for more mobile species. In contrast, the ESA has been interpreted to focus on individual species currently in jeopardy and for which the protection of natural ecosystems has not yet been enough.

Two of the more common situations leading to endangerment are (1) the species in question require a unique habitat or a large amount of common habitat that is not included in enough protected areas, and (2) the species has been extirpated from its remaining suitable habitat and then exists in much reduced numbers only in unsuitable marginal habitat. Both of these situations occur together when habitat is fragmented, so that smaller and smaller units of population are separated from each other into unviable populations subject to genetic inbreeding, and habitat quality diminishes with reduction in size and conflicting human uses of the landscape. It was to remedy such situations that each listed species required a Habitat Conservation Plan (HCP) based upon a determination of critical habitat. In 1982 the U.S. Congress amended the ESA to require that at the time a species is listed, critical habitat would be designated only to the maximum extent prudent and determinable. This places the burden of proof on the listing agency, so relatively few HCPs have been completed.

Progress toward recovery of endangered species has been slow due to the magnitude of the task of listing species, the determination of requirements for recovery, the resolution of conflict between ESA goals, and the different managerial goals of federal agencies and private landowners. Critics point toward inadequate funding. Some 600 Category 1 species await processing, while some 3000 Category 2 species await research and assessment. Of course, more funds would allow the services to hire more employees for research and assessment. But environmentally ignorant politicians often, usually, reduce environmental budgets.

The concept of saving wild species from extinction is attractive to urbanites, and so it is politically popular. But the actual implementation of this concept requires a huge effort that encounters opposition from many quarters. The responsible services respond by emphasizing work on "charismatic," i.e., "glamour" species—those most likely to be known and supported by the politically powerful urbanite. Yet even when this strategy results in increased funding for efforts to restore such wild species, these efforts can be thwarted by regulatory or land management agencies with conflicting agendas. Courts tend to defer to decisions made by agencies so long as they are not unconstitutional or "arbitrary and capricious." To demonstrate in court that an agency action is arbitrary and capricious requires time, money, effort, and factual information beyond the listing services' usual means. Furthermore, by imposing a more rigorous standard of review, decisions of often technical scientific issues are shifted from an agency with substantial biological expertise, to judges who have none.

It might be expected that in cases with no obvious economic values at risk, progress would be easier on behalf of endangered species. But scarcely a case exists without threat to economic interest, including the economic livelihood of the persons and agencies involved. In a culture of public employees, every player must be aware, for welfare of self and dependents, that he/she is vulnerable. The higher people advance in the agency, the more they have to lose. On their own behalf, then, as well as their belief in the virtue of their organization, they will tend to place the welfare of their organization above any different good.

Recovery of endangered species requires basic fact-finding, often no easy matter even for the best researchers, and a challenge for youthful enthusiasts. How the discovered facts are interpreted and applied to the advance of recovery programs tends to be the business of agency administrators. In a substantial number of cases, the on-the-ground researchers who are best acquainted with the needs of individual endangered species rather consistently report that normal bureaucratic behaviors impede endangered species recovery.

Biologists closest to the natural behavior of endangered species have encountered the natural behavior of government agencies and its negative consequences for species recovery. In a broader view, it seems that practically all human entities involved in an endangered species recovery program will benefit most, materially, as long as the species does not become extinct but never recovers to a viable population level. Then public interest will keep the financial support flowing. The optimist will find that the saving grace in this situation is not species recovery, but species survival. The biologist will see the ultimate, though perhaps prolonged, decline of the species to extinction.

Problems recognized might lead to problems solved. A need exists to curb some agency behaviors. In some cases the agencies concerned with an endangered species have been subject to oversight, as by the Marine Mammal Commission for the Florida manatee. Such a committee can keep continual pressure on the agency to produce benefits for the endangered species by encouraging fact-finding and timely action based on fact, and discouraging diversion of funds and energy toward agency custom and welfare. An independent federal "Endangered Species Recovery Committee" or individual committees with enough status and expertise could provide advice for a recovery program if authorized to recommend improvements to the program's organization and operation. Improving the organization, operation, and scale of success in the U.S. Endangered Species program should be a major national goal in the immediate future. Delay will only deepen the problem.

Many species have become endangered because current habitat conditions are unfavorable for their welfare. Some other species have become too abundant from the human perspective, because current habitat conditions and often legislative protection are favorable for their welfare.

In earlier chapters we noted that with development of agriculture and pastoralism some 10,000 years ago, humans had to protect their crops and herds from depredations of wild creatures. This led to the common opinion that there were good animals and bad animals. This lingered long through the European settlement of Canada and the United States, and is not yet completely extinct. But public opinion in the post-World War II years began to shift toward nonmaterial values and become increasingly concerned with the welfare of species formerly condemned. This shift was gradually reflected in both state/provincial and federal legislation. Until almost the mid-1900s, predatory birds and mammals could legally be killed by anyone, in some cases with inducement of bounties or with agency funded efforts. For example, by the 1960s the western states were phasing out bounties for cougars and the federal program of livestock predator control was being seriously questioned.

Meager successes of the endangered species program have occurred. The American alligator, peregrine falcon, and bald eagle are among these. The alligator of the southeastern United States has been subject to human predation for thousands of years, principally for its meat. During the 1800s the skin was at times commercially valuable, particularly from about 1860. Heavy commercial harvesting continued through the first decades of the 1900s, resulting in ever smaller alligator populations, annual take, and individual size.

Subsequent moves toward recovery can be traced in the state of Louisiana, rich in alligator habitat. That state recognized the overharvesting problem and in 1962 banned alligator hunting. In 1967 the alligator received federal listing under the Endangered Species Act. Total legal protection lasted from 1962 to 1972, during which time intensive study had provided a firm biological base for management aimed at recovery and ultimate controlled harvest. Simultaneously, a sustainable use program was developed.

Since most of the alligator habitat in Louisiana is in private ownership, one aim of management was commercial profit. Another was compatibility of alligator recovery with the biodiversity of the habitat, and ultimate harvesting. As alligator populations recovered, harvest was gradually begun. By 1981 alligators were no longer in need of federal protection. Controlled commercialization had two aspects in the late 1990s: harvesting from the wild population and production from alligator farming. The wild harvest amounted to about 25,000 annually in the 1990s. Production of wild plus farmed alligators available for commercial use has been large and predictable enough to meet a sustained market demand for skins and meat. Despite annual fluctuations in marketplace value, this sustainability translates into some economic stability, in contrast to the earlier history of overharvest and depletion of the wild population.

Cold-blooded animals such as alligators are easier to restore than warm-blooded birds or mammals because the former can endure temporary environmental setbacks through decline of metabolic rate and need for nourishment, whereas the latter need constant nourishment to maintain a constant metabolic rate. But successes have occurred in restoring declining populations of birds and mammals too. Birds at the top of their food chains include the peregrine falcon (duck hawk), bald eagle, and brown pelican which declined sharply during the era in which DDT was used widely in the United States. With the banning of DDT for most uses and, in the case of the falcon, extensive captive breeding and release into the wild, all three species have recovered enough to be removed from the list of endangered species (delisted) to the improved category of threatened (i.e., still in some, but less extreme, peril).

More species are still in jeopardy. For example, some 65 forms of mammals are on the U.S. Fish and Wildlife list for the United States as of the year 2002 (another 251 in other countries), and more are candidates for consideration but still are beyond the current capability of that agency. Similarly long lists exist for other endangered vertebrates in the United States (birds-78, reptiles-14, amphibians-12, fishes-71), invertebrates-148 (clams, snails, insects, spiders, crustaceans, etc.), and plants-596. A difficult task indeed, one never before attempted by humankind, will be to obtain enough biological knowledge about the needs of these and future endangered forms on which to base recovery plans integrated with the needs of national sustained land management.

As an auxiliary measure to maintain viable populations of larger species, for which protected units of habitat are generally too small, captive breeding is naturally thought of as a possibility. More than one large species has been perpetuated in captivity while it declined toward extinction in the wild, the American bison being a classic example. Increasing numbers of bison in captivity today provide stock for translocation to some of their original habitats, where they prosper. The concept of conservation of endangered wild species not in the wild, but in captivity, has the attraction of showing obvious results in the form of expanded facilities and visible animals, and diverting attention from degrading human uses of natural habitats. But it also has flaws which should be seriously considered.

First of all, to maintain a species in captivity requires recognizing and identifying the species and being familiar with its needs. The first part, recognizing and identifying, sounds simple enough. But the conservation aim is to maintain all currently living species and subspecies in perpetuity. How can we maintain in captivity species or subspecies that we have not even discovered yet? Many of these, small and obscure but undeniably true species yet undiscovered, certainly exist in the wild. From 10 million to 100 million species of life probably exist on earth, but only 1.4 million have been named and classified. With our changing world, many are thought to become extinct, almost daily, without even our awareness of their existence, except sometimes in the fossil record. One of the functions of maintaining natural areas is the survival of inconspicuous species little known or still undiscovered.

Second, our aim of conserving all wild gene pools (genetic assemblages) requires that enough individuals of each species survive to maintain genetic adaptability to natural conditions. Genetic variation and its consequences for successful survival are continuous, with some serving to fit each species into an often dynamic environment. If we place a species in captivity, even in large numbers, the course of genetic adaptation will be toward the new habitat of captivity rather than the former habitat in nature. Particularly if a species must be maintained in captivity with the aim of reintroducing it into the wild, the fewer generations that occur in captivity the better will be its re-adaptation to the wild environment.

Even if the aim of conservation narrows to the maintenance of endangered wildlife in captivity, two perennial problems would be (1) to avoid small population genetic maladies (inbreeding) through massive exchange programs, and (2) to avoid an ever-expanding list of endangered wildlife to be included in the captive populations. This program would be both costly and inadequate, except for a few species of special interest.

It is clear from the above that maintenance of wild habitats will be needed for effective programs of wildlife conservation. Sometimes adequate habitat exists from which some wild mammal species have been extirpated by overharvest; these possibly can be restored by transplanting captive-bred individuals if none from wild habitats is available. This is where zoos and large wildlife park enclosures can play a role. In each case, of course, success depends in large part on control of those human pressures that wiped out the native population in the first place.

The United States has an Endangered Species Act, but no Endangered Habitat or Ecosystem Act. The restoration of currently endangered species includes the need to at least protect, and often restore, the wild habitats needed to encourage their survival and increase. The same need for maintenance of natural habitats is imperative for survival of many obscure creatures not yet even identified.

Both the United States and Canada have large areas of publicly owned land, under the administration of federal and state/provincial agencies. It is on these rather than on most privately owned lands that management favoring threatened species is most immediately feasible. Particularly in the United States, with its large areas under administration of the U.S. Forest Service and the U.S. Bureau of Land Management, the 1970s saw the emergence of public concern about how these areas were managed with respect to the restoration and maintenance of threatened species.

Bibliography

Alvarez, H. 1993. Twilight of the panther: Biology, bureaucracy and failure in an endangered species program. Myakka, Sarasota, FL.

Bear, D. 1996. The promise of NEPA. Pages 178–188 *in* W. Snape and O. Houck, editors. Biodiversity and the law. Island Press, Covelo, CA.

Boardman, R. 1981. International organization and the conservation of nature. Indiana University Press, Bloomington.

Carson, R. 1962. Silent spring. Houghton Mifflin, New York.

Clark, J. A. 1994. The Endangered Species Act: Its history, provisions, and effectiveness. Pages 19–43 *in* T. W. Clark, R. P. Reading, and A. L. Clarke, editors. Endangered species recovery. Island Press, Washington.

Clark, T. W., R. P. Reading, and A. L. Clarke, editors. 1994. Endangered species recovery. Island Press, Washington.

Coggins, G. C. 1991. Snail darters and pork barrels revisited: Reflections on endangered species and land use in America. Pages 62–74 *in* K. A. Kohm, editor. Balancing on the brink of extinction: The Endangered Species Act and lessons for the future. Island Press, Covelo, CA.

Colborn, T., and C. Clement. 1992. Chemically-induced alterations in sexual and functional development: The wildlife-human connection. Princeton Scientific Publishing, Princeton, NJ.

Colborn, T., D. Dumanoski, and J. P. Myers. 1996. Our stolen future: Are we threatening our fertility, intelligence, and survival—a scientific detective story. Dutton, New York.

Cole, B. P. 1989. Recovery planning for endangered and threatened species. Pages 201–209 *in* U.S. Seal, E. T. Thorn, M. A. Bogen, and S. A. Anderson, editors. Conservation biology and the black-footed ferret. Yale University Press, New Haven, CT.

Clough, J. 1984. Property: Illusions of ownership. Gann, Portland, OR.

Decker, D., and G. Goff, editors. 1987. Valuing wildlife: Economic and social perspectives. Westview Press, Boulder, CO.

Easter-Pilcher, A. 1996. Implementing the Endangered Species Act. BioScience 46:355–363.

Easterbrook, G. 1995. A moment on Earth: The coming age of environmental optimism. Viking, New York.

Findley, R. W., and D. A. Farber. 1995. Cases and materiels on environmental law. West Publishing Company, St. Paul, MN.

Fitzgerald, S. 1989. International wildlife trade: Whose business is it? World Wildlife Fund, Washington.

Gilbert, F. F., and D. G. Dodds. 2001. The philosophy and practice of wildlife management. 3rd edition. Krieger, Malabar, FL.

Gottlieb, R. 1993. Forcing the spring: The transformation of the American environmental movement. Island Press, Covelo, CA.

Greve, M. S. 1996. The demise of environmentalism in American law. AEI Press, Washington.

Grumbine, R. E. 1992. Ghost bears: Exploring the biodiversity crisis. Island Press, Covelo, CA.

Harris, L. D., and P. C. Frederick. 1990. The role of the Endangered Species Act in the conservation of biological diversity. Pages 99–117 *in* J. Cairns and

T. Crawford, editors. An assessment: Integrated environmental management. Lewis, Chelsea, MI.

Hemley, G. 1994. International wildlife trade: A CITES sourcebook. Island Press, Washington.

Hickey, J. J., and D. W. Anderson. 1968. Chlorinated hydrocarbons and eggshell changes in raptorial and fish-eating birds. Science 162:271–273.

Holdgate, M. 1996. From care to action: Making a sustainable world. Taylor and Francis, Washington.

Institute of Medicine. 1993. Veterans and Agent Orange: Health effects of herbicides used in Vietnam. Institute of Medicine, National Academy of Sciences, Washington.

IUCN. 1994. IUCN Red List categories. International Union for Conservation of Nature and Natural Resources, Gland, Switzerland.

IUCN, UNEP, WWF. 1991. Caring for the Earth: A strategy for sustainable living. The World (International) Conservation Union, United Nations Environmental Programme, and WorldWide Fund for Nature, Gland, Switzerland.

Keohane, R. O., and M. A. Levy, editors. 1996. Institutions for environmental aid: Pitfalls and promise. MIT Press, Cambridge, MA.

Kohak, E. 1984. The embers and the stars: A philosophical inquiry into the moral sense of nature. University of Chicago Press, Chicago.

Lawton, J. H., and R. M. May, editors. 1995. Extinction rates. Oxford University Press, Oxford, UK.

Lee, K. N. 1993. Compass and gyroscope: Integrating science and politics for the environment. Island Press, Covelo, CA.

Littell, R. 1992. Endangered and other protected species: Federal law and regulation. Bureau of National Affairs, Washington.

McNease, L., and T. Joanen. 1978. Distribution and relative abundance of the alligator in Louisiana coastal marshes. Proceedings of the annual conference of the Southeast Association of Fish and Wildlife Agencies 37:182–186.

Meadows, D. H., D. L. Meadows, and J. Randers. 1992. Beyond the limits. Chelsea Green, Post Mills, UT.

Milbarth, L. W. 1984. Environmentalists: Vanguards for a new society. Albany State University Press, New York.

Miller, K. R., and S. M. Lanou. 1995. National biodiversity planning: Guidelines based on early experiences around the world. World Resources Institute, United Nations Environmental Programme and The World Conservation Union, Gland, Switzerland.

Newmark, W. D. 1995. Extinction of mammal populations in western North America national parks. Conservation Biology 9:512–526.

O'Shea, T. J., B. B. Ackerman, and H. F. Percival. 1995. Population biology of the Florida manatee. National Biological Service, Washington.

Payne, N. F. 2002. More wildlife on your land: a guide for private landowners. Barberie Publications, Plover, WI.

Reading, R. P., and B. J. Miller. 1994. The black-footed ferret recovery program.

Pages 73–100 *in* T. W. Clark, R. P. Reading, and A. L. Clarke, editors. Endangered species recovery. Island Press, Washington.

Rubin, C. T. 1994. The Green Crusade: Rethinking the roots of environmentalism. Free Press, New York.

Schorger, A. W. 1973. The passenger pigeon: Its natural history and extinction. University of Oklahoma Press, Norman.

Scott, J. M., S. A. Temple, D. L. Harlow, and M. L. Shaffer. 1994. Restoration and management of endangered species. Pages 531–539 *in* T. A. Bookhout, editor. Research and management techniques for wildlife and habitats. The Wildlife Society, Bethesda, MD.

Tober, J. A. 1989. Wildlife and the public interest: Nonprofit organization and federal wildlife policy. Praeger, New York.

Chapter 13

HOLISTIC CONSERVATION ON PUBLIC LANDS

Through the first two centuries of European colonization of the United States and Canada, the balance of forces heavily favored economic development, with some consequences described earlier. The impact of economic development on the natural world was not lost on the more perceptive citizens. In reference to the natural environment, as early as 1864 one thoughtful critic (Marsh) wrote that Americans are breaking up the floor, doors, and window frames of their house as fuel for warmth and cooking. Widespread popular support must exist for large-scale social and political action. Almost a half century later popular support for the natural world had become strong enough to support further political action.

From modest beginnings, public opinion toward constraining the less acceptable consequences of unfettered economic development began to shift more rapidly in the post-World War II years. Polluted water flowed in the rivers and appeared in wells, polluted air became more common, rural landscapes became more monotonous, farmed soil eroded into wetlands and streams, marine marshes were converted into recreational marinas, old-growth timber (more than 100 years old for most species) was clearcut far beyond sustainable levels, public lands were narrowly managed for private interests, and in similar ways it became increasingly clear that the natural environment, not only for wild creatures, but for humans as well, was being destroyed for short-term profit.

During 1945 to the 1960s management of public forestland and rangeland, like that of private farmland, remained largely focused on material production. The surviving old-growth timber was largely in the unroaded mountains. Powerful new machinery facilitated mountain road building, and sale of newly accessible publicly owned timber paid the costs. Forest management of the day aimed at replacing ancient "stagnant" forests with vigorous monocultures of the most economically valuable species which produced a uniform product in as short a time as possible. To achieve this goal, management included planting preferred seedlings, suppressing forest fires, and controlling insect damage. Simplification of forest habitats reduced the diversity of plant and animal species that could live in them. On the one hand, clearcutting stands temporarily encouraged ground-level vegetation such as shrubs, grasses, and forbs—food for the popular grazing and browsing deer and elk. And the new roads facilitated hunter access. The annual kill of big game species adapted to simplified forest habitats rose steadily from 1945 onward. On the other hand, species requiring old-growth habitat, such as lichen-eating woodland caribou, declined.

The focus on production that dominated the post-World War II years in many ways was exhibited too by the professional wildlife conservationist. Little official interest existed in any but principal game species. For these, the aim was to sell the most licenses possible and take the biggest annual harvest that could be maintained—the maximum sustained yield. Developed in fisheries management, this concept led big game managers to fashion systems of harvest that directed hunting pressure toward "underharvested" populations. Success in managing abundant wild big game in the United States and Canada was recognized abroad; the 1950s and 1960s saw many North American biologists advising on the ranching of wild hoofed mammals for sustained meat production in other continents.

The emphasis on increasing material production from lands managed by private business and governmental agencies faithfully reflected a preponderant post-World War II attitude in the United States and Canada. But from 1945 to the 1960s the focus of managers on narrow production goals was raising public uneasiness about the unintended side effects of their programs on human environments. Simultaneously, the rapid spread of television into private homes fueled concern with news of human-caused calamities from burning rivers (Ohio's Cuyahoga River in 1969) to mountain landslides. As a general measure of apprehension grew, it was augmented by clear calls for remedy. One of the first of this era was biologist Rachael Carson's book, *Silent Spring*, in 1962 (see chapter 10).

Humans were struck by the implications of *Silent Spring*, both for themselves and for the great number of wild species that depended upon insects and other invertebrates as food. Infant birds, in general, require the high-protein bodies of invertebrates for survival, even though they sometimes prosper as seed-eaters when adult. It took little imagination to conceive that the current liberal use of DDT on farm and forest might kill nontarget wild species.

Research on the unintended damage caused by insecticides soon revealed that a major problem with many of the most effective was their affinity for storage in fat, and their interference with normal functioning of bodily hormones, rich in fatty acids. Suppose that a human being ate toxin-carrying flesh? Indeed, DDT bio-accumulation in breast milk from American mothers contained 4 times the level of DDT considered by the federal government to be safe for human consumption.

A state biologist studying blue grouse on national forestland wondered what current DDT spraying to control insects damaging trees would have on his grouse chicks and, then, on grouse hunters and their families eating grouse. He queried the U.S. Public Health Service and the answer he received recommended removing fat from the birds before cooking. Publication of this response in the local newspaper elicited public opposition to the local use of DDT in the local public forest—and the speedy end of that managerial practice. The pressure of the public against their perceived misuse of managerial practices on public lands, illustrated by this example, became ever greater as more specific information became available. Species endangerment provided an easily grasped threat, and response focused on public lands.

Many little-noticed species, and well-known species too, were soon found to be in some danger of extinction and in addition, many did not occur in protected areas such as national parks. In fact, since national parks were first established for scenic values and located in mountainous regions, they tended not to include many other wildlife habitats: grasslands, marshes, coastlines, deserts, and fertile lowlands, for example.

Particular habitats for perpetuating threatened species in the United States have been established on public land on a small scale since 1903, when President Theodore Roosevelt created the Pelican Island Refuge in Florida for the benefit of "plume birds." Other efforts in that direction included the American Bison Society's establishment of the National Bison Range, and its stocking. But by the 1970s many endangered species of plants and animals existed as yet without protected habitat; that realization stimulated much more extensive efforts toward habitat protection. This was a cause that appealed to the protective tendencies of well-to-do urbanites; established in 1951, the U.S. Nature Conservancy flourished from the start. In many cases this nongovernmental organization (NGO) could act quickly to purchase valuable special habitats, which it then held until slower-moving governmental agencies could, in turn, acquire them. As an NGO, it could buy as well as sell when some of its lands proved more valuable for development than for conserving endangered species.

The urban interest in protecting habitat for rare and endangered plants and animals was continually augmented with up-to-the-minute information on additional threats and needs. Among these were the results of scrutinizing national parks with respect to wildlife. Was emphasis on recreation and protection causing damage to perceived park values? Such concerns inevitably led to a look at other public lands. Could these be managed better for values of the human environment as well as for conservation quality?

Focused by NGOs on public lands, an aroused public interest was concerned about the extent that these lands sheltered, or could potentially shelter, endangered species. Management of public lands had historically been strongly product-oriented. National forests produced wood, with wildlife an incidental product; national rangelands produced forage for livestock, with wildlife an incidental product; national wildlife refuges were managed largely for game, particularly waterfowl, with other wildlife an incidental product.

Each of these sorts of public land and product had its closely knit group of traditional stakeholders: the responsible agencies, university teachers, makers of related industrial products, users of the products, supportive legislators, and so on. Each of these resource-oriented coteries had been managing its resource for decades to its own satisfaction.

Now, urban interest was growing in environmental quality for endangered species and humans. Long enthusiastic about protected areas such as national parks, that urban interest began to look at other public lands and waters, since many endangered plants and animals were found in aquatic habitats. Traditional managers, product-oriented, obviously were ignorant of much knowledge or concern about endangered species. Aroused urban concern grew, produced plentiful

NGO support, and exerted increasing pressure on traditional governmental public land agencies through legislation and litigation.

The problem that these NGOs and their supporters faced was, fundamentally, impediment of bureaucratic custom. For many decades public agencies charged with conserving natural resources had done just that, according to their own philosophies. But the public's philosophies, largely nonmaterialistic, were diverging from utilitarian agency philosophies. To make agencies broaden their managerial philosophies to more closely parallel public concern, NGO staffs scrutinized and modified legislation. When agencies did not carry out legal directives, they could be sued; where enabling legislation needed revision, NGO lobbyists could work toward revision in legislatures.

Adversarial relationships are integral to rich industrial democratic cultures. Urban constituencies with increasing demands on traditionally rural resource uses are well armed with money and influence. They attempt to pursue their goals through changes of direction within the groups that have long been formed around each resource—the traditional resource coteries. But the traditional resource coterie tends to resist change. It has a high level of internal coherence and devotion to a well-defined philosophy, and is led by individuals educated in an earlier age. Custom saves energy by providing accustomed solutions to familiar problems. But public concern is focused not on familiar problems but on a newly recognized one. Are public lands being managed for restoration and maintenance of all wild species? Pressing this question is a dramatic way of attempting to reorient public land management toward restoration of natural habitats—a goal attractive to the urban mind. Emotional content for the necessary fundraising in this political drive can be enhanced by demonizing traditional national resource coteries: ruthless clearcutters, selfish overgrazers, and hoodlum ("slob") hunters, among others. This exacerbated relations between dominant urban political forces and their own rural citizenry, long accustomed to using the natural resources for material gain.

As mentioned, the three goals of international conservation are preservation of species, integration of economic development and nature conservation, and effective cooperation of rural local people in wildlife conservation. On the national level in the United States are the Endangered Species Act (ESA), legislation aimed at preservation of species, and the National Environmental Policy Act (NEPA), legislation aimed at integrating economic development with nature conservation. For both of these acts, and regulations aimed at implementing them, it has been necessary to identify the wildlife species involved, their population status, and ecological requirements and circumstances. Unfortunately, those species still unknown were estimated to be numerous, especially the smaller forms. For them the obvious need was preserving the natural habitat in which they had so far survived.

In 1971 the United Nations launched the Man and the Biosphere (MAB) Program. This recognized the need not only to protect natural values, as in parks and reserves, but also to conduct research on integrating economic development and nature conservation, and to gain the cooperation of local people around protected areas for sustained nature protection. The designation—biosphere reserve—was given to major natural landscape units, often already under national protection but also sometimes newly protected under this program. The biosphere reserve concept joined all three goals of international conservation—species preservation, integration of development with nature conservation, and cooperation of local people in wild species conservation. This third goal had no comprehensive, guiding, national North American legislation such as NEPA and ESA. Ultimately, the program was intended to protect examples of as many natural habitats as possible and address the problem that the intended conservation functions of protected natural areas were often weakened by activities of rural people living nearby. The program, then, was designed to develop a basis for rationally using and conserving the biosphere's resources and for improving the relationship between people and their environment.

The U.S. MAB statement uses the terms "protected area" to describe a park or similar area, "managed use area" for the surrounding territory, and adds a third "zones of cooperation," where stakeholders of biosphere reserves cooperate and educate each other in connecting conservation, economic, and cultural values. Such stakeholders comprise managing agencies, local governmental agencies, scientists, economic interests, nongovernmental organizations, cultural groups, and local citizens.

The term *biosphere reserve* can be applied to any protected area of sufficient size and ecological representation. Since no "protected" area is truly adequate to maintain viable populations of all species, particularly large mobile ones (elephant, tiger, grizzly bear, rhinoceros, to name a few), the conservation of each biosphere reserve was conceived to include a region around the protected "core area" within which human activities should be conducted in such a way as to support the conservation purposes of the reserve. A nature reserve surrounded by hostile environment is much like an island surrounded by ocean. Its wildlife populations are confined and isolated; the prospects for successful emigration or immigration are poor. For a species requiring much space per individual, the total population will necessarily be low, with the chance of inbreeding depression rising as the population declines. These undesirable results can be overcome by three sorts of remedies: (1) increasing the population of a species in the reserve by changing its habitat within the reserve for the better; (2) improving the chances for species in the reserve to expand and survive beyond the boundaries of the reserve; and (3) introducing "new blood" from a different gene pool to help avoid inbreeding depression. Proposals for managing biosphere reserves and their surrounding buffer zones are obviously relevant to points (1) and (2) above. Point (3) can be met in two sorts of ways. The best long-range solution is to provide for dispersal of individuals out of and into reserves via interconnecting belts of habitat, i.e., corridors or landscape linkages, so that reserves or other units of habitat-supporting populations exchange genetic diversity. The short-range solution is to transport individuals artificially between populations—an expensive program that will help only if introduced individuals become successful breeders.

In 2001, of 393 biosphere reserves in 94 countries, 47 occur in the United States and 10 in Canada. Those in the United States are variously administered by seven governmental and nongovernmental agencies, often in cooperation with local government and private landowners. These reserves had administrative titles such as Wildlife Refuge, National Preserve, National Park and Preserve, National Park, National Seashore, National Lakeshore, National Scenic River, National Monument, National Forest, State Forest, Experimental Forest, Experimental Range, Research Natural Area, Biological Station, Wilderness, Experimental Forest and Scenic-Research Area, and Biosphere Reserve. One reserve on the Canadian and another on the Mexican borders are administered cooperatively with the United States.

To date few examples exist of full development of the biosphere reserve concept sketched above. And in rural areas some citizens profess to believe that the international listing means international control of some sort over the national territory, a mistaken notion but one that casts a revealing sidelight on the territorial feelings of rural residents.

Viewed objectively, the nationally controlled protected natural area surrounded by a benignly developed area promoting the welfare and cooperation of local people is one quite viable vision of how to move toward the sustained existence of all wild species. Contemporary examples suggest that a key element in progress is control of the land. Where the unit of landscape (protected area and its surroundings) is "owned" by one entity, stakeholders (major interested groups) are few. For the simplest example, a region of aboriginal land has a single owner-stakeholder, and a single governmental stakeholder. The owner is mainly concerned with local human welfare; the government is concerned with sustained conservation of all wild species. Between them they can learn to deal successfully with each other in coping with the possibilities of production and development. Even so, the necessary change in the posture of government agencies from regulating in a command-and-control mode to regulating in a cooperative mode requires changes in individuals and agencies.

Fortunately, this process of comanagement is beginning to occur in various areas, particularly in those areas still inhabited by aboriginal people. The northern regions of Canada provide a compelling example. Rural populations there mostly consist of aboriginal people. Parts of their traditional territories have become national parks, and parts of the natural landscape have been altered by pressures from the more industrial southern Canada. The Canadian aboriginals and other native populations around the world face two paths: merge with the dominant industrial culture or adapt their traditional culture to new conditions. Many have chosen the second path, which will save them from cultural disintegration if successfully followed, and also will save wildlife and habitat of their territory from overexploitation and deterioration. But major change from aboriginal times has been the centralized government's modern assumption of authority over resource use by aboriginals.

Governments have cultures too, and today's governments tend to manage different natural resources through separate agencies, each focused on a particular resource, such as forests, water, wildlife, and so on. Each of these agencies is accustomed to developing and enforcing regulations guiding resource use. The result is that a particular regional landscape is generally managed or the activities of its human inhabitants and other users regulated by more than one government agency (see chapter 9).

For comanagement to develop, government agencies must be willing to share a measure of decision-making with local communities and, equally important, must provide representatives who are knowledgeable about local customs and values, and sympathetic to the needs of local communities. For Canada's Northwest Territories, these guidelines have been followed with growing pains and an increasing measure of success. Such a conflict of cultures has been described as the "state system" and the "indigenous system." According to this characterization, the state system is one in which the government assumes responsibility for managing resources available to all citizens, authority is centralized and flows from the top down, and management of fish and wildlife resources is functionally separate from management of the lands and waters that sustain them. The indigenous system is one in which the local residents assume a common ownership in such resources as wildlife, and practice management by consensus. The experience of every aspect of harvesting, such as traveling, searching, hunting, skinning, butchering, and eating, develops knowledge accumulated and shared intimately and constantly by everyone, and handed down to each generation. Important management data include historical experience and a long-range conception of the future as well as immediate observations of direct cause and effect.

Canada recognized that much was to be gained by cooperative integration of the necessary parts of the state and the indigenous systems. Canada moved toward comanagement of a specific geographic area, involving agreement between government agencies and user groups that provides: (1) those interested in the resource with a system of rights and obligations; (2) rules describing actions to be taken under various circumstances; and (3) procedures for collective decision-making by government representatives, user organizations, and individual users. Under comanagement, government agencies do not have to transfer or relinquish any legal authority or jurisdiction; but public authorities must share decision-making power with user groups. On 1 April 1999 a large section of Canada's northeastern Northwest Territories was redesignated Nunavut and given to the Inuit to administer under these general guidelines.

Comanagement shares the Man and the Biosphere goal of harmonizing biodiversity, cultural values, and socioeconomic development through developing partnerships among stakeholders. It has a formal history of 2 or 3 decades. It has been applied in and around protected areas in Canada and Alaska where aboriginal people gain part of their livelihood from wildlife but are willing to modify their harvest practices to restore and maintain currently overharvested populations.

An aspect of nonlocal stakeholder participation in North America is widespread public concern about possible extinction of species currently endangered, as expressed in national legislation and international treaties and conventions.

When in recent years populations of four species of geese in Alaska were declining toward extinction, the reasons were identified as local harvest of birds and eggs on the northern breeding grounds, and hunting and habitat degradation on the goose winter range far to the south. A management plan was developed and agreed upon by responsible government agencies, local native groups, and stakeholders (sportsmen and conservationists) on the wintering grounds. This plan called for reduction or cessation of harvest on the breeding grounds in the north and the wintering grounds in the south. Its successful implementation through comanagement was supported not only by the original participants but also by additional stakeholders including the National Audubon Society and other major national environmental and waterfowl hunting organizations. Similar local comanagement plus wider public support have resulted in restoration of populations of caribou, walrus, narwhal, bowhead whales, and other large mammals in North America, all of them important in sustained welfare of indigenous people.

An important biological aspect of comanagement of wildlife populations and habitats is that these exist in natural patterns on the landscape, for example as year-round population ranges, complete watersheds large enough to support wide-ranging wildlife species and those needing large habitat interiors, and the like. But even if gap analysis through geographic information systems can identify and suggest corrections in habitat gaps, often such landscape units are economically or politically fragmented by ownership or administrative authority. This complicates arrangements needed for comanagement by the number of stakeholders involved. Although difficult, learning how to overcome such impediments is essential for success.

An analysis of the evolution of wildlife comanagement in Quebec indicated that difficulty occurred because members of the comanagement committee were widely divided in values and cultural background regarding native practice and scientific management. This has caused reduced motivation; membership has changed often. Members should be selected based on positive attitudes toward other cultures. Nevertheless, Quebec succeeded in coordinating the technical expertise of government and the cultural traditions of the local people toward the mutual goal of large mammal restoration, maintenance, and use. One result was recovery of the beluga (white whale) and another the recovery of a major caribou population. The conclusion of the analysis was that comanagement has potential for wildlife managers because it can combine information from scientific and traditional origins to determine a species' status at the local level. Comanagement also allows discussion and establishment of joint management objectives, and development of joint action plans. Less enforcement is needed because controls are created and implemented locally, and will have greater compliance and better results. But some form of external independent presence and follow up are needed to implement cooperatively prepared management plans.

Developing contemporary comanagement programs will inevitably encounter local impediments. A current example is found in the region east of an international biosphere reserve: Waterton Biosphere Reserve (Canada) which is linked with Glacier National Park Biosphere Reserve (United States). The Waterton Biosphere Reserve includes Waterton Lakes National Park in Alberta. The adjacent managed use area is occupied by commercial activities such as forestry, ranching, farming, and oil and gas extraction. An active program of cooperation began in 1982 with the intent to use environmental research and to monitor public information and education to encourage integrated use, development, and conservation of natural resources. In this area, three large mammal species range between the protected and the managed use areas in culturally or economically significant numbers: the Rocky Mountain elk, the plains (gray) wolf, and the grizzly bear. Elk are potential competitors for food with domestic livestock and share some diseases and parasites. Since an adequate knowledge base existed, investigation of a potential elk-livestock conflict was quickly conducted, and a mutually satisfactory program of joint elk-livestock management was accepted and implemented. In contrast, the current perceived threat to livestock and humans by wolves and bears has impeded their successful integration into the managed area program. Research and education are continuing to support the cooperative activities of the stakeholders, but it is obvious that the land-use culture and the biological goals of the program are still at odds.

A greater measure of integrating potentially conflicting human values is being achieved in the southern United States portion of the Glacier-Waterton Biological Reserve as well as in Yellowstone National Park. There the wolf was once exterminated but has recently returned from Canadian populations. As an endangered subspecies, it has been allowed to spread and increase. Damage to livestock is compensated by NGO funds, in this case from the National Wildlife Federation. Chronic livestock predation is controlled by removing offending wolves.

Under federal protection as an endangered species, the grizzly bear is being more broadly distributed by reintroduction, and conflict with humans is being reduced by public education (removal of attractive foods, more prudent human behavior) and removal of offending bears. The stakeholders in this case consist of representatives of federal and state agencies and NGOs, all of whom can work together effectively as long as wide public support exists for their aims and methods. Different publics exist, some near and some far away. The ones within the area in which the situation exists, that is, the local public, can and do take a personal part in seeking acceptable wildlife conservation aims and programs to achieve them. But the distant public also plays a part, through their support of the endangered species protective legislation, since both the wolf and the grizzly are, by law, entitled to restorative programs.

Sustaining renewable natural resources in an industrial nation is not confined to protected areas and their environs. But protected areas are certainly useful. They not only provide some opportunity for recovery of overexploited plant and animal populations; they also improve continued existence of many other plant and animal species, some still unknown to science, which might otherwise be eliminated by the habitat changes that human economic activities often cause. Protection of little-known aspects of nature, such as biodiversity, invites study of the natural functioning of ecosystems, which provides clues regarding the restoration and potential sustained uses of nature. So research institutions are commonly among the stakeholders in and around a protected area.

The comanagement effort is a continuous one, since it requires an ongoing process of education on both sides, local and governmental, and a continuous process of adaptation to an ever-changing situation. Early participants must bring along their replacements for the inevitable moment when their own exhaustion nears. The interest and intelligent guidance of government must be maintained perpetually, despite changes of political party or national goals.

Equally important for success is that comanagement provides material improvement in the welfare of the local people involved. While government, in an early moment of enthusiasm, can provide economic supports for early comanagement efforts, the time will come when funds are short and budgets must be cut. Then comanagement that pays its own way will survive and prosper while comanagement that requires constant subsidy will collapse.

A little-recognized difficulty is the general indifference of comfortable urbanites to the welfare of rural human populations. City people are easily informed of threats to natural communities of plants and animals, but often show little concern about threats to the local human cultures that share those communities. This is unfortunate because pursuit of wildlife conservation in rural areas is largely controlled by local humans who can either cause problems or participate in solutions.

Even within the United States, where the "Yellowstone Model" has resulted in routine prohibition of extractive uses by local peoples in national parks generally, some adaptations to local needs are occurring. For example, accommodation is growing between Grand Canyon National Park and the Havasupai Indians, who inhabited that area for over 900 years before the park was established. The imposition of government power during establishment and early administration of the park has left a high level of distrust among the Indians. But more positive relations have been developed through involvement of mediators fully aware of the goals and values of all participants. Traditional activities such as hunting, gathering, and livestock grazing are permitted within designated park areas.

Aboriginal American cultures were not completely erased by the dominant European culture. In modern times a resurgence of aboriginal cultural customs and values has occurred. These include the need for wild game in various ceremonies. These, such as funerals, do not occur at predictable times, and so the season for hunting by the dominant culture—the fall season—is not inclusive enough for the native tribesmen's needs. But when American Indians take game out of season, a culture clash occurs with the dominant culture, a resentment of special privilege for the American Indians despite treaties allowing it.

Success in gaining cooperation of local people is becoming more widely recognized as a worthy goal by land management professionals such as agricultural, forestry, watershed, and wildlife specialists in the United States and Canada. To the technical staff, the biological information base seems generally adequate to coordinate improvements for nature conservation. But progress in establishing cooperative conservation programs shared jointly by local people and protected-area administrators has been slow. Common impediments are reluctance of government to share administrative authority, long-established distrust and hostility between local people and agents of government, lack of understanding by local people of how changes could improve their welfare, lack of understanding by government agents of the culture and values of local people, lack of experience in community action among local people, rivalry between culturally different local (tribal) people, and rivalry between different government agencies.

Each biosphere reserve can provide a theoretical merging of local and national objectives by discovering ways to harmonize biodiversity, cultural values, and socioeconomic development, and thus become a full partner in the process of integrating conservation and sustainable development locally. The U.S. and Canadian Biosphere Reserve Program can develop partnerships and promote mutual education among stakeholders and expand the constituency for developing shared goals for management and use of ecosystems in a changing environment. Cost sharing, coordination, and public support for government and private programs can be facilitated with greater participation to enhance stability and continuity, which should help stakeholders in a biogeographic area find practical ways to address resource problems.

The merging of local and national interests faces some obvious impediments. Not only are local people often still little understood by agency managers, but agencies themselves are diverse, with diverse personnel and concepts of primary mission.

Applying the biosphere reserve concept to national parks of the United States and Canada shows that current management programs fall somewhat short of the intended scope of the biosphere reserve potential. The traditional park philosophy focused on protecting nature within park boundaries. Research on natural systems within the park is tolerated. But the concept of integrating the nature reserve (park) with a surrounding buffer zone has not been actively pursued, even though a number of large parks of the United States were carved out of national forestlands, and the remaining portions of national forest are situated next to or even around them in classic buffer zone design. The national parks in the United States lie within jurisdiction of the U.S. Department of Interior; the national forests lie within jurisdiction of the U.S. Department of Agriculture. The administrative difficulties of this arrangement have impeded collaborative conservation programs. Past experience suggests that if enough public understanding exists of the benefits, say, to Yellowstone grizzlies, the political process will begin to exert pressure toward more intensive and effective integration of administratively different areas. Even now, discussions are in progress and maps have been drawn about regional matrices of national parks and corridors, e.g., the Yellowstone Network (Wyoming, Montana, Idaho), southern Appalachian Highlands Network (North Carolina, Tennessee, Georgia), North Cascades Network (Washington), and Sierra Network (California).

While the biosphere reserve concept focuses on large units of landscape, the total area of other public (federal, state/provincial, and county) lands is much larger, and hence has greater potential for conserving environmental values. Such are the lands administered in the United States by the U.S. Forest Service and the U.S. Bureau of Land Management. Typically, these are intermingled with each other, and with land in other ownerships—sometimes state and county, but more often private.

As urban environmental interest grew and hence became more politically effective through the 1960s, management of public lands was more closely scrutinized. The long period of management mainly for timber and grass was questioned. Was it satisfactory as far as the quality of aquatic and terrestrial habitats were concerned? With the ESA in place, was business as usual on public lands consistent with the perpetuation and restoration of endangered forms?

A major consequence of endangered species legislation was its impact on management of public lands such as national forests, grasslands, wetlands, and parks. The federal agencies were required to consult with the U.S. Fish and Wildlife Service when contemplating any managerial action that might infringe on the welfare of an endangered form or its habitat, a requirement that placed an unprecedented restraint on agencies hitherto guided largely by their professional coteries (see chapter 12). Viewed in this way, the legislation reflected the growing popular urban-centered concern about leaving the protection of nature in the hands of the traditional natural resource managers. Urbanites who thought of wildlife as a valuable part of human environments were roused to political action by such terms as *endangered, threatened*, and *biodiversity*.

Establishing a legal basis for species restoration was a necessary first step, gratifying to the interested public. To carry out the intent of the law was naturally more difficult, since on occasion this would conflict with long established managerial values and practices.

The basic mandates intended to guide the managerial programs of major public land management agencies in the United States have evolved in response to changing public values and demands. Beyond these mandates, shifting over time, is the actual practice on the ground that results from these changes.

A well-reported example of the early difficulties of accommodation is provided by the case of the spotted owl. By the 1970s this bird was thought to require old-growth forest for its survival. This focused attention on the remaining old-growth timber, almost entirely on public lands. In the early 1970s the U.S. Forest Service refused to deal with the spotted owl issue, claiming that multiple-use principles would be violated when land was set aside to protect the owl. In the early 1980s the agency tried not to deal much with the owl. Its regional guide for planning in national forests of the Pacific Northwest stated that final decisions regarding planning for the 13 owl forests in the Northwest would be mandated by the National Forest Management Act. But environmental groups appealed to the agency's nondecision, forcing it to treat seriously the issue of the spotted owl.

By the early 1990s the U.S. Forest Service acknowledged that the welfare of the spotted owl, now listed as an endangered species, required that old-growth timber be saved, not logged. That acknowledgment was nullified by decisions from the executive branch of government. Nongovernmental organizations kept up the political and legal pressure on the federal agencies most involved—the U.S. Forest Service and the U.S. Fish and Wildlife Service.

It was a classic case of agency tradition carried into a new political environment. The traditional agency clienteles in the Pacific Northwest forests were the logging towns, the lumber industry, the rural citizens who used the logging roads, and the rural communities that received payment in proportion to the value of logged timber and could afford to provide jobs such as additional schoolteachers to support the logging-driven economy. The new clientele consisted of outside groups with broader interests, the very groups that had supported new federal legislation such as the ESA.

Full and speedy implementation of endangered species legislation would be possible only if such legislation were fully supported by all. But interested parties will continue efforts to weaken or delay achievement of goals set forth in endangered species legislation while the urban population broadly supporting those goals will continue to become more politically powerful. Additional species will become extinct while the struggle between efforts to implement endangered species recovery and efforts to avoid its consequences continue.

As stated previously, in listing endangered species, the responsible agencies were denied economic considerations—a major deviation in federal directive. Federal government has a long history of promoting economic considerations of all sorts. Federal land management agencies assiduously pursued ways of weighing managerial decisions on cost/benefit scales. Economic analysis was a major element in managerial decisions and a persuasive argument in their justification. If some desired public good had little economic justification, it was easy to favor one that had much. With its deliberate avoidance of economic consequences, the ESA was well outside the agency frame of managerial reference. For example, in 1980, well after the ESA was in effect, a planner for the U.S. Forest Service could discuss the wildlife of the forest as just another economic entity.

The U.S. Forest Service is interested in the values associated with wildlife because such values indicate the benefit to people if wildlife is favored in the use of public monies. Of course, to guide such expenditures adequately, we also must know all costs that would be incurred. Multiple-use agencies generally require data on out-of-pocket expenditures and trade-offs with values of other resources. Thus, standard economic analyses can be used to decide on investments, to the extent that wildlife values can be measured on the same scale of these costs (appendix A).

The endangered species legislation never could be justified on standard cost/benefit grounds, and yet it was the law. Reinforcement of its goals in the United States was provided by the Forest and Rangeland Renewable Resources Planning Act in 1974 and the National Forest Management Act in 1976. Where endangered species management threatened to cause the heaviest economic losses, the agency resistance was understandably most intense; such a case was the conflict between the survival of the wild species dependent on the ancient forest of the

United States Pacific Northwest and the traditional functioning of the federal land management agencies responsible for that forest.

Large areas of mature forest dominated by Douglas-fir exist on lands administered by the U.S. Forest Service and the U.S. Bureau of Land Management. Huge areas also exist in private ownership. The original forests on private lands had been largely cut by the 1960s, and it was foreseen that a sawlog shortage would exist on those lands before the next generation of trees was ready for harvest—a 20-year timber gap. Presumably, federal lands would provide the sawlogs needed to keep the lumber industry going during the gap years.

When endangered species legislation came into force, in the late 1960s and early 1970s, federally controlled forests were found to support a number of species that apparently would lose essential habitat if the ancient forest was harvested and replaced with new plantings. Some were fairly well studied and some only recently noticed. Given the need to deal with the new protective legislation, federal agencies generated task forces to propose means of accommodation. To provide the focus for analysis, the Oregon Endangered Species Task Force of scientists and managers chose the northern spotted owl as a fairly well-known species, and one for which needed new information could be readily obtained.

Bringing together old and new information, the task force reported in 1973 that this owl was indeed dependent on its ancient forest habitat. Later analyses showed that of the original (pre-European settlement) ancient forest spotted owl habitat, perhaps only 10% remains, and that this remnant is almost entirely under the administration of the two U.S. federal land management agencies.

The initial response of the U.S. Forest Service, in the early 1970s, was to claim that its earlier mandate to practice multiple use would prevent it from preserving spotted owl habitat, while the U.S. Bureau of Land Management appeared to ignore the question. By the 1980s the U.S. Forest Service proposed to defer managerial response to the future planning proposals of the 13 owl forests.

As yet, the owl was not listed officially as an endangered species. But in 1987 an environmental group petitioned the U.S. Fish and Wildlife Service to list it. When the director of that agency intervened to block such listing, the case went to court, where the question "what was the basis for the decision?" could not be answered convincingly and therefore the decision itself was found to be "arbitrary and capricious." In 1990 the northern spotted owl was indeed listed, but the U.S. Fish and Wildlife Service claimed that it could not identify critical habitat. This claim was challenged by environmental groups, and in 1991 the U.S. Fish and Wildlife Service announced that 11.6 million acres, reduced in 1992 to 6.9 million acres, needed to be protected as critical habitat.

As the northern spotted owl was listed in 1990, an Interagency Scientific Committee was formed to make recommendations for integrating spotted owl population viability with managerial programs in the ancient forest. The recommendations produced by this committee (called the "Thomas Committee" because Dr. Jack Ward Thomas, U.S. Forest Service wildlife scientist, chaired it) were first locally proposed to be adopted, but opposition from U.S. President

George Bush (Republican), among others, blocked that proposal. In the resulting lawsuit in 1991 brought by the Seattle Audubon Society and other NGOs in U.S. District Court in Seattle, judgment was against the public land management agencies, with the judge stating:

> "More is involved here than a simple failure by an agency to comply with its governing statute. The most recent violation of NFMA (National Forest Management Act) exemplifies a deliberate and systematic refusal by the Forest Service and the FWS (U.S. Fish and Wildlife Service) to comply with the laws protecting wildlife. This is not the doing of the scientists, foresters, rangers, and others at the working levels of these agencies. It reflects decisions made by higher authorities in the executive branch of government."

The U.S. Bureau of Land Management also is responsible for much northern spotted owl habitat, and suffered similar pressures from environmental NGOs. In response, the Bureau of Land Management appealed directly to the national Endangered Species Committee (commonly call the "God Squad," consisting of seven presidential cabinet-level federal administrators) for an exemption from the demands of the ESA. The exemption was granted in 1992. But environmental groups appealed the decision, and the courts agreed that the exemption was improperly given.

These developments forced the federal land management agencies to comply with measures for conserving endangered species without considering economic consequences, and affected traditional agency beneficiaries—forest industry corporations, employees, and communities, as well as traditional agency programs of management. At present, three broad results can be discerned. Agencies responsible for managing public lands are adapting their programs to the demands of current endangered species legislation. Rural communities suffering economic loss from the agency shift toward nonmaterial values resentfully blame the agencies and the environmental NGOs encouraging that shift, sometimes advertising their resentment by offering "Spotted Owl Gumbo—10¢" at a roadside diner. And the corporate-political entities favor a profitable shift back from nonmaterial to material agency goals, and try in state and federal legislatures to weaken or overturn the laws that caused all this disturbance. That segment of society with a direct economic agenda in old-growth forest had difficulty understanding that the spotted owl was more than an endangered (and overtly noneconomic) species. It was also an indicator or umbrella species representing other species of animals and plants associated with old-growth forests. In addition, some of society also did not recognize—or chose to ignore—the fact that old-growth forests are essentially a nonrenewable resource in danger of extinction in the West as in almost all of the eastern United States.

From the wildlife perspective, these developments also have consequences. Conservation of the spotted owl in its natural habitat would conserve a host of other species, known and as yet unknown, that depend on that same habitat. Since management of public lands is continuous, even if it sometimes consists of leaving it alone, every management decision should be made with reasonable knowledge of its consequences for wild species, particularly those endangered forms under federal protection. This means that new ecological knowledge must be constantly provided by land management agency biologists. Federal agencies charged with recognizing, listing, and conserving habitat of endangered species will continually add to the list also, and so continually add to the concern of land management biologists and administrators. If these activities meet with broad public approval and support, funds for stimulating progress will be provided. But if that support is weak, the process will be steadily impeded by budgetary attrition.

Wildlife conservation on public lands, difficult as it is, will not answer as an adequate national policy. The movement is toward wildlife conservation on all lands, private as well as public.

Bibliography

Batisse, M. 1997. Biosphere reserves: A challenge for biodiversity conservation and regional development. Environment 39(5):7–15, 31–33.

Bean, M. 1983. The evolution of national wildlife law. Praeger, New York.

Berkes, F., P. George, and R. J. Preston. 1991. Co-management: The evolution in theory and practice of the joint administration of living resources. Alternatives 18(2):12–18.

Beuter, J. H., K. H. Johnson, and H. L. Scheurman. 1976. Timber for Oregon's tomorrow: An analysis of reasonably possible occurrences. Research Bulletin 19. Forest Research Laboratory, School of Forestry, Oregon State University, Corvallis.

Boardman, R. 1981. International organization and the conservation of nature. Indiana University Press, Bloomington.

Burnham, P. 2000. Indian country, God's country: Native Americans and the national parks. Island Press, Covelo, CA.

Byers, B. A. 1996. Understanding and influencing behaviors in conservation and natural resources management. Biodiversity Support Program, Washington.

Canadian Model Forest Program. 1999. Achieving sustainable forest management through partnerships: Canada's Model Forest Program. Canadian Forest Service, Ottawa.

Carson, R. 1962. Silent spring. Houghton Mifflin, Boston.

Cooper, M. E. 1987. An introduction to animal law. Academic Press, San Diego.

Daily, G. C., editor. 1997. Nature's services: Societal dependence on natural ecosystems. Island Press, Covelo, CA.

deKlemm, C. 1993. Biological diversity conservation and the law. International Union for Conservation of Nature and Natural Resources, Gland, Switzerland.

Drolet, C. A., A. Read, M. Breton, and F. Berkes. 1987. Sharing wildlife management responsibilities with native groups. Transactions of the North American Wildlife and Natural Resource Conference 52:389-398.

Dwyer, J. 1991. Memorandum decision and injunction: Seattle Audubon Society et al. *v.* John C. Evans et al. Number C89-160WD. U.S. Court, Western District of Washington, Seattle.

East, K. M. 1991. Joint management of Canada's northern national parks. Pages 333-345 *in* P. C. West and S. R. Brechin, editors. Resident peoples and national parks. University of Arizona Press, Tucson.

Gregg, W. P., Jr. 1991. MAB Biosphere Reserves and conservation of traditional land use systems. Pages 274-294 *in* M. L. Oldfield and J. B. Alcorn, editors. Biodiversity: Culture, conservation, and ecodevelopment. Westview Press, Boulder, CO.

Grumbine, R. E. 1992. Ghost bears: Exploring the biodiversity crisis. Island Press, Covelo, CA.

Harris, L. D. 1984. The fragmented forest: Island biogeographic theory and the preservation of biotic diversity. University of Chicago Press, Chicago.

Hoban, T. M., and R. O. Brooks. 1996. Green justice: The environment and the courts. Westview Press, Boulder, CO.

Hough, J. 1991. The Grand Canyon National park and the Havasupai people: Cooperation and conflict. Pages 215-230 *in* P. C. West and S. R. Brechin, editors. Resident peoples and national parks. University of Arizona Press, Tucson.

Jacobson, S. K., editor. 1995. Conserving wildlife. Columbia University Press, New York.

Kellert, S. R. 1994. A sociological perspective. Pages 371-389 *in* T. W. Clark, R. P. Reading, and A. L. Clarke, editors. Endangered species recovery. Island Press, Washington.

Kohm, K. A. 1991. Balancing on the brink of extinction. Island Press, Washington.

Langenau, E. E., Jr., and C. W. Ostrom, Jr. 1984. Organizational and political factors affecting state wildlife management. Wildlife Society Bulletin 12: 107-116.

Lax, D. A., and J. K. Sebenius. 1986. The manager as negotiator: Bargaining for cooperation and competitive gain. Free Press, New York.

Lee, K. N. 1993. Compass and gyroscope: Integrating science and politics for the environment. Island Press, Covelo, CA.

Lund, T. A. 1980. American wildlife law. University of California Press, Berkeley.

Lyster, S. 1985. International wildlife law. Grotius, Cambridge, UK.

Maehr, D. 1996. The Florida panther. University of Chicago Press, Chicago.

Marsh, G. 1864. Man and nature; or physical geography as modified by human action. Scribner, New York.

McCorquodale, S. 1997. Cultural contexts of recreational hunting and native subsistence and ceremonial hunting: Their significance for wildlife management. Wildlife Society Bulletin 25:568-573.

Meadows, D. H., D. L. Meadows, and J. Randers. 1992. Beyond the limits. Chelsea Green Publishing, Post Mills, UT.

Nietro, B. No date. Chronology of events related to the spotted owl issue. U.S. Bureau of Land Management, Oregon State Office, Portland.

Noss, R. F. 1987. Protecting natural areas in fragmented landscapes. Natural Areas Journal 7:1-13.

Noss, R. F. 1992. The wildlands project land conservation strategy. Wild Earth Special Issue: 10-25.

Oreshenko, G. 1988. Sharing power with native users: Co-management regimes for native wildlife. CARC Policy Paper 5. Canadian Arctic Resources Committee, Ottawa.

Payne, N. F. 1998. Wildlife habitat management of wetlands. Krieger, Malabar, FL.

Payne, N. F., and F. C. Bryant. 1998. Wildlife habitat management of forestlands, rangelands, and farmlands. Krieger, Malabar, FL.

Payne, N. F., and F. Copes. 1986. Wildlife and fisheries habitat improvement handbook. U.S. Forest Service, Washington.

Ponting, C. 1992. A green history of the world: The environment and the collapse of great civilizations. St. Martin's Press, New York.

Primack, R. B. 1998. Essentials of conservation biology. 2nd edition. Sinauer, Sunderland, MA.

Quigley, T. M., R. W. Haynes, and R. T. Graham, technical editors. 1996. Integrated scientific assessment for ecosystem management in the interior Columbia Basin and portions of the Klamath and Great basins. U.S. Forest Service General Technical Report PNW-GTR 382.

Schweitzer, D. L. 1980. Wildlife values information: Forest Service requirements and availability. Pages 91-98 *in* W. W. Shaw and E. H. Zube, editors. Wildlife values. Center for Assessment of Noncommodity Natural Resource Values, Institute Series Report 1, School of Renewable Natural Resources, University of Arizona, Tucson.

Simmons, N. S., and G. Metro. 1995. Yukon land claims and wildlife management. Pages 161-174 *in* V. Geist and F. M. Cowan, editors. Wildlife conservation policy. Delselig Enterprises, Calgary, Alberta.

Snape, W. J., and O. A. Houck. 1996. Biodiversity and the law. Island Press, Covelo, CA.

Stegner, W. 1987. The legacy of Aldo Leopold. Pages 233-245 *in* J. B. Callicott, editor. Companion to A Sand County Almanac. University of Wisconsin Press, Madison.

Stelfox, J. G., and R. D. Taber. 1968. Big game in the northern Rocky Mountain coniferous forest. Pages 197-222 *in* R. D. Taber, editor. Coniferous forests of the northern Rocky Mountains. (Proceedings of a symposium.) Center for Natural Resources, University of Montana, Missoula.

Teer, J. G. 1993. Commercial utilization of wildlife: Has its time come? Pages 73-83 *in* A. W. L. Hawley, editor. Commercialization and wildlife management: Dancing with the devil. Krieger, Malabar, FL.

Thomas, J. W., E. D. Forsman, J. D. Lint, E. C. Meslow, B. R. Noon, and J. Verner. 1990. A conservation strategy for the northern spotted owl. Report of the Interagency Science Committee, Portland, OR.

U.S. Department of the Interior. 1992. Recovery plan for the northern spotted owl-Draft. Government Printing Office, Washington.

U.S. National Committee for Man and the Biosphere. 1994. Strategic plan for the U.S. Biosphere Reserve Program. Biosphere Reserve Directorate, U.S. Man in the Biosphere Program, Springfield, VA.

Usher, P. 1986. The evolution of wildlife management and the prospects for wildlife conservation in the Northwest Territories. CARC Policies Paper 3. Canadian Arctic Resources Committee, Ottawa.

Yaffee, S. L. 1982. Prohibitive policy: Implementing the Federal Endangered Species Policy. MIT Press, Cambridge.

Yaffee, S. L. 1994. The northern spotted owl: An indicator of the importance of sociopolitical context. Pages 47–71 *in* T. W. Clark, R. P. Reading, and A. L. Clarke, editors. Endangered species recovery. Island Press, Washington.

Yaffee, S. L. 1994. The wisdom of the spotted owl: Policy lessons for a new century. Island Press, Washington.

Chapter 14

DEVELOPING NATIONWIDE PATTERNS OF CONSERVATION

Between 1965 and 1993, the world's annual population growth rate declined by 18%, but during the same time the population rose by 72% from 3.2 billion to 5.5 billion, mostly in less developed countries. Most scientists agree that too many people exist in the world already, resulting in severe environmental, social, and other damage regionally and worldwide. China, with a human population of over 1.2 billion, the most populous country on earth, has implemented and enforced a birth rate of one child per family.

Populations, human or otherwise, grow via two methods: a higher birth rate than death rate, and more immigration than emigration. For example, although the birth rate in the United States has declined below or at replacement level since 1972, i.e., below or at the death rate, the population is still increasing from immigration. To reduce population pressures, some countries encourage emigration; only a few countries permit large annual increases in population from immigration—mainly Australia, Canada, and the United States.

Population growth in North America will have to be stopped if ecosystem simplification worldwide is to be stopped, because North Americans use land and energy resources from the rest of the world. Percapita consumption of natural resources by North Americans is several times that of people in poorer countries. Annual population growth rates are 1.2% in Canada and 1% in the United States, compared to about 0.4% in other industrialized countries. Reducing such growth in Canada and the United States means reducing immigration, because now that the birthrate is generally under control, the growth rate in the United States and Canada is driven mainly by immigration. To do this, science must get more involved with politics. "Give me your tired, your poor," a slogan on the Statue of Liberty, is now obsolete, with 281 million people in the United States. Canada has 31 million.

If the United States still had 135 million people as during World War II, it reportedly could meet current energy demands without importing oil or using coal, thus achieving energy independence and ending the massive damage caused by burning coal. Instead, human populations have swelled, and the defeat of Iraq by the U.S.-led oil-dependent coalition of 29 nations during the Gulf War in 1991 was largely over oil. In fact, some had referred to the impending Gulf War as the first environmental war, with the potential burning of Kuwait's oilfields causing climate change in the region. Indeed, Iraq's deliberate pumping of crude oil from

Kuwait's storage tanks into the Persian Gulf was the world's worst oil spill, resulting in the deaths of an estimated 1 million birds alone. The Gulf War was the first one in history over which environmental concerns were expressed in advance, unlike the Vietnam War (despite Agent Orange), Korean War, World War II (despite the atomic bomb) or the U.S. war in Afghanistan that began in 2001.

Clearly, human population growth is becoming critical relative to human welfare as well as animal welfare. Entire habitats and even ecosystems—our very life-support system—are disappearing before our very eyes. So, the ultimate conservation problem is the rapid rate of human population growth which threatens to overwhelm wildlife and subvert the functioning of ecosystems. About 1850 the world population of humans reached 1 billion after 3 million years had passed from the dawn of human evolutionary history. By 1930 the human population had doubled to 2 billion. By 1990 it stood at 5.25 billion. Ten years later, in the year 2000, it was a whopping 6 billion people. Half of them live in perpetual poverty and malnourishment, resulting in regional ecological havoc that has worldwide implications.

We apply the term *carrying capacity* to the capacity of habitats to support wild animals, but never consider that term, or better, *optimum sustainable population*, for humans, who are animals also. Instead, we apply the term *economic growth* to ourselves, implying infinite capacity on a finite Earth, despite evident environmental degradation and associated problems.

Politics can be a strong ally or a strong obstacle. Historically, in the United States, the Democratic Party tends to be more sympathetic with environmental issues than the Republican Party. In Canada, the Progressive Conservative Party is more so than the Liberal Party, although less difference exists there. In Canada, things are further complicated by the emergence of the New Democratic Party and the Alliance Party.

Governments can exercise a degree of control in the modern world unmatched by anything before in world history, with computers, electronic surveillance, bureaucracies, police, prisons, deportations, and chemical and psychological methods, among others. In democracies, only when extensive public support exists can environmental policies be established. Often, some needed policies have been blocked by the public tendency to prefer short-term personal gain over long-term benefits to society. Both ancient times and modern times reveal that society is not fully aware of its role in the natural environment regarding long-term welfare and even survival. History shows us many examples of ancient societies that failed because they failed to live in harmony with their ecosystems, instead exhausting their resources and polluting their environments. Today's societies need to use their technological capabilities to minimize the destructive impact on the natural environment and enhance a relationship with it which benefits both people and the environment.

The general philosophy of the World Conservation Strategy, that economic development and nature conservation will benefit from evenhanded, effective integration, seems the best available guide toward long-term maintenance of natural genetic diversity. It is worthy of our best efforts. But the way will not be easy, partly because of the innate complexity of ecological relationships and partly because of the human elements involved.

Most tropical nations are poor. Within their forests are the most threatened plants and animals. Their governments can support few professional wildlife conservationists. Often there is a nongovernmental group, wealthy and influential, which has strong proponents of the preservation of nature, and is hostile to the idea that nature conservation should in any way be allied with economic development. Often, too, this materially secure preservationist party is not sympathetic to the material needs of the humans who live near nature reserves and are tempted to poach their resources. This attitude can be counterproductive, for more could be accomplished if this group would spend more time and money in educating the masses in the principles and economic (tourist) value of nature conservation (appendix A), as in Kenya, where hundreds of wildlife clubs exist, thanks to early input of the Food and Agriculture Organization in the United Nations.

Just as wildlife populations have had their many effects on human welfare, so too has pursuit of human welfare had many consequences for wildlife populations. One thing most humans seem to agree upon in developed nations is that it is good to work toward ways to promote human welfare and wildlife conservation. By identifying the patterns of interaction, we improve our chances of recognizing and alleviating the points causing friction in the relationship. But in undeveloped nations, the record for nature conservation ranges from dismal to lukewarm, as conservationists fight a thus far losing battle with high birth rates, poverty, and the day-to-day struggle to survive. More developed nations have 22% of the world's human population, but use 88% of the world's resources, 73% of its energy, and generate most of its wastes and pollution. This suggests that more developed nations must share wealth and improve standards of living with less developed nations to help preserve the world's natural resources.

Through the decades following World War II, international protectionist thinking was leavened by the inescapable facts that poor nations were going to welcome economic development, and were not going to reduce their birth rates until their standards of living rose. Among rich industrialized nations with low human birth rates, traditional protectionist thinking was that the high birth rates in poor nations needed to drop to accomplish anything in the way of nature conservation, or all was lost. Inhabitants of poor nations took a different view; having many children provided their families with the sort of future support that was provided in rich countries by inheritance, salaries, pensions, social security (social insurance), investments, life insurance, nursing homes, and, at worst, public welfare. To accommodate these realities, international conservation organizations proposed favoring economic development as long as it was integrated with continued nature conservation. This view was refined by introducing the goal of sustainability in economic development and nature conservation.

In ever greater numbers and with ever greater powers, humans occupy national landscapes. In response to this fact, humans advance the concept of sustainability of species and of productive human communities. The emphasis on sustainability in a world dominated by human economic activity needs a note of explanation. Monetary investment hopes for maximum profit which can in turn be invested in some different enterprise. Maximum profit often can be made through maximum harvest of a living resource. The shorter the term of harvest, the lower the cost for harvesting. Competition between harvesters hastens the end consequence: commercial extinction. Examples abound: North American beaver, bison, sea otter, codfish, among others. Similarly, commercial depletion of a particular habitat can significantly reduce populations for which that habitat is essential. The old-growth coniferous forest of northwestern North America is one example. Another is the filling and drainage of wetlands, both interior and coastal, for many human uses, agriculture and construction among them. Still another is the deterioration of western streamside habitats by livestock and the streams from siltation by logging.

Classical economics terms the incidental damages involved in maximizing profit as being externalized if the source of the damage does not have to pay for them. And often this is the case, since under present circumstances it is very difficult to set a monetary price on the ultimate costs of habitat loss. Faced with these facts, conservation thinking took readily to the concept of sustainability, often explained as the use of a renewable resource at a level that allows natural increase to replace annual harvest.

Given the difficulty of conforming all wildlife values into concepts of everyday economics, conservation thinking has leaned toward measurable biodiversity rather than measurable monetary values. The path to this new unit of measurement—biodiversity—has been a long one. A century ago, attempts by conservation thinkers to justify the survival of wildlife in the face of massive economic development centered on the concept that wildlife provided economic goods: food and other products, and consumption of weed seeds and pestiferous insects. Much early investigation focused on the economic goods provided by wildlife, yielding abundant information on food habits of many wild species. The concept of economic value in wildlife influenced the success of protective legislation and judicial decisions in the early 1900s. It was also advanced at mid-century when new nations were emerging, often impoverished and eager for economic development of any kind. But easy as it was to promote the economic value of meat, trophies, and wildlife tourism, it was impossible to stretch this concept to every last mosquito, leech, and snake. It was then that the concept of preservation of all natural gene pools—all living forms—arose.

By the 1970s the need for measurable wildlife values became acute, particularly to guide managerial decisions resulting from the comparison of alternatives required by national and state or provincial environmental policy legislation. Classical economic concepts yielding measurable monetary amounts were sought in wildlife affairs without complete success (appendix A). Therefore, biodiversity became the preferred alternative.

Economic development often destroys or degrades habitats, rendering them less suitable to sustain the natural diversity of wild species. A measure, then, of the distance between ideal nature and present situation is the difference in diversity of native forms between pristine and present conditions. The utility of biodiversity as one measure of success in nature conservation began to affect international thinking and, ultimately, international agreements.

International agreements having consequences for wildlife and habitats have been made through the 1900s. For the first years they typically concerned a few nations faced with a joint problem. Typical examples are the Fur Seal Treaty of 1911, in which the United States, Canada, Japan, and Russia joined to conserve the northern fur seal (and sea otter), and the Migratory Bird Treaty of 1916 to 1918 in which the United States and Canada joined to conserve migratory birds. At mid-century, international agreements quickly became more numerous and steadily more comprehensive for three major reasons:

1. Establishment of the United Nations provided a permanently funded body concerned with the whole world and influenced by practically all nations, old and new, rich and poor.
2. Increasing prosperity in the industrial nations provided funding for nongovernmental organizations such as the International Union for the Conservation of Nature and Natural Resources and the World Wildlife Fund.
3. Growing public concern about deteriorating human and wildlife environments provided political pressure to pass national remedial legislation that often served to cast light on global needs.

Early agreements focused on protection of particular species (fur seals, migratory birds). This pattern was extended to additional species (whales, from 1931 to 1946; endangered species, from 1973). Protection of specific natural areas was promoted (the national park concept, biosphere reserves, wetlands of international significance). Such topics were major concerns for rich industrial nations worried about pressures being put on wildlife and habitats of poor (often tropical) nations; through their memberships in international organizations, the poorer nations argued that such global goals alone would not be acceptable until their material security approached that of the rich nations.

Needs of poorer nations began to be more clearly recognized in mid-century conservation thinking. Thenceforth, international proposals moved toward the need for integrating sustainable economic development with sustainable nature conservation, for conservation of human cultures, for equitable sharing of costs and benefits.

By 1980 more comprehensive national programs of conservation were envisioned in the World Conservation Strategy, which illustrated the relationship between land use and biodiversity by using an image of a three-part iceberg. The tip of the iceberg, the 10% showing above water, represents an obvious, important, but minor part of the whole biological conservation picture, namely, off-site protection of species in zoos, seed banks, and the like. The middle part of the iceberg is more important than the tip, but still inadequate for biological conservation, namely, on-site protected areas in parks and reserves. The bulk of the iceberg is its least obvious and most important part, namely, coexisting values of economics and biodiversity in most of the landscape not receiving special protection.

In the world of 1980 to 2000, international agreements were forged through interaction of international agencies, which generate proposals largely from professional expertise, and a host of representatives of individual nations, which examine proposals from the perspective of the welfare of their nations. A major international initiative characteristic of the 1990s was dubbed Agenda 21, which concerned the broad topics of sustained nature and human welfare. The Agenda 21 Conference presented basic national duties for consideration:

1. Shared responsibility of all nations for the survival and integrity of the Earth.
2. Avoiding harm to future generations.
3. Practicing the principle of precautionary/preventive actions.
4. Sharing responsibilities and benefits equitably.
5. Protecting individual rights to environment and development.
6. Protecting indigenous peoples.
7. Preserving biological diversity and optimum sustainable yield.
8. Promoting environmental education and awareness.

These general statements of national duties are needed to generate specific guidelines to be useful for national governments. The concept of biodiversity was one that appeared to lend itself to a separate agreement. This, the Convention on Biological Diversity committed signatory nations to work toward restoring and maintaining the biodiversity within their own borders and eventually the whole world. Each nation faced with implementing this agreement had to start with the fact that plant and animal (biotic) habitats existed in a complex mosaic, as also did the human activities that affected them. Further, the customary conservation patterns such as spots of protection, controlled harvesting, local control of overabundance, though useful in their ways, were not comprehensive enough for what was now agreed as the national, and by extension, global need.

Because biological resources have a potentially enormous sustainable yield of benefits, they constitute a capital asset. But to date, institutions and financial and human resources have been inappropriate or inadequate, even though devoted to conserving and sustained use of these resources. Moreover, market practice and mechanisms, even national policies, fail too often to provide incentives for conserving and using biodiversity sustainability; they even facilitate degradation of ecosystems and depletion of species.

Loss of the world's biodiversity has continued, despite mounting efforts over the past 20 years. Protecting ecosystems on the landscape is currently the most effective way to conserve biodiversity. This could mean reducing or abandoning certain activities.

The variety and variability of genes, species, populations, and ecosystems on our planet produces an abundant and essential supply of indispensable goods and services that provide our food and fiber needs and many of our medicines. In other words, biodiversity of our natural resources is our very life support system, no matter where we live. As such, research should be undertaken into its importance. Biodiversity is critically important to the healthy and sustainable functioning of ecosystems and their role in producing goods, environmental services, and other values supporting sustainable economic activities and development, as well as human social behavior and nutritional habits directly dependent on natural ecosystems. Such research should be conducted at national and local levels, with indigenous peoples and nongovernmental organizations (NGOs) participating. Data should be computerized into a biodiversity information system.

Governments at all levels should support the nongovernmental organizations and private landowners, especially farmers, women, and indigenous people, who manage key sites for biodiversity outside protected areas. As part of environmentally sound development, governments also should help indigenous peoples and local communities to conserve and manage ecosystems. Traditional knowledge of indigenous people should be used to conserve biodiversity and use natural resources sustainably. Other requirements for conserving biodiversity include conducting national surveys to establish baseline information on biological resources, identifying and developing biogeographic units, evaluating potential economic implications, staffing and funding existing institutions better, such as museums, herberia, and universities, for documenting and integrating biodiversity.

Before, during, and after the international conservation conference called Earth Summit, held in Rio de Janeiro in 1992, the United States contributed the United States of America National Report, and following it in 1994 Canada produced Biodiversity in Canada—A Science Assessment. The common thrust of these documents is that lands outside protected areas are essential to sustained survival and maintenance of all living forms as well as sustained welfare of human populations. How this thrust is to be manifested on the ground is a matter in which the United States and Canada are currently engaged.

Adherence to the international agreements embodied in Agenda 21 from the Rio Convention made the 1990s a period of innovative planning for Canada and the United States. Canada has the lower human population, larger land unit, and higher proportion of nonagricultural land. Canada has employed satellite imagery and geographic information systems to establish a base mosaic of ecoregions, each of which has a distinct pattern of climate, water, soils, and characteristic native plants and animals. Ecoregions are subdivided into ecodistricts, characterized by different human uses, occurrence of endangered species, and presence of protected natural habitats. This process focuses national attention on those landscapes suffering, in an ecological sense, the most severe trauma. Having identified those particular landscapes, Canada will be inclined to allocate most of the available managerial resources toward the remedy of the most severe cases.

Remedial action, though desirable, is not assured. The political will to act through appropriate land use policies and incentives might not exist. Without it, sustainable coexistence of Canada's economic base and biological diversity in areas of known concern will not be ensured. The areas of most pressing concern lie in the southern parts of Canada, the agricultural belt of Alberta, Saskatchewan, and Manitoba, the more heavily settled and industrialized part of Ontario, and the Maritime Provinces of Prince Edward Island, Nova Scotia, and New Brunswick. (The initial modeling that led to this conclusion might well have underestimated the ecological consequences of timber extraction.) It is in just these regions that natural populations of plants and animals are most heavily impacted by human cultures and in which human cultures are most complex and therefore difficult to modify and integrate with biodiversity.

Northern Canada is too cold for agriculture and inhabited largely by aborigines. There it has been possible to integrate the aims of the local people and those of the nation into patterns of comanagement of renewable natural resources. Since these patterns can be sustained only by continuous human effort on all sides, and since they are relatively new and experimental, they are not uniformly successful. But over time, humans can learn and adapt.

Ironically enough, one of the impediments to the northern comanagement pattern is the largely urban opposition to killing wild mammals, manifested in boycotts on the sartorial use of their furs and skins, an opposition that weakens the aboriginal economy. Northern people began to suffer economic hardship ever since the late 1970s, when Greenpeace mounted its campaigns to end the clubbing of juvenile harp seals in Newfoundland. Greenpeace made little distinction between harp seals in Newfoundland and ringed seals in northern Canada and Alaska. When movie star Brigitte Bardot got involved with the "Save the Seals" campaign, hardly anyone in the south was concerned about the arctic hunter camped on the ice, trying to earn some extra cash and feed his family by hunting an altogether different species of seal, the ringed seal, which number in the millions (as do harp seals), are readily censused on the ice, can sustain substantial harvest, and are easily managed. Further complications involve overfished cod stocks around Newfoundland, overfished capelin stocks—the main cod prey—mainly by the Japanese, and now an overabundance of harp seals—a predator of cod (although less than 1% of its diet is cod).

As though nothing had been learned, Garret Hardin's "Tragedy of the Commons" continues today. John Cabot noted the abundance of cod before 1500, and his son Sebastian later noted that cod were so abundant in coastal waters that they could slow progress of a ship. In a mixture of greed, politics, erroneous biology, and lack of enforcement, an area that once teemed with cod had been decimated. The cod population collapsed. The result: a moratorium on cod fishing around Newfoundland since 1992 putting thousands of fishermen and fish plant workers out of work, and cod stocks that are not recovering as fast as predicted. The ecology, and economy, are out of whack there.

Cod was the backbone of Newfoundland's economy; the closing was a disaster for fishing communities scattered along the harsh coast. Recent evidence indicates that populations of harp seals are now declining because Canada's restored total allowable catch is excessive and inconsistent with its stated management objective of maintaining stable seal populations while allowing a sustainable harvest. Ironically, that could help boost cod stocks, except that harp seals also eat fish that prey on cod.

This is but one example of how urban economic decisions can narrow the survival options of rural people, who live where natural biodiversity is greatest. Someone has said that you cannot erase prejudice from the human mind by reason, because that was not the way it got there. Perhaps this accounts for the failure of explaining the facts about arctic seals and arctic people to the wildlife sympathizers of Europe, their enthusiasm fanned not only by Greenpeace, but also such other NGOs as International Fund for Animal Welfare, the Friends of the Earth, the People's Trust for Endangered Species, and Defenders of Wildlife. Of course, the European communities intent on preserving distant, little known wildlife, which they did not consider essential food or supplemental income, were unimpressed by the anti-antiseal campaign.

Canada has attempted to move beyond reliance on economic values alone in the national desire to improve wildlife conservation prospects over the entire country. Developing measures that quantify biodiversity must be a major priority in the field of biodiversity conservation. Further, such measures must be at a scale appropriate for management decisions, for in their absence, society and its governments will make decisions based almost exclusively on other quantified values, most likely economic values—the dominant experience in Canada. Without practical quantified measures of biodiversity, economic and biodiversity values will not or cannot be maintained indefinitely. Such measurements are needed as explicit criteria for producing development plans, monitoring results, and modifying management practices.

Biodiversity is more prudently considered a useful first approximation, since a full range of biotic forms are only partially known. If biological knowledge is incomplete, it is best to err on the side of caution. For many of those species already known, as yet no economically practicable methods of quantification exist. Moreover, it often happens that certain species have been and are threatened with extinction even though they occur in habitat suitable for their survival and rich in biodiversity. Examples could include the great auk, the American beaver, and the bison, among many others.

The indefinite, or infinite, or sustained maintenance of economic and biodiversity values over the same landscapes will apparently require new methods to assess them. Continuous attempts have occurred to enlarge the economic scope to include measurable economic values traditionally ignored. Among many examples would be the loss of a river fishery through the inflow of human, livestock, or industrial waste. A related approach has been to identify and measure the values of what are termed ecosystem services, which are values produced by nature (a functional river fishery, for example), which cost virtually nothing to maintain but which would cost a great deal to replace. Such analyses focus on major patterns of ecosystem service and function and on each major biome (e.g., forest, grassland, desert, tundra, wetlands, lakes/rivers, etc.). By quantifying services by biome, such analyses arrive at an economic value of the total ecological services by each area of each biome. With knowledge of the extent of each biome within its borders, any nation could arrive at an estimate of the economic value of the total annual production of ecosystem services. Such an analysis reveals what had hitherto been largely ignored: the ultimate costs of environmental damage or deterioration incidental to human activities.

If Canada faces a difficult task in its attempt to live sustainably with the native plants and animals that share its landscape, the United States faces a task more difficult still, by virtue of its lesser extent of "natural" areas and its greater intensity of human impact on the landscape. But the United States has much heavier and diverse political pressure from NGOs, which tend to support restoration and conservation of environmental quality. To prepare for the United Nations Conference on Environment and Development (UNCED) in 1992 in Rio de Janeiro, the United States produced a statement on progress and prospects. This statement dwells on the period 1970 to 1990, within which major investments occurred in environmental quality, with some notable successes such as, for example, the steep decline in emissions of lead to the atmosphere. The integration of development and environmental quality progressed through those decades. Later conferences were held in New York in 1997 and Johannesburg in 2002.

With an unprecedented national affluence in the 1990s, memberships in conservation-minded NGOs and arrangements for sources of support beyond membership fees have provided substantial funding for investigations and programs that influence environmental legislation and programs of government agencies. Not surprisingly, as old problems have yielded to effective measures, new problems have emerged, such as the rising ozone levels in the lower atmosphere, air transport of pollutants to lakes and estuaries, deterioration of flowing waters through excessive additions of human and agricultural wastes, and the current global warming (and its international Kyoto Agreement of 1997, which U.S. President George W. Bush (R) refused to ratify although 98 other nations did, including Canada).

Some claims of improvement are based merely on a slowing of the rate of damage rather than recovery from damage. An example is energy consumption, which is said to be ever increasing but not as fast as it was. Clothed in misleading terms, such matters encourage complacency when a more realistic depiction would encourage an enthusiasm for continued remedial effort. Facing the prospect of more successfully integrating sustained development and biodiversity, U.S. planners describe current remedial trends as environmental education programs, risk-based environmental planning and regulations, pollution prevention programs, and market-based incentives for pollution reduction.

For successful risk-based managerial decisions, a sound base of biological knowledge is a starting point. But for continuous movement toward success, parallel knowledge is needed of human sociological patterns and potential ways of modifying these toward achieving goals of the Convention on Biological Diversity.

To prepare for the UNCED in 1992, the United States submitted a report summarizing the nation's efforts to protect and enhance the quality of the human environment as coordinated with economic well-being, including using economic incentives to achieve environmental restoration. Much effort, and some success, has characterized the effort to restore and perpetuate cleaner air and water through less damaging ways of waste disposal. Also, methods of pollution detection and monitoring are improving, with results feeding public concern and political pressure for improvement. Some pollutants are fairly easy to control (lead in gasoline, pesticides such as DDT), but continued research reveals ever more damaging entities such as dioxin. Disposal of persistent hazardous radioactive waste is increasingly difficult. Agricultural wastes from soil erosion, pesticide runoff, and livestock manure from large feedlots continue to grow. All of these, and others, contribute to the deterioration of lakes, streams, and estuaries. With ever-growing human populations, and ever-growing per capita consumption, such factors multiply.

The more or less natural habitats that native plants and animals depend upon for survival are degraded by many of the continuing pressures of an industrial society. Simultaneously, wild species from other continents are brought to North America, often to flourish in their new environments and so exert negative pressures on native populations. These exotics range from diseases and parasites to numerous weeds that thrive in environments lacking the population checks of their homelands.

As the decline of many native species continues, and one after another is threatened with extinction, public concern has grown. By the 1990s it became increasingly clear that a piecemeal conservation program, even if implemented more effectively, might help deal with problems as they emerged (e.g., species endangerment, loss of natural areas), but would not do much to keep problems from emerging in the first place. Accepting the twin goals of sustained economic development and sustained environmental quality (including sustained populations of all native plants and animals) would require the willing cooperation of the human occupants of every ecological region. These concepts were accepted by the nations that acceded to the Rio Convention and could be reflected on the actual national landscapes only by major technological and societal change.

Favorable circumstances exist. Technological advances provide satellite-derived data on surface features, atmospheric patterns, etc., that promote discernment of environmental trends that might be linked back to causes. General human prosperity, leisure, and environmental awareness constitute a strong public presence in conservation affairs. But the predominant urban characteristic, fired mainly by nonmaterial values, shows little regard for the rural humans whose actions respond more strongly to their material needs.

Particular groups of rural people are the indigenous American Indian and Inuit, whose reserved lands are geographically within states/provinces but not under those governments. Often such groups are poor and poorly educated. Still, their efforts to maintain or recapture their native cultures include reference to a oneness with nature that could underlie an integration of economic and biodiverse sustainability.

A growing appreciation of the place of local people in effective conservation marked the last 2 decades of the 1900s. The assumption that guidelines should rightfully come from the center and be enforced in individual localities was found to be workable mainly when backed by police power, producing a constant barrage of criticism from representatives of poor countries. Alternatives were considered and of these the most promising was that of developing cooperative local programs that integrated objectives of local people and people of the nation. Recent patterns of linkage between local welfare and nature conservation include farm programs providing payment for not farming certain areas (e.g., U.S. Conservation Reserve Program) and roughly similar programs that provide tax relief in exchange for agreement not to develop (e.g., conservation easements). Most other governmental programs encouraging nature conservation affect national rather than local welfare (e.g., protected natural areas, migratory wildlife conservation, endangered species protection, etc.).

In the United States, the concept of linking local human welfare to local nature conservation has developed in piecemeal fashion by state arrangements with sportsmen in one pattern and landowners in another. Canada also exhibits such arrangements, and in agreements with northern indigenous communities also has developed workable comanagement programs linking local welfare to local nature conservation. The United States responds to demands for local welfare, but resulting programs generally slight nature conservation (grazing and timber sales and motorized recreation on public lands, for example).

Nature conservation is generally promoted without regard for local welfare. National programs favoring endangered species, for example, are little concerned with local welfare and often generate local opposition. The same can be seen in proposed programs to increase the restoration of natural wildlife habitats on public land. Some of the more extreme NGOs push for ending locally enjoyed hunting and fishing (People for the Ethical Treatment of Animals [PETA]) or local economic gain from wild harvest (Greenpeace—harp seal; Sierra Club—public lands timber).

In contrast, the international agreement stemming from the Rio Agenda 21 Conference calls for developing sustainable cultural and natural resource conservation based upon the welfare and positive cooperation of the local community in every "homogeneous" ecological unit of landscape. In agreeing with this proposition, the United States accepted responsibility for major modifications (incorporating existing minor modifications) in the ways that the landscape (a mosaic of wildlife habitats) has been managed for 2 centuries.

While the situation in the United States has many parallels with that in Canada, some significant administrative differences exist. The Canadian government has signed and ratified the Convention on Biological Diversity, fully accepting (in theory at least) its national implications. The United States President (Bill Clinton, a Democrat) signed the Convention, thereby accepting its aims as far as federally controlled activities are concerned. But the United States Congress (Republican) refused to ratify it, thus avoiding its implications for activities not under federal control. The reason for this refusal, presumably, is politics and congressional concern for continued support from customary sources.

Several impediments to developing sustainable cultural and natural resource conservation have been mentioned in previous chapters. One of the more prominent is that most private land—over half the total—is managed on economic principles within short time frames, with no discernable concern for human welfare in other than monetary terms, or for ecological sustainability. Another is that government programs at every level are the responsibility of a multitude of separate regulatory agencies, each with a primary interest in self-preservation and continued customary service to its traditional clientele, and steadily supplied with new recruits from specialized professional curricula at universities.

The president of the United States has the power to direct the U.S. federal agencies that manage the public lands. Public lands under direct control of managerial agencies can be subject to changes in the goals and policies guiding management. These changes from traditional narrow material production toward the broader concepts can include sustainable production and use of native species. Society generally recognizes the importance of local human communities as potential partners with government in achieving sustained local welfare and sustained natural biodiversity. But the necessary fundamental shift in control from government to local communities is not widely manifested.

Still, a strong though vaguely expressed desire exists for comanagement enhancing local human welfare, i.e., material welfare. National goals include nonmaterial as well as material values and will have to be integrated with local concerns if comanagement is going to evolve. Humans have been a part of the ecosystem for some 100,000 years. But only in the last 100 years, mainly, has the blend of human encroachment and natural systems been particularly challenging on a grand scale. Since it appears that comanagement is the most likely approach to stem the loss of wild species and renewable natural resources, the resolution of the present tangle of impediments appears to be the appropriate conservation task of the 21st century.

Bibliography

Abernathy, V. D. 1999. Population politics. Transaction, Piscataway, NJ.
Allen R. 1980. How to save the world: Strategy for world conservation. Kogan Page, London.
Berkes, F., P. George, and R. J. Preston. 1991. Co-management: The evolution in theory and practice of the joint administration of natural resources. Alternatives 18:12–18.
Biodiversity Science Assessment Team. 1994. Biodiversity in Canada: A science assessment for Environment Canada. Environment Canada, Ottawa.
Byers, B. A. 1996. Understanding and influencing behaviors in conservation and natural resources management. Biodiversity Support Program, Washington.
Chapman, A. R., R. L. Petersen, and B. Smith-Moran. 1999. Consumption, population, and sustainability: Perspectives from science and religion. Island Press, Covelo, CA.
Constanza, R., R. d'Arge, R. de Grost, S. Farber, M. Grasso, B. Hannon, K. Limburg, S. Naeem, R. V. O'Neill, J. Paruelo, R. G. Raskin, P. Sutton, and M. van

den Belt. 1997. The value of the world's ecosystem services and natural capital. Nature 387:253-258.
Council on Environmental Quality. 1992. United States of America national report to United Nations Conference on Environment and Development. Council on Environmental Quality, Washington.
Daly, H. E. 1996. Beyond growth: The economics of sustainable development. Beacon Press, Boston.
Dudly, J. P., J. R. Ginsberg, A. J. Plumptre, J. A. Hart, and L. C. Campes. 2002. Effects of war and civil strife on wildlife and wildlife habitats. Conservation Biology 16:319-329.
Dyer, G. 1985. War. Crown, New York.
Ehrlich, P. R., and A. H. Ehrlich. 1996. Betrayal of science and reason: How anti-environmental rhetoric threatens our future. Island Press, Washington.
Gilbert, F. F., and D. G. Dodds. 2001. The philosophy and practice of wildlife management. 3rd edition. Krieger, Malabar, FL.
Gilbert, M. 1999. A history of the twentieth century: Volume three, 1952-1999. William Morrow, New York.
Gray, G. 1995. Wildlife and people: The human dimensions of wildlife ecology. University of Illinois Press, Urbana.
Hardin, G. 1968. The tragedy of the commons. Science 162:1243-1248.
Harris, M. 1998. Lament for an ocean: The collapse of the Atlantic cod fishery, a true crime story. McClelland & Stewart, Toronto.
Hughes, J. D. 1975. Ecology in ancient civilizations. University of New Mexico Press, Albuquerque.
International Union for the Conservation of Nature and Natural Resources. 1980. World conservation strategy: Living resource conservation for sustainable development. International Union for Conservation of Nature and Natural Resources, Gland, Switzerland.
Jackson, W. 2002. When strength through exhaustion fails. Conservation Biology 16:291.
Johnston, D. W., P. Meisenheimer, and D. M. Lavigne. 2000. An evaluation of management objectives for Canada's commercial harp seal hunt, 1996-1998. Conservation Biology 14:729-737.
Keating, M. 1997. Canada and the state of the planet: The social, economic and environmental trends that are shaping our lives. Canadian Global Change Program, Oxford University Press, Don Mills, Ontario.
Kerasote, T. 1993. Blood ties: Nature, culture, and the hunt. Random House, New York.
Knight, J., editor. 2001. Natural enemies: People-wildlife conflict in anthropological perspective. Routledge, New York.
Kolankiewicz, L. 1998. Is immigration an environmental issue? Carrying Capacity Network, Washington.
Lovins, L. H. 2002. Design failure and conservation. Conservation Biology 16: 292-293.
Meffe, G. K., A. H. Ehrlich, and D. Ehrenfeld. 1993. Human population control: The missing agenda. Conservation Biology 7:1-3.

Miller, G. T., Jr. 2000. Environmental science: Working with the Earth. 8th edition. Thompson, Florence, KY.
Miller, K., and S. M. Landau. 1995. National biodiversity planning. World Resources Institute, United Nations Environment Programme and the World Conservation Union, Washington.
Morison, S. E. 1971. The European discovery of America: The northern voyages A.D. 500–1600. Oxford University Press, New York.
Moulton, M. P., and J. Sanderson. 1999. Wildlife issues in a changing world. 2nd edition. CRC Press, Boca Raton, FL.
Orr, D. W. 2002. The events of 9-11: A view from the margin. Conservation Biology 16:288–290.
Paoletti, M. G., D. Pimental, and B. R. Stinner. 1992. Agroecosystem biodiversity: Matching production and conservation biology. Agricultural Ecosystem Environment 40:3–23.
Pearson, T. G. 1937. Adventures in bird protection: An autobiography by Thomas Gilbert Pearson. Appleton-Century, New York.
Ponting, C. 1992. A green history of the world: The environment and the collapse of great civilizations. St. Martin's Press, New York.
Powledge, F. 1998. Biodiversity at the crossroads. BioScience 48:347–352.
Prescott-Allen, C., and R. Prescott-Allen. 1986. The first resource: Wild species in the North American economy. Yale University Press, New Haven, CT.
Raven, P. H. 1990. The politics of preserving biodiversity. BioScience 40:769–774.
Robinson, N. 1992. Agenda 21 and the UNICED proceedings. Oceanea Publications, New York.
Robinson, N. A., editor. 1993. Agenda 21: Earth's action plan (annotated). IUCN Environmental Policy and Law Paper 27. Oceana Publications, New York.
Salonius, P. 1999. Population growth in the United States and Canada: A role for scientists. Conservation Biology 13:1518–1519.
Scherr, S. J., B. Frelinghuysen, R. Born, J. E. Blumenfield, and M. B. Nowlin, editors. 1993. One year after Rio: Keeping the promises of the Earth Summit: A country-by-country progress report. Natural Resources Defense Council, New York.
Sitarz, D. 1994. Agenda 21: The Earth Summit strategy to save our planet. Earthpress, Boulder, CO.
Wackernagel, M., and W. E. Rees. 1997. Perpetual and structural barriers to investing in natural capital: Economics from an ecological footprint perspective. Ecological Economics 20:3–24.
Walters, C. 1986. Adaptive management of renewable resources. Macmillan, New York.
Western, D., and M. Pearl, editors. 1989. Conservation for the twenty-first century. Oxford University Press, Oxford, UK.
Western, D., and R. M. Wright. 1994. Natural connections: Perspectives in community-based conservation. Island Press, Washington.
Wilson, E. O., editor. 1988. Biodiversity. National Academy Press, Washington.

Appendix A

ATTITUDES TOWARD WILDLIFE

Attitudes toward wildlife influence the various values present-day humans have for the wildlife resource. In his essay on "Wildlife in American Culture," Aldo Leopold (1966) wrote that a person cannot measure culture, but that most folks think cultural values exist in the customs, sports, and experiences of interacting with wild things. He listed three such values: (1) the value that stimulates awareness in history, i.e., national origins and evolution; (2) the value that reminds us of our interdependence with the soil-plant-animal food chain and its organization; and (3) the value in experiences exercising ethical restraints collectively known as "sportsmanship."

Some of the following attitudes toward wildlife overlap, and some people have more than one of these attitudes, which Kellert (1987, 1988, 1996) identified thus:

Ecologistic-Scientific = primary interest in the study of the structure and functioning of animals and their relationship with nature (e.g., scientific study, collecting, hobbies, conservation support, activism, and membership; ecological study)

Naturalistic = primary interest and affection for wildlife and the outdoors (e.g., outdoor wildlife-related recreation such as birding and wildlife photography)

Aesthetic = primary interest in the physical appeal and beauty of nature (e.g., nature appreciation, art, wildlife tourism)

Humanistic = primary interest in and strong emotional attachment and "love" for aspects of nature (e.g., pets, casual zoo visitation, wildlife tourism)

Moralistic = primary ethical concern and spiritual reverence for nature (e.g., kindness to animals, animal welfare support and membership)

Utilitarian = primary concern for the practical and material exploitation of animals or the animal's habitat (e.g., consumption of furs, meat hunting, bounties, raising meat or other animal products)

Dominionistic = primary interest in the mastery, physical control and dominance of animals (e.g., trophy hunting, animal spectator sports, selective breeding)

Negativistic = primary orientation toward fear, aversion, and alienation of nature (e.g., cruelty to animals, overt fear behavior, avoidance of animals)

Symbolic = primary interest in the use of nature for language and thought (e.g., use in talking, children's books)

Through history, the prevalence of these attitudes has changed. Presently in the United States, the most common attitudes toward animals are the humanistic, moralistic, utilitarian, and negativistic. Much of the current misunderstanding and conflict about issues involving humans and wildlife in American and probably similar societies can be explained by the relative popularity of these four often conflicting attitudes, as well as by the lack of environmental literacy reflected by the least common attitudes of ecologistic-scientific. (The dominionistic attitude is also among the least common attitudes.) King (1947) provided the best summation of the values that wildlife provides society as: (1) commercial; (2) recreational; (3) biological, i.e., the contribution of wild animals to productive ecosystems; (4) scientific and educational; (5) esthetics, i.e., wildlife and their habitats as objects of beauty or historical importance, and as they become part of literature, poetry, art, and music; (6) social, i.e., the community benefits economically, physically, and mentally, resulting in increased facilities, and a happier and healthier community; and (7) negative, which impacts society from such things as personal injury, disease transmission, and property damage.

The relationship between humans and wildlife is complex, including the values wildlife provides humans. Present day humans use and value wildlife in the following ways (Hoover 1976):

Direct user = a consumptive or nonconsumptive user of wildlife

Primary beneficiary = a business benefiting directly from the direct user's expenditures

Secondary beneficiary = a business benefiting from expenditures of a primary beneficiary

Option holder = one who is willing to pay a premium for some future use of a wildlife commodity

Vicarious user = one who benefits indirectly just by knowing wildlife is present in an area

Altruistic user = one who sees value in wildlife for the enjoyment of present and future generations

Environmentalist = one who considers wildlife an integral part of the overall concern for the environment

Alternative resource user = one who sees wildlife as negative values in terms of wildlife incompatibility with other resources

The various values of wildlife provide various and substantial social, economic, and ecological values to humans (Eltringham 1984, Decker and Goff 1987, Hawley 1993, Anderson and Hill 1995, Duda et al. 1998). About 10,000 BC, the world population was about 10 million humans, of which 100% were hunters (Lee and DeVore 1968). By about AD 1500, the world population was about 350 million, and only 1% were hunters. By about AD 1970, the world population was about 3 billion, and only 0.001% were hunters. In fact, as with primitive times, most of the daily intake of protein in much of the developing world continues to come from wildlife (Prescott-Allen and Prescott-Allen 1986). In developed countries such as the United States and Canada, wildlife recreation is big business; in 1996 expenditures in the United States alone for wildlife-related recreation was over $100 billion, although only 7% of adults hunted (U.S. Fish and Wildlife Service and U.S. Bureau of Census 1997)! In Canada it was $11.7 billion in 1996 (Federal-Provincial-Territorial Task Force on the Importance of Nature to Canadians 2000). Even these figures are ultraconservative because they do not include consumer surplus or the dollar multiplier factor. Furthermore, ecotourism is on the rise, making tourism the No. 1 or No. 2 industry in many countries of the world. Conserving the world's wildlife and wildlands is an investment in the future of humankind. In fact, economic incentives can be developed and used in the conservation effort (McNeely 1988, Swanson and Barbier 1992, Czech 2000).

References

Anderson, T. L., and P. J. Hill, editors. 1995. Wildlife in the marketplace. Rowman and Littlefield, Lanham, MD.

Czech, B. 2000. Shoveling fuel for a runaway train. University of California Press, Berkeley.

Decker, D. J., and G. R. Goff, editors. 1987. Valuing wildlife: Economic and social perspectives. Westview Press, Boulder, CO.

Duda, M. D., S. J. Bissell, and K. C. Young. 1998. Wildlife and the American mind: Public opinion on and attitudes toward fish and wildlife management. Responsive Management, Harrisonburg, VA.

Eltringham, S. K. 1984. Wildlife resources and economic development. Wiley, New York.

Federal-Provincial-Territorial Task Force on the Importance of Nature to Canadians. 2000. The importance of nature to Canadians: The economic significance of nature-related activities. Environment Canada, Ottawa.

Hawley, A. W. L., editor. 1993. Commercialization and wildlife management: Dancing with the devil. Krieger, Malabar, FL.

Hoover, R. L. 1976. Incorporating fish and wildlife values in land use planning. Transactions of the North American Wildlife and Natural Resources Conference 41:279–289.

Kellert, S. R. 1987. The contributions of wildlife to human quality of life. Pages 222–229 *in* D. J. Decker and G. R. Goff, editors. Valuing wildlife: Economic and social perspectives. Westview Press, Boulder, CO.

Kellert, S. R. 1988. Human-animal interactions: A review of American attitudes to wild and domestic animals in the twentieth century. Pages 137–175 *in* A. N. Rowan, editor. Animals and people sharing the world. University Press of New England, Hanover, NH.

Kellert, S. R. 1996. The value of life: Biological diversity and human society. Island Press, Covelo, CA.

King, R. T. 1947. The future of wildlife in forest land use. Transactions of the North American Wildlife Conference 12:454–467.

Lee, R. B., and I. DeVore, editors. 1968. Man the hunter. Aldine De Gruyter, Hawthorne, NY.
Leopold, A. 1966. A sand county almanac, with other essays on conservation from *Round River*. Oxford University Press, New York.
McNeely, J. A. 1988. Economics and biological diversity: Developing and rising economic incentives to conserve biological resources. International Union for Conservation of Nature and Natural Resources, Gland, Switzerland.
Prescott-Allen, C., and R. Prescott-Allen. 1986. The first resource: Wild species in the North American economy. Yale University Press, New Haven, CT.
Swanson, T. M., and E. B. Barbier, editors. 1992. Economics for the wilds: Wildlife, diversity, and development. Island Press, Covelo, CA.
U.S. Fish and Wildlife Service and U.S. Bureau of Census. 1997. 1996 national survey of fishing, hunting, and wildlife-associated recreation. U.S. Fish and Wildlife Service and U.S. Bureau of Census, Washington.

Appendix B

COMMON AND SCIENTIFIC NAMES OF ANIMALS AND PLANTS MENTIONED

*Extinct

Mammals

Common name	Scientific name
Alpaca	*Lama pacos*
Antelope, pronghorn	*Antilocapra americana*
Ape (in Africa)	Pongidae
Ass	*Equus asinus*
Aurochs	*Bos taurus*
Badger, American	*Taxidea taxus*
Badger, Old World	*Meles meles*
Banteng	*Bos javanicus*
Bat	Chiroptera
Bear	*Ursus* spp.
Bear, black	*Ursus americanus*
Bear, grizzly (brown)	*Ursus arctos*
Bear, polar	*Ursus maritimus*
Beaver, European	*Castor fiber*
Beaver, North American	*Castor canadensis*
Bison, American (buffalo)	*Bison bison*
Bison, forest (wisent)	*Bison bonasus*
Bison, giant*	*Bison latifrons*
Boar, wild	*Sus scrofa*
Bobcat	*Felis rufus*
Buffalo, African	*Syncerus caffer*
Buffalo, water	*Bubalus bubalis*
Camel, bactrian	*Camelus bactrianus*
Camel, dromedary	*Camelus dromedarius*
Caribou, woodland (reindeer)	*Rangifer tarandus*
Cat, domestic	*Felis cattus*
Cat, wild	*Felis sylvestris*
Cattle, domestic	*Bos taurus* and *B. indicus*
Cattle, wild (wild ox)	*Bos taurus*
Cheetah	*Acinonyx jubatus*
Cougar	*Felis concolor*

Coyote	*Canis latrans*
Deer, fallow	*Dama dama*
Deer, mule	*Odocoileus hemionus*
Deer, musk	*Moschus* spp.
Deer, roe	*Capreolus capreolus*
Deer, white-tailed	*Odocoileus virginianus*
Dog	*Canis familiaris*
Elephant, African	*Loxodonta africana*
Elephant, Asian	*Elephas maximus*
Elk (red deer, hart, stag)	*Cervus elaphus*
Ermine (stoat)	*Mustela erminea*
Ferret, European	*Mustela putorius*
Fox, red	*Vulpes vulpes*
Gaur	*Bos gaurus*
Gazelle	*Gazella* spp.
Goat, Bezoar	*Capra aegagrus*
Goat, domestic	*Capra hircus*
Goat, mountain	*Oreamnos americanus*
Gopher, pocket	Geomyidae
Gopher, pocket	*Thomomys* spp.
Guanaco	*Lama guanicoe*
Guinea pig	*Cavea porcellus*
Hare, snowshoe	*Lepus americanus*
Horse, domestic	*Equus caballus*
Horse, wild	*Equus ferus*
Huita	*Capromys* spp.
Human	*Homo sapiens*
Jackal (4 spp.)	*Canis* spp.
Llama	*Lama glama*
Lynx	*Felis lynx*
Macaque	*Macaca* spp.
Mammoth, Columbian*	*Mammuthus columbi*
Mammoth, imperial*	*Mammuthus imperator*
Mammoth, woolly*	*Mammuthus primigenius*
Manatee	*Trichechus manatus*
Marten	*Martes americana*
Mastodon, American*	*Mammut americanum*
Mink	*Mustela vison*
Mink, sea (giant)*	*Mustela macrodon*
Mongoose	*Herpestes ichneumon*
Moose	*Alces alces*
Mouflon, Asiatic	*Ovis orientalis*
Mouse, house	*Mus musculus*
Mouse, meadow	*Microtus pennsylvanicus*
Muskox	*Ovibos moschatus*

Appendix B

Muskrat.. *Ondatra zibethicus*
Narwhal... *Monodon monoceros*
Onager.. *Equus hemionus*
Opossum.. *Didelphis virginiana*
Otter, European.................................... *Lutra lutra*
Otter, river .... *Lutra canadensis*
Otter, sea... *Enhydra lutra*
Panda, giant .... *Ailuropoda melanoleuca*
Pig, domestic (swine, hog) .... *Sus scrofa*
Porcupine .... *Erithizon dorsatum*
Prairie dog .... *Cynomys* spp.
Pronghorn antelope (*see* Antelope).................
Rabbit .... *Sylvilagus* spp.
Rabbit, cottontail.................................. *Sylvilagus floridanus*
Rabbit, European (hare) .... *Oryctolagus cunicuclus*
Raccoon .... *Procyon lotor*
Rat, black (roof) .... *Rattus rattus*
Rat, Norway (house)............................... *Rattus norvegicus*
Rat, Polynesian .... *Rattus exulans*
Red deer (*see* Elk)................................
Rhinoceros....................................... *Rhinoceros* spp.
Sable (Europe).................................... *Mustela zibellina*
Sea cow, Steller's*................................ *Hydrodamalis gigas*
Seal, elephant (giant seal) .... *Mirounga angustirostris*
Seal, harp .... *Phoca groenlandica*
Seal, Juan Fernandez fur .... *Arctocephalus philippii*
Seal, northern fur .... *Callorhinus ursinus*
Seal, ringed...................................... *Pusa hispida*
Seal, southern fur .... *Arctocephalos* spp.
Sheep, bighorn .... *Ovis canadensis*
Sheep, domestic................................... *Ovis aries*
Skunk, striped .... *Mephitus mephitus*
Squirrel, fox .... *Sciurus niger*
Squirrel, gray .... *Sciurus carolinensis*
Tarpan (forest horse) .... *Equus caballus*
Tiger... *Panthera tigris*
Vicuña... *Vicugna vicugna*
Weasel... *Mustela* spp.
Whale, beluga (white).............................. *Delphinapterus leucas*
Whale, blue...................................... *Balaenoptera musculus*
Whale, bowhead.................................. *Balaena mysticetus*
Whale, gray...................................... *Eschrichtius robustus*
Whale, minke.................................... *Balaenoptera acutorostrata*
Whale, right .... *Eubalaena glacialis*
Whale, sperm .... *Physeter macrocephalos*

Wolf, gray .... *Canis lupus*
Woodchuck .... *Marmota monax*
Yak .... *Bos grunniens*

Birds

Common name   **Scientific name**

Auk, great* .... *Pinguinus impennis*
Bustard .... *Otis tarda*
Cahow (*see* Petrel, Bermuda) ....
Canary.. *Serinus canaria*
Chicken .... *Gallus gallus*
Chukar .... *Alectoris chukar*
Coot... *Fulica americana*
Crane... *Grus* spp.
Crow, American .... *Corvus bracyrhyncos*
Crow, carrion .... *Corvus corone*
Curlew.. *Numenius* spp.
Curlew, stone .... *Burhinus oedicnemus*
Dodo* .... *Raphus cucullatus*
Dove.. Columbidae
Duck .... Anatinae
Duck, black... *Anas rubripes*
Duck, Labrador* .... *Camptorhyncus labradorius*
Duck, wood... *Aix sponsa*
Eagle, bald .... *Haliaeetus leucocephalus*
Falcon .... *Falco* spp.
Falcon, peregrine (duck hawk) .... *Falco peregrinus*
Finch .... Fringillidae
Goose .... *Anser* spp. and *Branta* spp.
Goshawk .... *Accipiter gentilis*
Grebe, horned .... *Podiceps auritus*
Grouse, blue .... *Dendragapus obscurus*
Grouse, ruffed .... *Bonasa umbellus*
Grouse, sharp-tailed .... *Pedioecetes phasianellus*
Gull .... *Larus* spp.
Hawk .... Accipitrinae or Buteoninae
Hawk, Cooper's .... *Accipiter cooperii*
Hawk, sharp-shinned................................... *Accipiter striatus*
Hen, heath* .... *Tympanuchus cupido cupido*
Heron... Ardeidae
Honeycreeper, Hawaiian .... Drepanididae
Jay (in Europe) .... *Garrulus glanderius*
Jay (in North America) .... Corvidae
Jungle fowl, red .... *Gallus gallus*
Lark, horned.. *Eromophila alpestris*

Appendix B

Loon .... *Gavia* spp.
Moa* .... *Dinornis* spp. and *Megalapteryx* spp.
Ostrich.. *Struthio camelus*
Owl.. Strigidae
Owl, spotted .... *Strix occidentalis*
Parakeet, Carolina*............................... *Conuropsis carolinensis*
Partridge, gray (Hungarian) .... *Perdix perdix*
Peacock .... *Pavo* spp.
Pelican, brown .... *Pelecanus occidentalis*
Petrel .... Procellariidae
Petrel, Bermuda (cahow) .... *Pterodroma cahow*
Pheasant .... *Phasianus* spp.
Pheasant, English (ring-necked)........................ *Phasianus colchicus*
Pigeon, passenger* .... *Ecopistes migratorius*
Plover, ringed .... *Charadrius hiaticula*
Prairie chicken, greater (pinnated grouse).............. *Tympanuchus cupido*
Prairie chicken, lesser............................ *Tympanuchus pallidicinctus*
Quail, bobwhite .... *Colinus virginianus*
Rail .... Rallidae
Robin, American .... *Turdus migratorius*
Shrike, red-backed.. *Lanius collurio*
Snipe .... *Capella gallinago*
Solitaire*... *Myadestes townsendi*
Sparrow... Emberizidae
Swan .... *Cygnus* spp.
Turkey .... *Maleagris gallipavo*
Warbler .... Parulidae
Wheatear .... *Oenanthe oenanthe*
Woodcock .... *Scolopex minor*
Woodlark .... *Lullula arborea*
Woodpecker .... Picidae

Reptiles and Amphibians
Common name   **Scientific name**

Alligator .... *Alligator mississippiensis*
Snake.. Colubridae
Tortoise, Galapagos.............................. *Testudo elephantopus*
Turtle, sea .... Cheloniidae and Dermochelyidae

Fish
Common name   **Scientific name**

Capelin .... *Mallotus villosus*
Carp.. *Cyprinus carpio*
Catfish .... *Ictalurus* spp.

Cod .... *Gadus morhua*
Darter, snail .... *Percina tanasi*
Salmon... *Oncorhynchus* spp.
Trout .... *Salvelinus* spp.

Invertebrates

Common name   **Scientific name**

Budworm, spruce...................................... Choristoneura spp.
Clam .... Mollusca
Crustacean .... *Crustacea*
Cuttlefish .... *Sepia* spp.
Earthworm .... *Lumbricus terrestris*
Grasshopper... Orthoptera
Honeybee... *Apis mellifera*
Insect .... Insecta
Leech.. Hirudinea
Looper, hemlock .... *Lambdina fiscellaria*
Mosquito... Culicidae
Moth, gypsy .... *Porthetria dispar*
Moth, tussock .... *Hemerocampa plagiata*
Silkworm......................... *Bombyx* spp. and *Autheraea* spp.
Snail... *Helix* spp.
Spider .... Arachnida
Squid, giant.. *Architeuthis dux*

Plants

Common name   **Scientific name**

Apple.. *Pyrus malus*
Aspen .... *Populus tremuloides*
Barley .... *Hordeum vulgare*
Bean.. *Phaseolus* spp.
Beech.. *Fagus* spp.
Birch .... *Betula* spp.
Cherry.. *Prunus avium*
Clover .... *Trifolium* spp.
Corn (*see* Maize)..
Cotton.. *Gossypium* spp.
Date... *Phoenix dactylifera*
Douglas-fir .... *Pseudotsuga menziesii*
Fig .... *Ficus carica*
Flax .... *Linum usitatissimum*
Grape, wine .... *Vitis vinifera*
Grass .... Gramineae

Appendix B

Hawthorn .... *Crataegus* spp.
Lichen .... Algal-fungal association
Maize (corn)... *Zea mays*
Mesquite .... *Prosopis* spp.
Moss.. Bryophyta
Mushroom............................ Ascomycetes and Basidiomycetes
Oak .... *Quercus* spp.
Oak, scrub.. *Quercus prinoides*
Oak, shinnery... *Quercus harvardii*
Oats .... *Avena sativa*
Olive .... *Olea eropaea*
Orange... *Citrus sinensis*
Pea .... *Pisum sativum*
Peach .... *Prunus persica*
Pear .... *Pyrus communis*
Pumpkin .... *Cucurbita pepo*
Reed.. *Phragmites* spp.
Rye... *Secale cereale*
Sagebrush .... *Artemisia* spp.
Spruce .... *Picea* spp.
Squash... *Cucurbita maxima*
Sugarcane .... *Saccharum officinarum*
Sunflower .... *Helianthus annuus*
Tobacco.. *Nicotiana tabacum*
Turnip .... *Brassica napus*
Wheat .... *Triticum aestivum*
Wheatgrass, crested................................. *Agropyron cristatum*
Willow .... *Salix* spp.

*Extinct

INDEX

acid rain, 116
Afghanistan, 93, 176
Afghanistan War. *See* war
Africa, 1, 4, 5, 6, 52, 54, 60, 125, 126, 127, 131, 138
Agenda 21 Conference, 180, 181, 186
Agent Orange, 176
agricultural society, 118
agriculture
    chemicals (pesticide and fertilizer), 102, 104, 116, 120
    commercial, 56, 60, 101–102, 103, 111, 116
    crop rotation, 78
    departments, 104, 106, 107, 108, 109, 166
    development, 8, 14, 15, 19
    and diet, 24
    in Eurasia, 14–27, 35, 36, 67, 116
    expansion of, 10, 14–15, 19–21, 25, 67, 73, 99–102, 114, 115–116, 118
    federal programs, 101, 116, 186
    food production, 19
    forest farming, 20
    irrigation, 9, 19, 104
    reduction of, 103
    revolutions, 19
    slash-and-burn, 20, 22
    surplus and nonsurplus crops, 116
    traditional, 66, 67, 78, 99–101, 103
    and wildlife, 20–21, 21–22, 24, 73, 99–100, 102, 104, 109, 114, 115, 116–117
    See also grazing; rangeland
Alaska, 6, 48, 49, 57, 59, 66, 70, 130, 162–163, 182
Alberta, 73, 164, 181
Aleut. *See* Inuit and Aleut
Aleutian Islands, 48
Algonkian, 64
Alleghenies, 64, 66
Allen, Glover, 126
alligator, 16, 150–151
alpaca, 16, 18

American Bison Society, 158
American Committee on International Wildlife Protection, 126
American Game Policy, 94, 103, 110–111
American Revolution. *See* war
American Sportsman, 100
animal domestication, 14–27
animal rights activist, 143
Annals of Agriculture, 78
Antarctic, 48
antelope, pronghorn, 82, 115
ape, 54
Apocrypha, 30
Appalachian Highlands Network, 166
approbation. *See* attitudes toward wildlife
Arab, x, 42, 52
arboreta, 79–80
archer, 40–41
Arctic, 57
aristocratic hunt, 31–32, 42, 71
aristocratic status, 76–77
Arkansas Hot Springs National Reserve, 105
Asia, 1, 7, 11, 19, 116, 126, 127, 138
ass, 17, 18, 22, 32
Assam, 16
Assyria, 32
Atlantic coast, 57, 59, 66
attitudes toward wildlife
    approbation, x, 2–3, 8, 31, 38, 40, 71–72, 83
    and values, x, xi, 1–2, 191–194
Audubon club, 91
Audubon Society, 126, 163, 170
auk, great, 52, 54, 71, 183
aurochs. *See* ox, wild
Australia, 5, 79, 130, 175
automobile. *See* transport
Azores, 52
Aztec, 31, 59–60

Babylonia, 30, 31, 32
badger, 78, 82

203

Bali Action Plan, 136–137
Baltic Sea, 47
Banff National Park, 105
banteng, 18
Bardot, Brigitte, 182
Basque, 46
bat, 119, 120
bear
  black, 66, 68, 70, 82
  brown (grizzly), 36, 37, 38, 42, 73, 79, 93, 144, 160, 164, 166
  decline of, 66, 100
  extinction of, 79
  habitat for, 8, 68
  marketing, 82, 83
  polar, 130
  as predators, 37, 73, 93
  protection of, 36, 42, 130, 164
  tolerance for, 144
beaver
  decline of, 61–62, 66, 67, 73, 183
  extinction of, 65, 78, 79, 178
  hunting territory, 63
  marketing, 82
  value of, 51, 64
Benz, Karl, 101
Beringia, 6, 7, 15, 17
Bering Sea, 6, 47, 48, 50
Bering Strait, 17
Bermuda, 53
Bible, 30, 32, 33, 65
biodiversity, 127, 130, 133, 142, 162, 164, 166, 167, 178–184, 187
Biodiversity in Canada—A Scientific Assessment, 181
biological processes, 1–2, 180
Biological Station, 161
biological values, 192
biomes, 183
biosphere reserve, 160–166
Biosphere Reserve, 161, 166
biotic communities, 131–132
biotic potential, 108
bird conservation groups, 91
birds
  death of, 176
  decline of, 79
  domestication of, 16
  ducks. *See* waterfowl
  extinction of, 51, 53
  game birds, 77–78, 99, 104, 105 (*see also individual species*)
  marketing, 82, 83
  seabirds, 54
  shorebirds, 82
  songbirds, 22, 51, 77, 79, 82, 86, 90, 125
birth rates, 175, 177
bison
  abundance of, 57, 63, 64, 66
  commercial use of, 70–71
  decline of, 37, 38, 67, 72, 73, 78, 87, 183
  domestication of, 16, 18
  extinction of, 79, 87, 178
  during Interglacial Ages, 5, 6, 7, 8
  marketing, 82
  protection of, 42, 151, 158
Black Death, 57, 76
Blackfoot, 63
boar, wild, 16, 17, 32, 38, 42, 77, 119
boat and raft. *See* transport
bobcat, 82
bobwhite quail
  abundance of, 66, 68
  on farmland, 114
  grain for, 99
  marketing, 82
  study of, 94
Boone, Daniel, 66
Boone and Crockett Club, 126
Boston, 82
bounty, 93, 144
bow and arrow, 3, 28, 30, 40
Britain. *See* England
British House of Commons, 76
Bronx Zoo, 92
Bronze Age, 28
Brooklyn, 82
buffalo. *See* bison
buffalo, water, 18
Bush, George H. W., 170
Bush, George W., 184
bushmeat, 135
bustard, 79

Cabot, John, 45, 182
Cabot, Sebastian, 182
Caesar, Julius, 36
Cahokian, 10

Index

cahow. *See* petrel
California, 48, 49, 50, 70, 144, 166
Cambridge, U.K., 129
camel, 16–18, 22, 31
Campbell, Robert, 91, 107
Canada
   conservation laws, 83–85
   immigrants to, 7, 175
   nationhood, 66
   Parks Canada, 108
   political parties, 176
   population growth rate, 175
   wildlife management history, 85–86
Canada Agriculture Rehabilitation and Development Act, 101
Canada Conservation Act, 108
Canada Department of Agriculture, 106
Canada Department of Canadian Heritage, 108, 110
Canada Department of Interior, 91, 108
Canada Dominion Forest Reserves and Parks Act, 108
Canada Environmental Conservation Service, 110
Canada Forest Reserves Act, 106
Canada Forestry Branch, 91, 106, 107, 109
Canada Parks Branch, 106, 107, 108, 109
Canada Wild Animal and Plant Protection and Regulation of International and Interprovincial Trade Act, 89–90
Canadian Environment Act, 146
Canadian Wildlife Service, 88, 108, 110, 129
canary, 16
Cape Breton, 61
Cape Cod, 54
Cape Horn, 49
capelin, 182
Caribbean, 53, 55
caribou
   decline of, 70, 156
   domestication of, 18
   during Interglacial Ages, 6
   marketing, 82
   recovery of, 163
   See also reindeer
Carolinas, 62
carp, 102
carrying capacity, 176

Carson, Rachel, 120, 157
Cartier, Jacques, 45
cat, domestic, 18, 22, 53, 78
catfish, 16
cattle, 16, 17, 18, 22, 30, 53, 73, 93, 115, 118, 121
Central America, 16, 17, 31, 133
Chapman, Frank, 83
chariot. *See* transport
chase, 39
cheetah, 31
Chicago, 69
chicken, 16, 18, 77
China, 19, 30, 32, 42, 48, 49, 52, 93, 175–176
Chippewa, 4, 7, 63
Christian, 33, 42, 60, 61, 65–66
chukar, 93
Chukchi Sea, 50
Civil War, U.S. *See* war
Clark, William, 64
classification of species (survival status), 129
climatic change, 5–7, 35, 103
Clinton, Bill, 186
Clovis projectile point, 7 (*see also* weaponry)
cod (codfish), 54, 59, 61, 178, 182
Cody, Buffalo Bill, 83
Colombia River, 62, 103
Columbus, Christopher, 45, 52, 60
comanagement, 161–163, 165, 182, 187
command and control, 29, 161
Commission of Conservation, 108
commons, 38–39
Communal Areas Management Programme for Indigenous Resources (CAMPFIRE), 138
compass, 45
compensatory reproduction, 10, 121
Connecticut, 55
conservation. *See* wildlife conservation
conservation easement, 186
Conservation of the Wild Life of Canada, The, 107
Conservation Reserve Program (CRP), 116, 186
Constantinople, 52
Consultative Commission for the International Protection of Nature, 125

Convention on Biological Diversity, 180, 184, 186
Convention on International Trade in Endangered Species of Wild Fauna and Flora (CITES), 135, 136
Cook, James, 48, 49, 51
Cooperative Wildlife Research Unit, 95, 110
coot, 82
corn, 8, 9, 19, 59–60, 99
corridor, 160, 166
Cortés, Hernán, 59
Costa Rica, 131
cougar, 73, 92, 93, 144, 150
cow. *See* cattle
coyote, 92, 93, 121
crane, 82
Crete, 32
crow, 78, 93, 125
cultural change, 1–2
curlew, 79, 82
Cuyahoga River, 157

Daimler, Gottlieb, 101
Dakotas, 57
Dark Ages. *See* Middle Ages
Darling, J. N. "Ding," 95
DDT, 120, 143, 151, 157, 185
deer
  abundance of, 8, 66, 119
  albino, 54
  decline of, 67, 100
  domestication of, 16
  fallow, 38
  habitat for, 37, 68, 156
  increase in, 107, 115
  laws on taking, 86
  marketing, 82
  mule, 71, 82, 107, 115
  musk, 52
  protection of, 36, 42, 54
  reduction in, 108, 114
  roe, 30
  spread of, 38
  study of, 94
  venison, 82
  white-tailed, 66, 82, 107, 115
Defenders of Wildlife, 183
Denmark, 45, 54, 120

Depression, Great, 103, 109, 111
Ding Darling National Wildlife Refuge, 95
disease, 7, 24, 29, 57, 59, 60, 71, 139
DNA, 7, 15
Dodge City, 72
dodo, 52, 53
dog, 3, 15–16, 18, 21, 23, 30, 31, 35, 38, 67, 68, 77, 78, 79
domestication, 14–27
  methods, 16
  traits needed, 16
dove, 90
Drake, Francis, 55
duck stamp, 85, 95, 110
Dust Bowl, 103

eagle, 143–144, 150, 151
Earth Day, 142, 143
Earth Summit (Rio Convention), 181, 185
East Africa, 131
ecological services, 138
economic growth, 176
economics
  analysis, 143, 168, 183
  bison, 71–72
  considerations, 143, 145, 168, 183
  development, 159, 141, 156, 159, 162, 177–180
  ecotourism. *See* tourism
  endangered species trade, 135–138
  environmental, 145, 168, 192–193
  forest, range, and farm, 103, 116, 117
  fur. *See* fur trade
  imbalance, 116
  Indian, American, 57
  NEPA, 144, 159
  passenger pigeon, 69
  whales. *See* whaling
  wildlife, 70, 82–83, 114
  World Bank, 127
  World Conservation Strategy, 176–177
ecoregion, 181
ecosystem, xi, 148, 152, 176, 180, 181, 183
  (*see also* habitats)
ecotourism, 131, 193
Egypt, 30, 32
elephant, 16, 18, 31, 52, 134, 160
elk
  abundance of, 66, 71, 94, 115

Index

decline of, 37, 67, 100
habitat for, 68, 156
marketing, 82–83
protection of, 36, 42, 164
reduction in, 114
Rocky Mountain, 164
See also red deer
endangered species
classification of, 129, 136
interest in, 158–59, 171
legislation for, 127, 135, 164, 167–169, 179
number of, xi, 151
programs for, 186
recovery of, 130, 146–152
Endangered Species Committee. *See* "God Squad"
Endangered Species Recovery Committee, 149
England
climatic changes in, 35
commons in, 38–39
estates of, 67, 76–81, 82, 102, 132
exploration of, 45, 48, 53, 55, 70
hunting in, 39–42, 56
law, 83–84, 85, 86–87, 90, 125
pesticides in, 120
Roman influence, 36
trade with New World, 46–47, 51, 60, 62, 64
war, 64, 66, 83
environmental impact statement, 135, 145
Environmental Movement, 122, 142, 143
environmental quality, 145
environmental restoration, 184–185
epidemics, 57, 59, 60 (*see also* disease)
Eriksson, Leif, 45
ermine (stoat), 51
Errington, Paul, 108
estate, 56, 77–79, 87, 115
Ethiopa, 31
Etruscans, 31
Eurasia, 5, 11, 14–27, 30
Europe, 7, 20, 35–75, 107–108, 116, 119, 132
Experimental Forest, 161
Experimental Forest and Scenic-Research Area, 161
Experimental Range, 161
exploration, 19, 45–58, 59–75, 76

Extinct and Vanishing Birds of the World, 126
Extinct and Vanishing Mammals of the Old World, 126
Extinct and Vanishing Mammals of the Western Hemisphere, 126
extinction and extirpation
and classifications, 129
commercial, 47, 50, 51, 65, 70–71, 78, 178
protection programs, 125–140, 146–149, 168
and recovery, 9, 51, 148–149, 164, 179
of species, xi, 7–8, 21, 25, 31, 34, 38, 42, 48–49, 51, 52, 53–54, 65, 66, 67, 69–70, 72, 76, 93, 99, 100, 144, 151, 164
threat of, 29, 66, 82–83, 130, 134, 149, 150, 151, 167, 169–170, 183, 185
Exxon Valdez, 49

falcon, 54, 92, 120, 150, 151
farm game, 114–117
farming. *See* agriculture
Faroes, 45
ferret, 18
Fertile Crescent, 19
fertilizer, 22, 78, 109, 115–116, 185
feudalism, 36–37, 40–42
Field and Stream, 100
Finland, 121
fire
accidental, 69, 105, 107, 115
for agriculture, 19, 20–21, 22, 23, 67–68
by ancient warrior-ruler hunting, 30
Chicago Fire, 69
for cooking, 3, 6
by Indians hunting, 3–4, 66, 98
Peshtigo Fire, 69
for prospecting, 105
suppression, 156
war, 101, 175
firearms. *See* weaponry
fish and fishing, 6, 9, 16, 30, 41, 45, 54, 66, 79, 86, 102, 103, 110, 120, 121, 131, 147, 151, 182, 183
Food and Agriculture Organization (FAO), 127, 132, 177
Ford, Henry, 101
forest
abuse of, 36, 105–106, 178

clearcutting, 34, 156, 159
dead wood, 118
fragmentation of, 67–68, 101, 118, 156
lumber industry, 118–120, 167–169
management of, 90–91, 156, 158
mountain, 105–106
old growth, 119, 156, 167, 169, 170, 178
protection of, 39–40, 107, 169
sawlogs, 107, 168
subclimax, 107, 114
timber production, 118–120, 156
Forest and Stream, 100
forestland, 109, 111, 114, 115, 117–120, 156
fox, 51, 77, 78
fragmentation. *See* forest
France, 36, 41, 42, 45, 46, 54, 55, 61, 62, 64, 79, 126, 132
free-warren, 41
French and Indian War. *See* war
French Revolution. *See* war
Friends of Animals, 143
Friends of the Earth, 183
fund-raising, 134
Funk Island, 54
fur, 36, 38, 39, 57, 87
Fur Seal Treaty, 51, 90, 125, 128, 179
fur trade, 36, 48–51, 55–56, 57, 59–66, 73, 99, 103, 143

Galapagos, 50
game birds. *See* birds
game farms, 92, 93
"game hog," 100
Game Law of England, 41
Game Management, 94, 107, 108
game production, 93–94
game warden systems, 88
gap analysis, 163
gardens, 79–80
Gaul, 36
gaur, 16
gazelle, 30
Geer *v.* Connecticut, 85
gene pool, 152
Geneva, 135
Gentiles, 30
genus system, 56
geographic information system, 163, 181
Georgia, 55, 166

Germany, 35, 90
glacier, 6, 8, 14
Glacier National Park Biosphere Reserve, 164
goat
  domestic, 16–18, 20, 30, 53
  mountain, 82
"God Squad," 147, 170
Gomez, Estevan, 61
gopher, pocket, 121
"grace under pressure," 38
Graham, Edward, 131
Grand Canyon National Park, 165
Grand Coulee Dam, 103
grazing, 14, 19–21, 22–24, 29, 34, 68, 78, 108, 115, 116, 159, 165 (*see also* rangeland)
Great Lakes, 62, 69
Great Plains, 3, 57, 63, 71, 72, 73, 103
grebe, horned, 82
Greece, 31, 32
Green Bay, 69
Greenland, 45
Green Movement. *See* environmental movement
Greenpeace, 143, 182, 183, 186
Greenway, James, 126
grouse
  abundance of, 66, 68
  blue, 157
  and DDT, 157
  decline of, 100
  grain for, 99
  habitat loss, 104
  increase in, 107
  and insecticides, 120
  marketing, 82
  ruffed, 66, 68, 94, 107, 120
  sharp-tailed, 99, 100, 104
  study of, 94
guanaco, 18
guinea pig, 16
Gulf of Mexico, 62
Gulf of St. Lawrence, 45
Gulf War. *See* war
gull, 82
gunpowder, 42, 58, 60, 66 (*see also* weaponry)
Guyana, 133

Index

habitat
  carrying capacity, 176
  conserving, 84–85, 141–155
  after Interglacial Ages, 6–7, 35
  and land use, 3–4, 14, 19, 21–22, 23, 24, 38, 65, 66, 67–68, 73, 78, 92, 98, 102, 107, 115, 156
  loss of, 37, 60, 67, 69, 104, 105, 118, 156, 158, 176, 178, 185
  protection of, 42, 131–132, 146, 148, 150, 156, 158, 160, 179–181
  and reproduction, 100
  restoration of, 117, 146
  (*see also* agriculture; fire; forest; grazing; rangelands; wetlands)
Habitat Conservation Plan (HCP), 148
Hardin, Garret, 182
hare. *See* rabbit and hare
Harkin, James, 106, 107
Harper, Francis, 126
harvest, commercial, 45–58, 60–66, 69–73, 82–83, 150, 178
Havasupai, 165
Hawaii, 49, 51
hawk and falcon, 78, 93, 125
  Cooper's hawk, 92
  goshawk, 92
  sharp-shinned hawk, 92
  peregrine falcon, 92, 121, 150, 151
heath hen, 66, 86, 99
Hemingway, Ernest, 38
Henry, King, 40
herbicide. *See* pesticide
heron, 83
Hewitt, Gordon, 106–107, 122
"high guns," 83
historical categories of wildlife management in the U.S. and Canada, 85
hog. *See* pig
Hohokam, 10
Holland (Dutch), 46, 47, 55, 60, 62, 63, 79, 126, 132
Homo sapiens, 1
honeybee, 16, 116
honeycreeper, 51
Hood, Robin, 39
Hornaday, William, 92–93, 107
horse
  breed development, 78

  domestication of, 17, 18, 57
  extinct, 7
  for farming, 36, 73, 102
  herds of, 73
  for hunting, 31, 32, 56, 57, 77, 79
  tarpan (forest horse), 42
  for transport, 17, 22, 32, 57, 66, 70
  for warfare, 31, 37, 57, 60
Hudson Bay, 55
Hudson River, 62
Hudson's Bay Company, 55, 61, 63, 64
huita, 53
human and wildlife relationships, xi, 11, 65, 191–192
human evolution, 1
human population
  expansion of, 4–5, 14, 32, 37, 64, 67, 86, 135, 175–178, 192–193
  in groups, 2–3, 5, 6, 10–11, 15, 19, 110
  size, 5, 15, 24, 45, 59, 60, 71, 138, 175–176, 177, 192
human relationships, 10–11
human territoriality, 4–5, 8–9, 14, 24, 37, 60, 63, 64, 65, 89, 98, 125, 161
Hungary, 93
hunting
  bag limits, 87–89, 91, 114
  bands
    aspects of, 4–6
    decline of, 21
    and farmers, 24
    location of, 7, 19–20
  demographics, 117, 192–193
  effects on wildlife, 1–3
  and gathering, x, 1–13, 14–15, 19–20, 21, 24, 28, 29, 35, 98
  license, 87–89, 91, 114, 115
  market hunting, 87, 88
  meat consumption, 5, 33, 35, 192
  meat storage, 5, 35
  in medieval Europe, 38
  method constraints, 87, 88, 89
  preserves, 32–33
  records, 30–31, 33
  seasons for, 87, 88, 114–115
  as sport, 31, 32, 40, 56, 57, 77–78, 79, 87, 91
  as training for war, 30
Hutchins, John, 70
Huxley, Julien, 127

Iceland, 45, 54, 130
Idaho, 166
illegal trade, 136
Illinois, 99, 100
immigration concerns, 175
incentive payments, 116
India, 16, 28, 31, 52, 54, 93, 126, 137, 138
Indian, American
  citizenship of, 84
  decline of, 10, 45, 59, 60, 71
  and fire, 3-4, 66, 98
  and fur trade, 48, 54, 61-65
  and horses, 57
  and human expansion, 1-13
  land of, 67, 99
  macrocontact, 57
  microcontact, 57
  pacification of, 67, 71, 72, 101
  Paleo-Indian hunter, 7, 9, 15, 69
  removal of, 67, 101
  on reservations, 73, 84
  spirituality of, 33, 165
  and sustainability, 185
  territory of, 63, 65, 98, 133
  weapons of, 3, 9, 60, 65
  See also names of individual tribes
Indian Wars. *See* war
indigenous system, 162
Industrial Revolution, 19, 56
industrial society, 118
insecticide. *See* pesticide
Interagency Scientific Committee (Thomas Committee), 169
Interglacial Ages. *See* Pleistocene
international agreements, 179-180
International Council on Bird Preservation (ICBP), 125-126, 128, 129, 131
International Fund for Animal Welfare, 183
International Nature Protection, 126, 128
international programs, 127-138, 141
International Union for the Conservation of Nature and Natural Resources (IUCN), 128-132, 134-136, 141, 179
International Union for the Protection of Nature (IUPN), 128
International Union of Biological Sciences, 126
International Whaling Commission (IWC), 121, 130

International Wildlife Protection, 126
Inuit and Aleut, 1, 8, 10, 11, 35, 45, 46, 50, 59, 162, 185
inversity, 108
Iowa, 87, 89, 100
Iran, 32, 131
Iraq, 19, 31, 175-176
Iron Age, 28
Iroquois, 63
Islam, 52
Israel, 52
Italy, 45, 52, 90

jackal, 15
Japan, 51, 90, 130-131, 179, 182, 184
jay, 78, 93
Jefferson, Thomas, 64, 101
Jew, 30
Journal of Wildlife Management, 110
Judeo-Christian religion, 33
jungle fowl, 18

Kamchatka, 47
Kansas, 72
Kentucky, 66
Kenya, 177
Korean War. *See* war
Kuwait, 175-176
Kyoto Agreement, 184

Labrador, 46
Lacey, John, 89
Lake Ontario, 62
Lake States, 69
land ownership, 34, 35-36, 67, 76-79, 82-84, 95-96, 98-99, 103, 105, 108-109, 156-174, 181 (*see also* estate)
landscape linkage. *See* corridor
language, 1, 2, 7, 76
L'Anse aux Meadows, 45
lark, 86
"Last Refuges of the World, The," 131
Latin America, 138
Laurier, Wilfred, 107, 108
law
  Canadian responsibilities, 85-86
  divisions, 84-85
  goals, 84
  U.S. responsibilities, 85

Index

See also wildlife conservation
leather, 38
Leopold, Aldo, xiii, 94, 107, 108, 122, 191
Lewis, Meriwether, 64
lion, 31, 32, 56
Lives of Game Animals, 107
llama, 16, 18
loon, 82
Louis XIV, 62
Louisiana, 62, 64
Louisiana Purchase, 64
Louisiana Territory, 62
lynx, 51

macaque, 53
Macedonia, 32
Madagascar, 52
Magna Carta, 39
Maine, 62, 86, 88
maize. *See* corn
mammoth, 5, 6, 7
Man and Nature, 106
Man and the Biosphere (MAB) Program, 159–160, 162
manatee, 47–48, 149 (*see also* sea cow)
Manifest Destiny, 66, 67, 70
Manitoba, 73, 181
Manual of Game Investigational Techniques, 122
manure, 22, 78, 185
Marine Mammal Commission, 149
Maritime Provinces, 73, 101
"market hunters," 87, 88, 100
Marsh, George, 105, 156
marten, 73, 119
Maryland, 87
Mascarene Islands, 52
Massachusetts, 83, 86, 88, 93
mastodon, 6, 7
material satisfaction, x–xi
maximum sustained yield, 121, 157
medieval Europe, 35–44, 76, 80
Mediterranean, 33–35, 36, 52, 105
Mexican War. *See* war
Mexican Revolution. *See* war
Mexico, 8, 9, 19, 31, 45, 48, 49, 59, 66, 70, 90
Michigan, 63, 93
Middle Ages, 35–44, 76
Middle East, 14–15

Midwest, 73, 94, 101, 103
Migratory Bird Hunting and Conservation Stamp, 95 (*see also* duck stamp)
Migratory Bird Hunting Permit, 95
Migratory Bird Treaty, 89, 90, 93, 107, 125, 128, 144, 179
migratory game, 86, 90, 179
mink, 16, 73, 92, 99, 101
mink, sea, 54
Minnesota, 63, 93
Mississippi River, 55, 62, 64, 70, 71
Missouri, 63, 71
Missouri River, 57, 63, 72
moa, 52
Monaco, 130
mongoose, 18
Montana, 72, 166
moose
  decline of, 67, 70
  extirpation of, 79
  laws on taking, 86
  marketing, 82
  protection of, 42
Mosby, Henry, xiii, 122
mouflon, 16
mouse. *See* rat and mouse
Muir, John, 91, 106, 123
multiple use, 85, 121, 133, 138, 142, 158, 167, 168, 169
museums, 79–80
muskox, 5, 6
muskrat, 65, 73, 82, 101, 108
"Myth of Superabundance," 83

National Audubon Society, 91, 126, 163, 170
National Bison Range, 158
National Forest, 161
National Lakeshore, 161
National Monument, 161
National Park and Preserve, 161
national parks, 63, 94, 105, 106, 114, 131, 132, 133, 136, 138, 139, 158, 160, 161, 165, 166, 179
National Resources Defense Council, 143
National Scenic River, 161
National Seashore, 161
National Wildlife Federation, 110, 143, 164
natural resources, ix, 83, 122, 161–162, 177

Nature Conservancy, 143, 158
nature conservation, 159, 186 (*see also* wildlife conservation)
Near East, 16, 17, 19, 33, 52
Nebuchadnezzar, 32
Nelson, Gaylord, 142
Netherlands. *See* Holland
New Amsterdam, 55
New Brunswick, 182
Newfoundland, 45, 46, 54, 55, 59, 182
New Hampshire, 88
New Jersey, 55, 87
New Orleans, 71
New Spain, 55
New York, 55, 62, 82, 83, 86, 87, 128
New Zealand, 49
Nimrod, 30
nongovernmental organizations (NGOs)
  funding for programs, 133-34, 164, 179, 184
  global conservation, 128
  pressure from, 145, 168
  and public lands, 158-159
  and research, 142-143, 181
Normandy, 39
North Africa, 42
North America
  American Indians. *See* Indians, American
  conflicts in, 56-57
  hunting bands, 4-6, 7, 11
  immigrants to, 7
  and Spanish explorers, 55
  wildlife conservation in, 82-124
North American Wildlife Conference, 110
North Carolina, 53, 67, 166
North Cascades Network, 166
North West Company, 61, 64
Northwest Territories, 162
Norway, 45, 50, 130
Nova Scotia, 182
Nunavut, 162

oceanic wildlife, 45-51
Ohio, 100, 157
oil spill, 49, 176
Ojibwa. *See* Chippewa
onager, 17, 18
Ontario, 70, 86, 181

opossum, 82, 92
optimum sustainable population, 176 (*see also* maximum sustained yield)
Oregon, 95, 169
Oregon Endangered Species Task Force, 169
Orient, 52, 57
ostrich, 32
otter
  river, 82, 120
  sea, 48-51, 61, 64, 78, 178, 179
Our Vanishing Wild Life, 107
owl, 78, 93, 125, 167, 169-170
  spotted, 167, 169-170
ownership, communal, 35-36, 39
ox
  domestic, 17, 22, 36
  wild, 16, 17, 37-38, 42

Pacific coast, 49, 55, 62, 64
Pacific Northwest, 49, 167-169
Pakistan, 28, 93, 126
Paleolithic. *See* Stone Age
panda, 134
parakeet, Carolina, 68, 69-70
Parks Canada, 108
Parmentier, Jean, 60-61
Parmentier, Raoul, 60-61
partridge, 30, 38, 77, 93, 104
pastoralism, 22-23, 29 (*see also* grazing)
peacock, 32, 54
Pearson, T. Gilbert, 126
pelican, brown, 151
Pelican Island Refuge, 158
People for the Ethical Treatment of Animals (PETA), 186
People's Trust for Endangered Species, 183
Persia, 31, 32
Persian Gulf, 176
pesticide, 93, 104, 109, 116, 120, 121, 143-144, 151, 156, 157, 185
petrel, 53
pheasant, 32, 38, 77-78, 93, 104, 115
Philadelphia, 82
Philippines, 48
pig (swine, hog), 16, 17, 18, 20, 39, 53
pigeon, passenger, 69, 70, 82, 87
Pinchot, Gifford, 90-91, 106, 122, 123
pinnated grouse. *See* prairie chicken

Index

Pittman, Key, 95
plague, 57, 76
Plains Indians, 72
planet, dependence upon, ix
plants
   classification of species, 129
   domestic, 8, 9, 14, 15, 16, 19, 20, 21, 22, 36, 59, 60, 78, 99
   domestication of, 19
   scientific names of, 200–201
Pleistocene, 5–7
plover, ringed, 79
plume market, 83, 89, 158
poaching, 39–42, 49, 80, 82, 90, 92, 94, 103, 105, 131, 132, 136, 137
politics, 76, 176
pollution, 34, 116, 120, 143, 156, 157, 184–185
Polynesia, 7, 45, 51
pope, 52, 55
populations. *See* human populations; wildlife populations
porcupine, 82
Portugal, 52, 60, 61
prairie chicken, 66, 82, 87, 99, 104
prairie dog, 93
prairie grouse. *See* prairie chicken; sharp-tailed grouse
prairie provinces, 73, 101
predation, 4, 21, 23, 25, 29, 37, 38, 73, 77–78, 90, 92–93, 100, 120, 121, 125, 144, 164
predator control, 73, 92–93, 121, 144, 164
Preservation of African Fauna, 125, 126
Preservation of the Fauna of the Empire, 125, 126
Pribilof Islands, 90
Prince Edward Island, 182
Prince William Sound, 49
private land, 105, 114–120 (*see also* land ownership)
Project Tiger, 137
Protection of Colonial Fauna, 126
public lands
   holistic conservation on, 156–174
   management of, 105–111, 114–115, 158–159, 167, 169–171
   See also land ownership
Puget Sound, 49

quails. *See* bobwhite quails
Quebec, 55, 62, 70, 76, 163

rabbit and hare
   abundance of, 66, 68
   domestication of, 16
   on farmland, 22, 114
   hunting, 30
   marketing, 82
   spread of, 38
   stocks of, 53
raccoon, 65, 73, 82, 92
rail, 82
railroad. *See* transport
Ramsar Convention on Wetlands of International Importance, 131–132
rangeland, 109, 111, 114, 115, 117, 120, 156 (*see also* grazing)
Rapidan River, 101
rat and mouse, 22, 30, 51, 53, 68, 78
Red Data Books, 129, 146
red deer, 30, 32, 36, 37, 38, 42, 79 (*see also* elk)
refuge, 24, 80, 95, 131, 158, 161
Regent's Park, 80
reindeer, 5, 6, 18–19, 22, 79 (*see also* caribou)
religion, 2, 9–10, 30–31, 32, 33, 36, 37, 65–66
Renaissance, 42, 52, 76
reproduction, 10, 100, 108, 121
Research Natural Area, 161
resource management, 122
rhinoceros, 160
Rhode Island, 86
rifles, 53, 66–67, 71 (*see also* weaponry)
Rio Convention (Earth Summit), 181, 185
Rio de Janeiro, 181, 184
Rio Grande River, 59
Robertson, A. Willis, 95
robin, 86, 120
Rocky Mountains, 65, 78, 93
Rocky Mountains Park, 105
Roman Empire, 33–34
Rome, 32, 33–34, 36, 52, 80, 83
Roosevelt, Theodore, 91, 122, 158
rural residents, 138–139, 141–142, 161, 185–186
Russia, 46, 47–49, 51, 61, 66, 70, 90, 130, 179

sable, 51
salmon, 103–104
sanctuaries, 24, 80, 95, 131, 158, 161
Sand County Almanac, A, 122
San Francisco Bay, 50
Sanibel Island, 95
Saskatchewan, 73, 181
Scandinavia, 45, 47, 54
scientific names, 195–201
Scotland, 54
sea cow, 47–48, 51
seal, 52
   elephant, 49–50
   harp, 182, 186
   Juan Fernandez, 50, 78
   northern fur, 48, 49–51, 90, 179
   ringed, 182
   southern fur, 49–50, 78
   See also Fur Seal Treaty
Seattle Audubon Society, 170
Seton, Ernest Thompson, 107
settlement, westward, 64, 67–70, 82, 99
settlement and trade, 59–75
Seven Years War. *See* war
sheep
   bighorn, 82
   domestic, 15–18, 20, 30, 73, 82, 93
   mouflon, 16
Sherwood Forest, 39
Shetlands Islands, 50
ship. *See* transport
Shoemaker, Carl, 95
shotguns, 77–78, 86 (*see also* weaponry)
shrike, red-backed, 79
shrubland, 114
Siberia, 5, 6, 47, 51
Sierra, 166
Sierra Club, 91, 106, 186
Sierra Network, 166
Sifton, Clifford, 107
Silent Spring, 120, 157
Sioux, 4, 63
skunk, 73, 82, 92
slash-and-burn agriculture. *See* agriculture; forest
slavery, 3, 20, 28, 36, 60
slob hunter, 159
smallpox, 29, 57 (*see also* disease)
snail darter, 147

snipe, 82, 86, 90
Soil Bank, 116
solitaire, 53
songbirds. *See* birds
South America
   and agriculture, 19
   camels in, 17–18
   immigrants to, 7
   primitive mammals from, 53
   seals in, 49
   sea turtles in, 133
Southeast Asia, 18
South Georgia, 50
South Korea, 130
Spain, 46, 48, 49, 52, 55, 60, 61, 64
spear and spear-thrower (atlatl), 3, 6, 7, 28, 30, 31, 38 (*see also* weaponry)
species
   of birds, xi
   classification of, 129, 135–136, 147, 148, 151
   common and scientific names, 195–201
   endangered, xi, 151 (*see also* endangered species; threatened species)
   introductions, 51, 93, 104, 135
   of mammals, xi
   sustainability, 177–178, 184–187
species system, 56
spiritual world, 2, 9–10, 33, 36, 65 (*see also* religion)
Spitzbergen, 46
Sporting Arms and Ammunition Manufacturers Institute, 91–92, 94, 95, 110
sportsmen, 87, 91, 191
squirrel, 68, 82, 119
State Forest, 161
state system, 162
state wildlife agencies, 85, 88, 95, 107, 114
St. Augustine, 59
Steller, Wilhelm, 47–48
St. Helena, 53
stirrup, 37
St. Johns, 59
St. Lawrence River, 55, 62
St. Louis, 63, 71
Stoddard, Herb, 108
Stone Age, x, 1–13, 14–16, 18, 24, 28–29, 35, 60, 64

Index

sugarcane, 56, 60
Survival Service Commission (SSC), 129, 136
Sweden, 45, 56
Switzerland, 90, 135
Syria, 32

Tellico Dam, 147
Tennessee, 147, 166
Tenochtitlán, 59
Texas, 72
Thomas, Jack Ward, 169
Thomas Committee, 169
threatened species
    classification of, 129, 147, 148
    interest in, 158
    legislation for, 167
    number of, xi
    recovery of, 146–147
tiger, 32, 134, 137, 160
Titus, 34
tobacco, 19, 60
tortoise, Galapagos, 50
tourism, 105, 131, 177, 178, 191, 193
trade
    and exploration, 45–58
    and settlement, 59–75
    in Stone Age, 28–29
    and wildlife commerce, 136
Trade Records Analysis of Flora and Fauna in Commerce (TRAFFIC), 136
trade routes, 29, 45–52
trading posts, 62–63
"Tragedy of the Commons," 182
train. *See* transport
transport
    automobile, 94, 101, 116, 118, 156
    boat and raft, 6, 59, 62, 63, 66, 70, 71
    camel, 17
    chariot and cart, 17, 32, 60
    dog and travois, 57
    elephant, 18
    foot, 6, 7, 70
    horse and donkey, 17, 22, 32, 57, 66, 70
    ox, 17
    reindeer, 18
    ship, 45–50, 55, 59, 60, 62, 76, 87, 182
    sled, 6

train, 70–71, 72, 82, 83, 87, 94, 101, 105, 118
trap, steel leghold, 61, 143
trespassing laws, 84, 96, 103, 111
trout, 120
Tudor era, 76–77
tundra ecosystem, 18–19
turkey, wild
    abundance of, 8, 66, 68
    decline of, 67
    domestication of, 16
    grain for, 99
    marketing, 82
turtle, sea, 133
Tyler, Wat, 41

Udall, Stewart, 83
United Nations, 127, 131, 132, 137–138, 141, 159, 177, 179
United Nations Conference on Environment and Development (UNCED), 184
United Nations Development Program (UNDP), 127
United Nations Educational, Scientific and Cultural Organization (UNESCO), 127, 128
United Nations Environmental Program (UNEP), 127, 130
United States
    conservation laws, 83–88
    immigrants to, 7, 175
    nationhood, 67
    political parties, 176
    population growth rate, 175
    wildlife management history, 85–86
United States of America National Report, 181
university, 95, 101, 102, 104, 109, 122, 181, 187
U.S. Agency for International Development (USAID), 127
U.S. and Canadian Biosphere Reserve Program, 166
U.S. Animal Damage Control (ADC) (Wildlife Services), 93
U.S. Army Corps of Engineers, 109
U.S. Biological Survey, 93
U.S. Bureau of Biological Survey, 95

U.S. Bureau of Indian Affairs, 84
U.S. Bureau of Land Management, 108, 109, 111, 117, 152, 167, 169, 170
U.S. Bureau of Reclamation, 109
U.S. Bureau of Sport Fisheries and Wildlife, 110
U.S. Civil Service Act, 122
U.S. Conservation Reserve Program, 186
U.S. Department of Agriculture, 104, 106, 108, 166
U.S. Department of Commerce, 147
U.S. Department of Interior, 84, 93, 106, 108, 110, 147, 166
U.S. Dingle-Johnson Act, 110
U.S. Endangered Species Act (ESA), 84, 86, 146–151, 152, 159–160, 164, 167, 168
U.S. Fish and Wildlife Service, 87–88, 95, 108, 109, 110, 146, 147, 148, 151, 167, 168, 169, 170
U.S. Forest and Rangeland Renewable Resources Planning Act, 168
U.S. Forest Reserves Act, 106
U.S. Forest Service, 91, 106, 107, 108, 111, 117, 152, 167–168, 169, 170
U.S. General Mining Law, 101
U.S. Homestead Act, 101
U.S. Indian Removal Act, 67, 101
U.S. Lacey Act, 85, 89, 90
U.S. Morrill Act, 101
U.S. National Council on Environmental Quality, 145
U.S. National Environmental Policy Act (NEPA), 84, 135, 144–145, 159–160
U.S. National Forest Management Act (NFMA), 167, 168, 170
U.S. National Marine Fisheries Service, 147
U.S. National Park Service, 108
U.S. Natural Resources Conservation Service, 108, 109, 131
U.S. Office of Indian Affairs, 84
U.S. Pacific Railroad Act, 101
U.S. Pittman-Robertson Act, 95, 110, 117
U.S. Public Health Service, 157
U.S. Soil Conservation Service. *See* U.S. Natural Resources Conservation Service

U.S.S.R., 130 (*see also* Russia)
U.S. Taylor Grazing Act, 108
U.S. Timber and Stone Act, 101
U.S. War Department, 84
Utah, 115

values. *See* attitudes toward wildlife
van Tienhoven, P. G., 126
vicuña, 18
Vietnam, 121
Vietnam War. *See* war
Viking, 45
Virginia, 60, 101
von Liebig, Justus, 78
von Linn, Carl, 56

Wales, 40
war
   Afghanistan, 176
   American Revolution, 64, 78
   English civil war, 83
   French Revolution, 42
   Gulf War, 175–176
   Indian Wars, 71
   Korean War, 176
   Mexican Revolution, 49
   Mexican War, 66, 70
   Seven Years War (French and Indian War), 62, 64
   U.S. Civil War, 60, 65, 70, 72, 101
   Vietnam War, 121, 176
   War of 1812, 62
   World War I, 93, 94, 100, 125
   World War II, 104, 111, 114, 115, 116, 117, 121, 126, 134, 135, 141, 150, 156, 157, 175, 176
warbler, 120
warfare, 4, 8, 9, 10, 20, 23, 28–34, 36–37, 40–42, 57, 63, 65
War of 1812. *See* war
warrior-ruler class, 29
warriors, 28–34
Washington, 100, 103, 144, 166
waste, 35
waterfowl
   abundance of, 101
   conservation of, 90, 109, 110, 125
   decline of, 116

Index

duck
  black, 86, 116
  Labrador, 54
  wood, 86
duck factory, 73
goose, 68, 82, 89, 99, 163
grain for, 99
habitat for, 73, 94–95
hunting laws, 86
hunting of, 115
and insecticide, 120
killing of, 89
marketing, 82
prairie pothole region (duck factory), 73, 101
swan, 82
watershed, 163
Waterton Biosphere Reserve, 163–164
Waterton Lakes National Park, 164
weaponry
  of American Indians, 2, 3, 9, 62
  development of, 3, 7, 40, 53, 60, 66–67, 71, 72, 87
  and gunpowder, 42, 59, 60, 66
  restrictions of, 88–89, 90, 91
  skill with, 23, 30, 38, 71, 83
  types of, 3, 6, 7, 9, 28, 30, 31, 38, 40, 42, 53, 60, 62, 66, 71, 86
weasel, 78, 92
weather. *See* climatic change
West Indies, 45, 52
wetland, 21, 65, 94–95, 102, 110, 131, 156, 158, 178 (*see also* waterfowl)
whale
  beluga, 163
  blue, 47, 51
  bowhead, 50, 51, 163
  gray, 50, 51
  minke, 130
  narwhal, 163
  right, 46
  sperm, 46
whaling, 45–47, 48, 50, 121, 130–131, 179
wheatear, 79
wheel, 10, 17, 57, 60
White Sea, 46, 47
wildlife
  agencies, 85, 88, 95, 107, 114

attitudes toward, 191–194
  commercial harvest. *See* harvest, commercial
  domestication of, 16–22
  hunting. *See* hunting
  ownership of, 67, 82
  populations, 2–3, 20–24, 32, 37, 42, 45, 51, 67–68, 83
  programs, 108–111, 114
  sanctuaries, 24, 80, 95, 131, 158, 161
wildlife conservation
  broadening, 141–155
  in Colonial period, 76–81
  elements, of, 85
  government responsibilities, 85–86, 91
  history, 85
  holistic conservation, 156–174
  international goals, 142, 159, 160
  international issues, 125–140
  land use to 1945, 98–113
  laws and regulations, 29–30, 32, 33, 36, 38–39, 40, 41, 42, 51, 67, 82–97, 101, 105–106, 108, 110, 159, 169, 178
  from 1945 to 1970, 114–124
  in North America, 82–124
  patterns of, 175–189
  urgency for, 142–143
Wild Life Conservation in Theory and Practice, 107
"Wildlife in American Culture," 191
Wildlife Management Institute, 95, 110
Wildlife Refuge, 161
Wildlife Society, The, 110
William the Conqueror, 39
Wisconsin, 63, 69, 93
wisent, 37–38, 42 (*see also* bison)
wolf
  decline of, 77, 144
  extinction of, 79, 93, 164
  as game, 38
  as predator, 4, 21, 25, 37, 73, 92, 93, 164
  protection of, 42, 129, 164
  reintroducing, 144
  taming of, 15–16
woodchuck, 82
woodcock, 82, 86, 90
woodlark, 79

woodpecker, 118
World Bank, 127
World Conservation Monitoring Centre (WCMC), 129–130
World Conservation Strategy, 176–177, 179–180
World Conservation Union (WCU), 129, 130
World War I. *See* war
World War II. *See* war
World Wide Fund for Nature (WWF), 130, 134–135, 179
World Wildlife Fund (WWF). See World Wide Fund for Nature

writing, 1, 33, 39–40
Wyoming, 166

yak, 18
Yellowstone Model, 165
Yellowstone National Park, 62, 63, 94, 105, 164, 165, 166
Yellowstone Network, 166
Yosemite National Park, 106

zones of cooperation, 160
zoo, 31, 55, 69, 70, 79, 80, 92, 134, 151–152, 179, 191